WITCH HUNT

WITCH HUNT

HISTORY OF A PERSECUTION

BY

NIGEL CAWTHORNE

BARNES
& NOBLE
BOOKS

NEW YORK

This edition distributed by Barnes & Noble Books

This edition published in 2004 by
Chartwell Books,
A division of Book Sales, Inc.,
114 Northfield Avenue
Edison, New Jersey 08837

First published by Arcturus Publishing Limited

British Library Cataloguing-in-Publication Data: a catalogue
record for this book is available from the British Library

© Arcturus Publishing Limited, 2003
26/27 Bickels Yard, 151–153 Bermondsey Street, London SE1 3HA

ISBN 0-7607-5858-1

Edited by Paul Whittle
Cover & book design by Alex Ingr
Cover image: *The Trial of George Jacobs* (1855) by T. H. Matteson,
Peabody Essex Museum, Salem, USA/Hulton Archive

Printed in China

Contents

O Christian Martyr Who for Truth could die
When all about thee Owned the hideous lie!
The world, redeemed from superstition's sway,
Is breathing freer for thy sake today.

Words written by John Greenleaf Whittier and inscribed
on a monument marking the grave of Rebecca Nurse,
one of the condemned 'witches' of Salem.

Introduction

T HERE HAVE BEEN NUMEROUS attempts to explain the witch-hunting mania that swept the western world in the sixteenth and seventeenth centuries. Why was it that suddenly people saw witches flying on broomsticks and dancing naked at sabbats with the devil? According to one theory, a grain fungus spread across Europe, which worked like a psychedelic drug, giving hallucinations to those who consumed it. A similar theory has also been advanced for the sudden collapse of the early English colony on Roanoke Island.

Others see it as a product of sexual hysteria. Many of the witchcraft cases in this book have a strong sexual element, often involving young women in the throes of puberty, as in many poltergeist cases.

Was the witch hunt part of a misogynist agenda, a giant conspiracy among men to persecute women? Or was witch-hunting thinly disguised anti-Semitism? Were attention-seeking children the cause? There are sometimes hints of what we now call paedophilia. Could this be the explanation? Or was it all of the above?

But any of these explanations would be wrong. They all see the events of the sixteenth and seventeenth centuries though twenty-first century eyes. The cases I have related in this book can only really be understood in their own terms. True, many people confessed to being witches and named others under unspeakable torture. Yet others confessed voluntarily, even though they knew that their confession would result in a horrible death. While some people plainly made accusations for material gain, others had unimpeachable motives.

Some said that they had seen things and done things that, in our eyes, are clearly impossible. Plainly old women do not fly on broomsticks; the devil does not penetrate thick prison walls to make love to unwilling victims. People do not turn into wolves. But many good, honest and sincere people reported such things – and they were believed.

Imagine what it was like to live in a society where everyone believed in witchcraft. Imagine living in a society where, even if you had not seen people flying or dancing naked at sabbats, everyone believed that such things went on. Both the witch-burner and the witch – and often one became the other – had the same mindset. They believed that Satan was present on the earth, and that his purpose was to corrupt good Christian people by any means necessary. If one had, let's say, a dream with an explicit sexual content, it would be easy to interpret it as the work of the devil. Surely, if you are a good, upright and sexually continent person, such ideas in your mind must be the work of the devil? It is not hard to see some of the confessions as what is now known in child sexual abuse cases as 'false memory syndrome'. If the sexual abuse of a child by its parents has disturbing effects in later life, then if you are a disturbed adult, it is not hard to believe that your parents must have abused you and that you have blocked this unpleasant fact from your mind. Then, with a little creative therapy, it is possible to fill in the ghastly details.

Likewise if all sin proceeds from the devil then, if you are sinful – as we are told we all are – then you must be in league with him. Surely Satan could have visited you one night, whisked you off to a sabbat, then forced you to forget about it? In that case how can you trust your own memory? After all, those who are trying to obtain a confession from you are trying to save your immortal soul. Might it be that the allegations they are making are right?

The collective madness we see in these witch-crazes also has echoes in events that are closer to our own time. In the witch-burning in

Germany, there are disturbing harbingers of the Jewish holocaust.

And such frenzies can even occur in the most liberal of societies. In 1950s America, there were the aptly named witch hunts where Senator Joe McCarthy and other leading politicians in Washington sought out Communists and 'fellow travellers' in the movie industry and other walks of life. Many innocent people were imprisoned, and Julius and Ethel Rosenberg paid with their lives.

It is not difficult to understand how America could be gripped by an anti-Communist fever in those post-war years. Throughout the twentieth century, Communists had been vehemently opposed to the rampant capitalism of the United States, and Russia was a long-term enemy. In the wake of the First World War, the Soviet Union had taken over half of Europe. Then in 1949, China, the most populous country on earth, became Communist, and Communists were also on the march in Korea, Vietnam, Laos, Malaya and, closer to home, in Cuba. The Soviet Union had also recently developed its own atomic bomb and had missiles that could deliver enough explosive power to wipe out an American city. For the first time since the war of 1812, mainland America was under threat.

The playwright Arthur Miller made the comparison between the McCarthyite witch hunts and the Salem witch-craze in his play *The Crucible*. He showed how a society could turn in on itself in the face of a pervasive external threat. New England society in the late seventeenth century was beset by fears of attack by Native Americans and the French, and there was also the ever-present fear of disease, crop failure and economic hardship.

By and large, the witch-crazes in Europe sprung up at times when countries were beset by religious wars. France and Germany, particularly, were torn apart by armed struggle between Catholics and Protestants. Cities and whole regions would change their religious affiliation overnight, sometimes more than once. In the face of such uncertainty, a collective madness sets in. We now live in such uncertain times.

I have presented the cases in this book using court reports, depositions, letters, confessions, torture records and other written material from the time. I have reported the evidence without comment so that the reader can make up his or her own mind how such things can happen. Any attempt on my part to explain these cases in twenty-first-century terms would risk explaining them away. In some cases, the victim faced a terrible dilemma: either confess and be burnt to death or stay silent and die horribly under torture. One can only hope that the victims found their religion a comfort in such extremis. But others freely confessed to flying, turning into wolves or other animals or making love to the devil himself. Their evidence cannot merely be discounted because, rationally, such things do not happen in the real world. Their real world was different from ours. It is worthwhile remembering that many things we believe now will look just as absurd in three or four centuries' time.

Giles Corey confronts his accusers at his trial for witchcraft in Salem, 1692. Eighty-two-year-old Corey refused to plead, and was pressed to death as a result.

The Crucible

THE DEVIL WAS ABROAD in New England in 1692. The colonial powers England and France were at war. The Indians were on the warpath. Pirates were hindering trade. Smallpox was raging. The winter was cruel and taxes were crippling. To the Puritans of New England, such a litany of misfortune could only be the work of the devil and his agents on Earth – witches.

The witch problem came to light when a group of young girls gathered in the house of the Reverend Samuel Parris in Salem village to listen to the West Indian tales of the slave woman Tituba. Two of them, the Reverend's 9-year-old daughter Elizabeth and her 11-year-old cousin Abigail Williams, got so excited that they suffered fits of sobbing and convulsions, and Elizabeth threw a Bible across the room. This was not the first time that the two girls had drawn attention to themselves, both being known as somewhat wilful and headstrong: it would, however, gain them more attention than they had perhaps bargained for.

The two girls' hysteria spread to others. Ten girls, aged between twelve and twenty, began making odd gestures, striking poses and making ridiculous speeches that neither they nor others could understand. One, 17-year-old Elizabeth Hubbard, was the niece of the local physician Dr. William Griggs. He began to believe that they were possessed. It was not long before the local ministers diagnosed witchcraft.

Another sufferer, 20-year-old Mary Warren, worked for Elizabeth and John Proctor, who discovered a cure for Mary's fits: they stopped as soon as John threatened to thrash her. Mary Sibley, the aunt of 16-year-old Mary Walcott, had another remedy. She got Tituba's husband to make a 'witch cake'. Barley was mixed with the children's urine, then fed to a dog. This was supposed to transfer the children's affliction to the unfortunate animal.

It was Tituba who first talked of spectres in the shapes of neighbours trying to win the girls to the devil. Plainly this had to be investigated. But when the question 'What torments you?' brought no answer, various names were suggested to the girls. The suspects, perhaps predictably, were those who lived on the fringes of society – a pipe-smoking beggar named Sarah Good, the thrice-married cripple Sarah Osborne, Martha Corey who had given birth to an illegitimate mixed-race son and Tituba herself.

Sarah Good was the first to suffer. On 29 February 1692, she was charged with the felony of using 'certain detestable arts called witchcraft and sorcery', causing three of the girls – Elizabeth Hubbard, Ann Putnam and Sarah Bibber – to be 'tortured, afflicted, pinned, consumed, wasted, and tormented'. At a preliminary hearing on 1 March, Mrs Good said that she had no contact with the devil, denied hurting the children and claimed that she had been falsely accused. When the girls were called to testify, they began to cry out in pain, complaining that her spectre was pinching, biting and paralysing them. The judge was convinced and demanded that Mrs Good give the names of her accomplices.

Soon other names were mentioned and fresh hearings held. Again the girls went into contortions. At the examination of William Hobbs, Abigail Williams said that he was going after Mercy Lewis, the 19-year-old servant of Mr and Mrs Thomas Putnam, who was immediately seized by a fit. Abigail then cried that he was going after 16-year-old Mary Walcott, who also had a seizure.

Elizabeth Booth accused John Proctor. Mary Walcott accused Abigail Faulkner. Ann Putnam named the Reverend George Burroughs, Rebecca Nurse and her two sisters, Elizabeth Proctor, 80-year-old Giles Corey and many others. She named more witches than any of the others and it seems she was coached by her parents. Fourteen years after the trial, Ann confessed that she had been deluded by Satan into making false accusations.

Thirty-year-old Mrs Putnam was also free with her accusations. As was 36-year-old Sarah Bibber, who made depositions against ten people, usually backing what the girls themselves had said. For example, she testified that she had seen 'the apparition of Rebecca Nurse...most grievously torture and afflict the bodies of Mary Walcott, Mercy Lewis and Abigail Williams by pinching them and almost choking them to death'. She also cried out in the courtroom saying that Rebecca Nurse had pinched her, though Rebecca's daughter swore that she had seen Sarah stab herself with a pin. The widow Sarah Holt also testified against Rebecca Nurse because her husband had died soon after Rebecca had chastised him when his pigs had strayed into her field. Rebecca was 71 years old and bedridden. She and one of her sisters, Marty Esty, were convicted and hanged. The other sister, Sarah Cloyce, confessed and was reprieved.

Fifty-five of the 150 accused confessed, as a confession automatically meant a reprieve. Those executed at Salem were put to death not because they were witches, but because they denied it. The girls did not go into convulsions when those who confessed gave their testimony and, when Tituba confessed, both Ann Putnam and Elizabeth Hubbard said that, 'She left off hurting me and has hurt me little since.' However, Samuel Wardwell, who confessed and later retracted his confession, was one of those to die.

Sarah Churchill, the 20-year-old servant of George Jacobs, refused to testify against him when he was arrested. The other girls immediately turned on her and accused her of being a witch too. She changed her mind, but later poured her heart out to Sarah Ingersoll, the spinster daughter of the local deacon and keeper of the local inn. But when Sarah filed a deposition, it was ignored. Sarah Bidder also testified to this. Sarah Ingersoll also said that, when one of the girls had complained that Elizabeth Proctor was afflicting her when she came to the inn, she told the girl that she lied, as there was nothing there. 'Then the girl said she did it for sport.'

Like Sarah Churchill, Mary Warren could not bring herself to testify against her employer. With John and Elizabeth Proctor in jail, however, Mary found herself on her own, looking after the Proctors' five children – with the Proctors' property already impounded by an overzealous sheriff. Fifty-two neighbours got up a petition saying that John Proctor was innocent, and Mary expressed her doubts to her girlfriends, Ann Putnam, Mercy Lewis, Mary Walcott and Abigail Williams. They simply denounced her as a witch. She stuck to her guns for three weeks, then confessed that John Proctor's apparition had afflicted her and she admitted signing the devil's book. John Proctor was further condemned for this sceptical attitude towards witchcraft.

When the deputy constable of Salem Village John Willard, who had made the first arrests, suggested that it was the girls who should hang not those they accused, he quickly realised his mistake and fled. He was captured ten days later, and six girls and Mrs Putnam testified against him on seven indictments, more than against any other defendant. He was tried on 2 August and hanged on the 19th.

Reverend George Burroughs – the only clergyman accused in the witch hunt – had had a falling out with Salem Village some years previously, over the non-payment of his stipend, and had left the village in 1683. He also seems to have had a bitter monetary dispute with John Putnam at the same time. It was John Putnam who instigated Burroughs' arrest and return to Salem to stand trial for witchcraft. He was accused by Ann Putnam and Mercy Lewis, whom Burroughs had brought to the Putnams' house as a waif to be their servant. There was talk of broomstick rides and feasts featuring 'roast and boiled meat...red bread and red wine like blood' – most Puritans considered transubstantiation the work of the devil.

Ann testified that, as well as choking her, Reverend Burroughs had tried to get her to sign a book giving her soul to the Devil. When she refused, she stated, he tortured her. Later she accused him of murdering both his first and second wives. Mercy Lewis said Burroughs had taken her up to a high place and shown her all the kingdoms of the world, and told her that they would be hers, if she signed his book. He also said that he could raise the devil and, if she testified against him, she would see his two – dead – wives at first hand.

Another girl, Abigail Hobbs, said that the devil in the shape of Reverend Burroughs had given her wax dolls, and he was no mere apparition – she had touched him. At the time Abigail was in jail and Burroughs was eighty miles away in Maine. Again he had urged her to sign his book.

Benjamin Hutchinson testified that he had been with Abigail Williams when she had seen Burroughs' spectre in front of Ingersoll's tavern. When he threw a pitchfork at the place where she said it stood, she fell into a fit. However, she recovered quickly because, she said, the pitchfork had only torn Burroughs' coat. She had heard it tear, she added. They then went into the inn and Abigail saw the spectre again. It transformed into a grey cat. Although Hutchinson was unable to see this either, he lashed at it with his rapier – and Abigail collapsed in a fit. This same tale was told four months before by Mary Walcott with Bridget Bishop providing the spectre and her brother Jonathan striking at it·so that 'he tore her coat in striking, and she heard it tear'.

Six of the girls testified against Burroughs, along with eight people who had confessed to being witches. Nine depositions – including only two eyewitnesses – spoke of Burroughs' unnatural strength. He had been an athlete at Harvard. More evidence came when the girls claimed that he was biting them. He was brought from jail, his mouth pried open and his teeth were found to match the marks on their bodies. However, Burroughs had already condemned himself out of his own mouth.

'There neither are nor ever were witches that having made a compact with the Devil can send a devil to torment other people at a distance,' he said. Denying the existence of witchcraft was proof of being a witch.

On the scaffold, on 19 August 1692, Burroughs recited the Lord's Prayer so flawlessly that some of the onlookers began to believe he was innocent, as an inability to recite the prayer was considered a sure sign of a witch. The local witch-hunter Cotton Mathers warned them that the devil was all the more dangerous when he appeared as an angel of light, and ensured that Burroughs was hanged, along with Martha Carrier, John Willard, George Jacobs, Sr. and John Proctor.

When they began to run out of suspects in Salem Village, the girls began to cast their net further afield and the centre of witchcraft moved to Andover. But the chief accusers, Ann Putnam and Mary Walcott, had a problem as they did not know the names of people there. So a new test was introduced. Suspects were lined up. When the girls fell into one of their fits the suspects had to touch her. If she miraculously recovered the person who touched her was a witch.

John Ballard asked the two girls to investigate the cause of his wife's illness, which had defied diagnosis or cure. They found that she had been bewitched by Ann Foster, her daughter Mary Lacy, and her granddaughter Mary. They confessed to save themselves, naming others to show that they were co-operating with the court. Nevertheless Mrs Foster died in jail from exposure and maltreatment.

After issuing forty warrants, the judge in Andover, Justice Dudley Bradstreet, refused to sign any more. This made him a witch. He was indicted for nine murders and fled. His brother was also indicted for inciting his dog to afflict the girls. The dog was tried and hanged as a witch.

Then the girls' attention turned to Boston where the Lieutenant Governor of Massachusetts signed a warrant against the famous Indian fighter Captain John Alden. When he appeared in court, the girls mistakenly identified another man in his place. When he was correctly identified, he was made to stand on a chair and the girls fell flat on their faces. Then when his hand was placed on them, they recovered. Later in the proceedings he asked, 'What is the reason you don't fall when I look at you? Can you give me one?'

He was accused of selling powder and shot to the Indians and the French, sleeping with Indian squaws and fathering Indian children. Stripped of his sword, he was jailed, but escaped after fifteen weeks. The nearby town of Gloucester called for the girls' services in October, but they only managed to identify four witches there. They were called back the following month, but the panic caused by the attacks of the Indians and the French in July was now subsiding. On their way, in Ipswich, they went into fits at the sight of an old woman, but the people of Ipswich ignored them and the witch scare was over.

Of the 150 accused, only thirty-one were brought to trial in 1692, six of whom were men. Nineteen were hanged. Two others – Sarah Osborne and Ann Foster – died in jail. Eighty-year-old Giles Corey was pressed to death. Thomas Putnam – Ann's father – had testified that the witches that afflicted his daughter had threatened to press her to death in front of Giles Corey. A ghost in a winding sheet had told her that Corey had pressed him to death and Corey, Putnam said, had entered into a covenant with the devil that he should not hang. Corey refused to plead. He was taken out into a field beside Salem jail and subjected to 'peine forte et dure', a treatment used to force unwilling defendants to plead, where weights were heaped on the unfortunate victim's naked body. Corey withstood this torture for two days before he died, still refusing to plead. Although this punishment was technically legal in England until 1827, it was outlawed in Massachusetts by the 1641 Body of Liberties.

Mary Bradbury escaped from jail after sentencing. Elizabeth Proctor and Abigail both pleaded pregnancy, which delayed their execution long enough to get a reprieve. Tituba was held indefinitely without trial and five other condemned witches confessed and were, consequently, reprieved.

Elizabeth Clarke (l) names her five 'familiars' in this seventeenth-century woodcut. The other woman is probably Anne West. The baleful figure of Matthew Hopkins lurks behind the two women.

2

Witchfinding in England

WITCH TRIALS such as those at Salem were by no means unique. There had been others in New York and Long Island between 1665 and 1670, and nine witches were hanged in Connecticut between 1647 and 1662. In England, there was a long history of witch hunts stretching back to the late seventh century when the punishment for witchcraft prescribed by the Archbishop of Canterbury Theodore was a period of fasting. In the eighth century, the Archbishop of York, Ecgberht, made the punishment for slaying by incantation a fast of seven years. In the tenth century King Athelstan introduced the death penalty for murder by witchcraft, but William the Conqueror reduced this to banishment. The death penalty returned under Henry VIII, but only for a second offence.

In 1525, twenty men were acquitted of murder by the use of a wax doll. In 1560, eight men – including two clergymen – confessed to sorcery. Swearing not to do it again, they were sentenced to a brief appearance in the pillory. In 1563, Elizabeth I signed a new witchcraft act which was particularly hard on fortune-tellers – especially those who foretold her death. Under it 535 bills of indictment were drawn and eighty-two people were executed. Chelmsford became a centre of witch trials and, of the 291 witches tried at the Essex assizes between 1560 and 1680, only twenty-three were men. Eleven of those were tried in connection with a woman.

Three witches were tried in Chelmsford in 1566, one of whom was hanged. A second was hanged after being tried in 1579, along with another condemned witch. In 1582, thirteen witches from St. Osyth, Essex, were tried at Chelmsford, accused of bewitching to death. Two were hanged. The rest reprieved or acquitted. That same year, a notorious sorceress found guilty in Durham was sentenced to sitting in the market square 'with a paper on her head'. Nevertheless the idea of witchcraft was beginning to take a grip on the English psyche. In 1593, in Huntingdon, 76-year-old Alice Samuel, her husband John and daughter Agnes were convicted of murder by witchcraft. Their accusers were the children of a local squire who suffered from, perhaps, epilepsy but certainly hysteria. When Mrs Samuel visited their house, they told her that their fits would stop if she told them to. To humour them she did so, and when the fits stopped, she was promptly accused of being a witch. Later, the children said that their fits would only stop if she confessed that she was a witch and she had killed Lady Cromwell, a local dignity. On this evidence the Samuels were hanged. The unmarried Agnes was urged to save herself by claiming she was pregnant – an unborn child cannot be executed for the crimes of its mother under English law.

'That I will not do,' she said. 'It shall never be said that I was both a witch and a whore.'

In 1596 in Burton, Alice Gooderidge confessed after being tortured by a 'cunning man' who put a new pair of shoes on her and 'set her close to the fire till the shoes became extremely hot... She being thoroughly heated, desired a release and she would disclose all.' She was sentenced to a year's imprisonment and died in jail. Her accuser, Thomas Darling admitted lying when he said she had bewitched him, though he too may have been threatened with torture. His fits were caused by worms, a doctor who examined him said. In 1603 Darling was sentenced to be whipped and have his ears cut off for libelling the vice-chancellor of Oxford University.

That same year, James VI of Scotland became James I of England. Having personally led witch hunts in Scotland, he signed a draconian Witchcraft Act in 1604 which stayed on the statutes until 1736. Soon the whole country was looking for witches. In 1605, three women were tried in Abingdon after being accused by a fourteen-year-old girl named Anne Gunter. The King himself sent £300 towards the costs of the proceedings. Unfortunately the girl confessed that she had feigned her hysteria. However, in 1607, a total of forty-one people were executed for witchcraft.

The Pendle Witches

In March 1612, a local justice in Lancashire named Roger Nowell examined a blind, disfigured 80-year-old woman named Elizabeth Sowthern. Known as Old Demdike, she was said to be a witch. She admitted as much, confessing that she had become a witch in 1560 when a 'spirit or devil came to her in the shape of a boy'. Five years later, this 'wicked firebrand of mischief' had persuaded her friend and neighbour Ann Whittle – know as Old Chattox – to join her in her 'most barbarous and damnable practices, murders, wicked and devilish conspiracies'. Sowthern also implicated her granddaughter Alison Device, who was indicted for using witchcraft to lame a peddler. Old Chattox was charged with bewitching Robert Nutter of Greenhead to death in the Forest of Pendle with the help of her daughter Anne Redfearne and Old Demdike's daughter Elizabeth Device.

While these Anne and Elizabeth were still at large, they called a meeting of the two families to try and free the other three women who were being held in Lancaster Castle. About eighteen women and two or three men turned up and dined on 'beef, bacon and roasted mutton'. This dinner party was portrayed as a witches' sabbat, which are traditionally much more orgiastic affairs. Over dinner, they planned to kill the jailer and blow up the castle. However, this came to the ears of Justice Nowell, who had nine of them arrested. The rest fled.

Two of Elizabeth Device's children – 20-year-old James and 9-year-old Jannet – gave evidence. James confessed stealing communion bread to give to a hare that disappeared when he crossed himself, while Jannet testified that a 'spirit in the likeness of a dog' named Ball helped her mother kill people. This prompted their mother to confess. They also identified all those at the family meeting as witches. For good measure,

Jannet named her brother James a witch, saying he employed a dog called Dandy to bewitch people to death. In jail, he too confessed.

Anne Redfearne was acquitted on the charge of killing Robert Nutter for lack of evidence. This displeased the mob, so she was tried again for killing his father Christopher Nutter. This time she was found guilty, on evidence that was largely hearsay and gossip. However, James Device testified that his grandmother had said that Alice Nutter, Christopher's widow and Robert's mother, was a witch. Jannet also testified that her mother had said Alice was a witch, and Elizabeth Device said that she and Alice had bewitched a man to death. Alice Nutter went to her death protesting her innocence. The rest were convicted on evidence scarcely less flimsy.

Old Demdike died in jail. Ten of the others were hanged, including Old Chattox – who also confessed – her daughter Anne Redfearne, Elizabeth Device, her son James and her eleven-year-old daughter Alison. Two others were sentenced to a year in jail with four appearances in the pillory.

While the trial was underway, it was interrupted by the trial of three women from Salmesbury accused of being witches. Under cross-examination their accuser, a young girl, admitted being coached by a Roman Catholic priest who was angered by their conversion to Protestantism. But this did not sway the judge in the Old Demdike case. In 1607, 4-year-old John Smith, the son of Sir Roger Smith of Husbands Bosworth in Leicestershire, began accusing a number of women of bewitching him. It seems he too suffered from epileptic fits. No one took any notice of his accusations until 1613, when a case of possession in France became well known in England. Nine women were arrested and hanged in 1616. Soon after the King was in Leicester and summoned the boy 'whereupon John Smith began to falter, so the King discovered the fallacy'. Six other women were still in jail as a result of Smith's allegations. They were given a new trial and released, though one of them had died in jail in the mean time.

Another fraud was exposed in 1620 in Bilson, where it was discovered that William Perry had been coached by a Roman Catholic priest to feign possession by vomiting 'rags, thread, straw and crooked pins'.

He almost fooled Thomas Morton, the Bishop of Lichfield who was investigating the case, by passing black urine – until he was discovered tucking a piece of cotton saturated with black ink under his foreskin. The following year Katherine Malpas of Westham, Essex, was also found to be feigning possession when she accused two women of bewitching her. But still, they took things more seriously in Lancashire.

In 1633, at Hoarstones, again in the Pendle Forest, 21-year-old Mary Spencer was convicted because, on her way to the well, she would roll her pail down a hill, run in front of it and call for it to follow her. Her accuser was a 10-year-old boy named Edmund Robinson, who also said that when he had beaten two greyhounds which had failed to course a hare they turned into a woman and a boy. When he refused a bribe to keep quiet about this, the women took Edmund on the boy, who had now became a white horse, to a sabbat. Robinson's father endorsed this testimony.

Unfortunately, the boy did not know the names of any of the witches he had seen at the sabbat, so he was authorised to go around the county to see if he could pick any of them out. He would get money for each one he recognised. Among those he picked out was Jannet Device, whose testimony had led to the death of eleven others at the first Lancashire witch trials. However, the Reverend John Webster of Kildwick cast doubt on Edmund's testimony, asking him straight out whether his story of visiting a sabbat was true. Four of the accused – including Mary Spencer – were sent to London, along with Edmund and his father. King Charles I's physician, the sceptical Dr. Harvey, examined the accused and could find no devil's marks on them. 'Devil's marks' were blemishes in the shape of a figure, sometimes a toad's foot, on other occasions a hare, a spider, a puppy or a dormouse, with which the devil marked his followers. They were birthmarks, scars or tattoos which did not bleed when pricked. On men they were found in the armpits, on the lips, shoulder or anus. On women they were usually found on the breast or the private parts, often concealed under the pubic hair. As a result, suspected witches on the Continent often had to be publicly stripped and have their bodies shaved. When questioned, Edmund admitted that he had made the whole story up, at the prompting of his father, in the hope of making money.

Matthew Hopkins – The Witchfinder General

Then came a man who was altogether more serious about witchcraft. His name was Matthew Hopkins but more commonly he was known as 'The Witchfinder General', and was famously played by Vincent Price in a 1968 movie of that name. Throughout his fourteen-month reign of terror, he was responsible for the condemnations and executions of around 200 alleged witches, nearly as many as all the other English witch-hunters put together.

Hopkins was the son of a Puritan minister named James Hopkins of Wenham in Suffolk. He trained as a lawyer and earned a meagre living, practising first in Ipswich, then in Manningtree in Essex. It was there he found a much more lucrative way to make a living – witch-finding. In his book *The Discovery of Witchcraft*, first published in London in 1647, he related how he started: 'In March 1644, he had some seven or eight of that horrible sect of Witches living in the Towne where he lived, a Towne in Essex called Manningtree, with diverse other adjacent Witches of other towns, who every six weeks in the night (being always on the Friday night) had their meeting close to his house, and had their solemn sacrifices there offered to the Devil, one of whom this Discoverer heard speaking to her imps and bid them go to another Witch, who was thereupon apprehended'.

His first victim was the one-legged hag Elizabeth Clarke, whose mother had been hanged as a witch before her. She was thrown into prison where she was stripped and 'found to have three teats about her, which honest women have not'. Torture was illegal, but she was kept without food or sleep for three consecutive nights. On the fourth, she weakened and confessed to being a witch and worse. Hopkins recorded:

> *The said Elizabeth forthwith told this informant and one Master Stearne, there present, if they would stay and do the said Elizabeth no hurt, she would call one of her white imps and play with it on her lap. But this informant told her he would not allow of it. And that staying there a while longer, the said Elizabeth confessed she had carnal copulation with the*

devil six or seven years; and he would appear to her three or four times a week at her bedside, and go to bed with her and lie with her half a night together, in the shape of a proper gentleman, with a laced band, having the whole proportion of a man. And he would say to her, 'Bessie, I must lie with you.' And she never did deny him.

In all, Elizabeth had five familiars: a white kitten named Holt, a polecat called Newes, a black rabbit called Sack-and-Sugar, a spaniel named Jarmara, and Vinegar Tom, a long-legged greyhound with a head like an ox, broad eyes and a long tail. Eight other people, including Hopkins himself, swore they had seen these familiars. Clarke named her accomplices, who included Anne West and her daughter Rebecca; Anne Leech; Helen Clarke, and Elizabeth Gooding. With the except of Elizabeth Gooding, they too confessed. Others admitted consorting with imps and familiars called Elemanzer, Pyewacket, Peck-in-the-Crown and Grizzel Greedigut – 'names that no mortal could invent,' Hopkins said. Thirty-two people in all were implicated.

Their trials began at Chelmsford on 29 July 1645. The Presbyterian Robert Rich, the Earl of Warwick, was 'President of the Court', the ordinary assizes having been suspended with the Civil War raging. Twenty nine-people were condemned. Ten were hanged at Chelmsford. The others were executed in villages round about, further fuelling the witch hysteria.

After the Chelmsford trials, Hopkins quickly became the sought-after expert. He styled himself 'Witch-Finder General' and claimed to have special commission from Parliament to rid the country of witches. There was certainly no shortage of them in Puritan East Anglia during the Civil War. To cope with the growing demand, Hopkins, dressed fashionably in Puritan tunic and cloak, took on a team of assistants, two men and two women. The notorious 'witch-pricker' Jack Stearne was his second in command, while Mary 'Goody' Phillips made a specialty of finding devil's marks. They were assisted by Edward Parsley and Frances Mills. Hopkins was soon charging from £15 to £23 to cleanse a town of witches. It is estimated that together they made nearly a thousand pounds. At Stowmarket in Suffolk, the local authority levied a special tax to pay him and his assistants. They coughed up £28 3d, at a time when the average monthly wage was only sixpence, or 2.5p.

Hopkins went about his business by turning gossip and innuendo into formal accusations. His victims were usual poor, old, feeble – the most defenceless members of the community. He looked for those people who were unpopular and against whom others held grievances. Most villages had at least one old hag. To help him in his work he had a 'Devil's List', a coded roster of all the witches in the country.

Once he found a victim, he would have them locked into a isolated prison cell, stripped naked, beaten, starved and kept from sleep. Although torture was illegal, 'pricking' to try and discover devil's marks was allowed. Hopkins and his assistants turned this into excruciatingly painful ordeal by the use of evil-looking pins, needles and bodkins. Not above using trickery to prove guilt, Hopkins sometime used a knife with a retractable blade, so a mark would not bleed when pricked.

But what was really required was a confession. The victim was made to sit cross-legged on a table or stool, then bound in that position with cords and left alone for up to twenty-four hours. Or naked and barefoot they would be forced to walk up and down the cold stone floor of the cell without stopping. Once his victims had been worn down by humiliation and exhaustion, Hopkins would begin browbeating them, demanding to know how they became acquainted with the devil. A nod or a grunt would suffice as a confession. His assistants could fill in the details later. Hopkins was particular fond of getting people to confess to having signed a pact with the devil, but charges also included bewitching people or livestock to death, causing illness and lameness, and entertaining spirits or familiars, which usually turned out to be household pets.

Hopkins also used 'swimming' to discover witches. The accused was tied up and thrown into water. If they floated they were deemed to be guilty, if not they drowned. The idea was that, as a witch rejected the water of baptism, water would reject them and they would float in an unnatural manner. This method had been used in England since 1612 but Hopkins developed it into a public spectacle. He bent his victims double with their arms crossed between their legs, then tied their thumbs to their big toes. Another rope was tied around their waist and held by a man on either side, ostensibly to prevent the victim from drowning. Then they were lowered from into a river, pond or stream, and allowed to sink and rise three times. But whether they floated or drowned depended on the men handling the rope.

After the success of the Chelmsford trials, Hopkins moved on to Bury St. Edmunds where he discovered that the minister of Brandeston, 70-year-old John Lowes, 'was naught but a foul witch'. It appears he had been a quarrelsome old fellow, disliked by many in his parish. He was 'swum in the moat', kept awake for three days and nights, then forced to walk without rest until his feet were blistered. 'Weary of his life and scarce sensible of what he said or did', he confessed sorcery and was hanged. Denied the benefit of clergy, Lowes recited his own burial service on the way to the gallows.

Hopkins' specialisation seems to have been extracting confessions of witchcraft from elderly women with pets. Faith Mills, of Fressingham, Suffolk, admitted that her three pet birds, Tom, Robert, and John, were in reality familiars who had wrought havoc by magically making a cow jump over a sty, and breaking a cart. She was hanged.

By the end of 1645 Hopkins had some 200 people locked up awaiting trial in Suffolk. But his cruelty and greed began to attract resistance from the authorities. Some even began to question whether he actually had a commission from Parliament: a good question, as this appears never to have been substantiated. A special judicial commission – consisting of Sergeant John Godbolt, some local justices and two clergymen, Samuel Fairclough and Edward Calamy (the elder) – was formed to deal with the backlog of witchcraft trials. It ordered Hopkins to stop his 'swimming' until they could catch up. Trials began in earnest and eighteen people were tried and hanged in quick succession. However the sessions had to be broken off when the Royalist forces approached Bedford and Cambridge. But when they started again, another fifty witches were quickly despatched.

By 26 July 1646 Hopkins was in Norfolk where another twenty witches met their fate. In September he went to Yarmouth at the request of the council. He was recalled in December, and it is not known how many died. He also visited Ipswich, Aldeburgh and King's Lynn before moving on to Stowmarket, stopping at small towns and villages along the way. Again, it is uncertain how many died in his march across East Anglia.

However, the tide began to turn against him. When he tried to moved in Huntingdonshire, John Gaule, the vicar of Great Staughton, spoke out against Hopkins from the pulpit. Hopkins retaliated in a letter to one of Gaule's parishioners:

> *My service to your Worship presented. I have this day received a Letter, &c, to come to a Towne called Great Staughton, to search for evil disposed persons, called Witches (though I hear your Minister is farre against us through ignorance). I intend to come the sooner to heare his singular Judgment on the behalfe of such parties; I have known a Minister in Suffolke preach as much against their discovery in a Pulpit, and forced to recant it (by the Committee) in the same place. I much marvaile such evil Members should have any (much more any of the Clergy) who should daily preach Terrour to convince such Offenders, stand up to take their parts, against such as are Complainants for the King and suffers themselves, with their Families and Estates. I intend to give your Towne a Visit suddenly. I am to come Kimbolton this weeke, and shall bee tenne to one, but I will come to your Towne first, but I would certainly know afore, whether your Towne affords many Sticklers for such Cattell, or willing to gave and afford us good welcome and entertainment, as others where I have beene, else I shall wave your Shire (not as yet beginning in any part of it myselfe) and betake me to such places, where I doe, and may persist without controle, but with thanks and recompense. So I humbly take my leave and rest, your Servant to be Commanded, Matthew Hopkins.*

Then Gaule published *Select Cases of Conscience Touching Witches and Witchcraft* in London in 1646, exposing Hopkins' methods of torture.

Hopkins prudently avoided visiting Great Staughton and retaliated with his pamphlet *Discovery of Witches*, but the witch-scare was over and he retired to his home in Manningtree. Stearne feared public animosity in Manningtree and moved to Bury St Edmunds.

The story that Hopkins himself was charged with witchcraft and 'swum' seems apocryphal. In his book *A Confirmation and Discovery of Witch-craft*, published in London in 1648, John Stearne wrote that Hopkins passed away 'peacefully, after a long sicknesse of a Consumption'. He was buried in the nearby village of Mistley on the 12 August 1647.

After that, witch trials continued sporadically. In 1652, six witches were hanged in Maidstone. However, Elizabeth Hynes of Thorpe, who was indicted for employing two evil spirits in the likeness of a black and a white kitten called Katt and Bess, was acquitted. The others, though, were accused of bewitching to death and went to the gallows. After the Restoration in 1660, there were few executions. In the Norfolk sessions, between 1661 and 1679, there were fifteen indictments for bewitching. Six cases were thrown out. In eight, the accused was found not guilty. The other defendant died in prison. Of the fifty-two trials for witchcraft in the Western Circuit between 1670 and 1712, only seven resulted in conviction – and in one of those the condemned witch was reprieved. The last witch to be executed in England was Alice Mollard, hanged in Exeter in 1684, eight years before Salem.

In all, in England, around a thousand died. However in England, like America, witches were not burnt at the stake. That was the punishment for treason. Witches were hanged. And under English law – which applied in Colonial America – torture was outlawed, despite the excesses of Matthew Hopkins. But things were very different on the Continent and in Scotland, where over a hundred thousand perished in the flames.

Jacques de Molay (c. 1244–1314), the 23rd and Last Grand Master of the Knights Templar, is led to the stake to burn for heresy. He is shouting to Pope Clement V and King Philip IV that they will face 'a tribunal with God' within a year. They both died soon afterwards.

The Origins of the
Witch Hunt

WITCHCRAFT WAS WIDESPREAD in the ancient cultures of the Middle East. Figures who had magical power to heal sickness or perform other acts of sorcery appear in the literature of ancient Mesopotamia, Egypt and Canaan. Alongside it there was a fear of malevolent magic or sorcery, especially in Mesopotamia, and from the earliest times, people sought for some way to counteract it.

According to the Bible, the ancient Hebrews also knew about witchcraft, though the Hebrew terms for 'witch' or 'sorcerer' probably refer to what we would now call mediums or clairvoyants who had the power to divine the future. In the First Book of Samuel, King Saul consults the 'witch of Endor'. The Book of Ezekiel refers to women who can control the souls of others using veils and 'magic bands'. These women are clearly sorcerers or witches in the modern sense and are condemned for going against God. But in Exodus, chapter xxii, verse 18, in his long codicil to the Ten Commandments, God tells Moses, 'Thou shalt not suffer a witch to live.' This biblical injunction was regularly cited by witch-hunters.

Ancient Greece and Rome took a more liberal approach. Only those who intended harm were punished. Those intending good were praised and even received official approval. It was generally accepted that practitioners could damage others in their financial, political, athletic and amorous endeavours and even cause their death. Certain goddesses – particularly Diana, Selene, or Hecate – were associated with the performance of malevolent magic. Their rites took place at night and according to a fixed ritual involving various paraphernalia and spells. In the second century classic *The Golden Ass*, Lucius Apuleius tells how the women of Thessaly – a region notorious for its witches – would assume various animal forms and go about gnawing off bits of dead men's faces.

However, many of the fiendish things that witches are supposed to do were also ascribed to the early Christians. The second-century writer Minucius Felix wrote that Christians worshipped the head of a donkey – 'that most abject of beasts. Others say that they reverence the genitals of the presiding priest himself and adore them as though they were their father's.' Initiation involving the stabbing to death of a child wrapped in dough with 'invisible blows', after which 'they hungrily drink the child's blood and compete with on another as they divide his limbs.' There are also drunken, incestuous orgies held in the dark so that couplings occur purely by chance.

Minucius Felix was a Christian apologist and wrote these accusations down so that they could be rebutted. But such charges were often taken seriously. In 177, the landowners of Lyons decided to save the money needed to hire gladiators for the games by sacrificing Christians in the arena instead. After they had been stoned by a mob, the Christians were thrown in prison, and their slaves were tortured until they confessed that their masters killed and ate children and indulged in promiscuous and incestuous orgies. Such accusations, however, were regularly made about many other groups on the periphery of society, such as Jews.

The fear of witches was also widespread among the Germanic peoples, who spread throughout Europe during the decline of the Roman Empire. As in the Greco-Roman world, such powers were especially attributed to women, and the old hag who practised witchcraft became a common figure in literature. In Northern Germany, sacred women were venerated as tribal soothsayers as women were the conduit of nature.

The Saxons brought with them their devilish gods – Thor, Wotan and Loki – and the Valkyries, wild women who flew though the clouds on stormy night, and the very name 'witch' is derived for the Anglo-Saxon word 'wicca', meaning sorcerer or prophet.

In 747, Pope Zachary called the Second Council of Clofesho in England, which forbade all 'wizardry, sorcery, divinings, fortune-telling, periapts, spells, conjurations and incantations, which are the very filth of the wicked, yea, heathen falsehood and deceit'. In England, a ban on witchcraft appeared in the code of King Alfred, which also laid down 'Those women who are wont to receive enchanters and magicians, wizards and witches thou shall not suffer them to live.' The death penalty was also introduced for killing by magic, and the administration of drugs or love potions was forbidden, along with astrology – particularly when it involved foretelling the death of a king.

This prohibition became written into the law of Christian countries. Under the laws of King Aethelred, soothsayers, magicians and whores were urged to desist under pain of death and the Secular Laws of Cnut denounced those who 'love witchcrafts to ensue them, or contrive secret murder' – murder by the use of black magic – 'in anywise; or offer evil sacrifice' – Black Mass – 'or by soothsaying, or perform anything pertaining to such abominable illusions'. However, legal punishments where no actual injury was caused were light. Witches who did no harm were usually tolerated as a hangover from the old religion. The Church also partly shared in this relatively enlightened view. The *Canon Episcopi*, first recorded in 906, ordered that 'Bishops and their officials must labour with all their strength to uproot thoroughly from their parishes the pernicious art of sorcery and malifice invented by the devil, and if they find a man or woman follower of this wickedness to eject them foully disgraced from their parishes.'

The document conceded that 'certain abandoned women perverted by Satan, seduced by illusions and phantasms of demons, believe and openly profess that, in the dead of night, they ride upon certain beasts with the pagan goddess Diana, with a countless horde of women, and in the silence of the dead of night fly over vast tracts of country'. However, these women were suffering from delusions and so should not suffer anything worse than excommunication and exile. After all, God made everything – including witches – and anyone who does not believe that is 'beyond doubt an infidel'. Burning at the stake was reserved for such heretics.

Heretical sects

There had been heresy in the Christian church almost from the beginning. The first Montanism – the belief that the heavenly Jerusalem was about to descend from the sky in Phrygia, Asia Minor – sprung up in the year 156, only a century and quarter after Christ died. In 325, the newly converted Emperor Constantine called the Council of Nicea to hammer out a set of core beliefs that Christians would have to abide to. After the Council of Nicea the Gnostics, a mystical sect, found themselves persecuted. Gnosticism itself was split into a number of cults. One of the more extreme was the Manichaeans, who followed the third century heretic Mani – whose name has given us the word 'maniac'. He followed the Zoroastrians in their belief in a universe divided into light and dark, good and evil. His followers practised extreme asceticism. They were forbidden to kill any animal or plant for food and, if possible, they should not even break a single twig. Arrested in 276, Mani was crucified and his corpse flayed.

By the twelfth century, the doctrine of the Church was pretty much settled, but the Church itself was a mess. Services were conducted in Latin which few of the congregation could understand. Most people were illiterate and could not read the Bible for themselves. But they could see that the Church was corrupt. The clergy lived a life of luxury. Many clergymen lived openly with their mistresses as ecclesiastical marriage had recently been banned.

In 1176, a wealthy French merchant called Peter Waldo started his cult which aimed to clean things up. He was even given a dispensation to preach by the Pope, provided that he obtained a licence from his local bishop. However, as the Bishop of Lyons was one of the fat cats Waldo wanted to denounce, the licence was refused and, in 1184, Waldo and his followers were excommunicated.

The Waldensians then became evangelical ascetics and went on the road. Over the years, they became more radical. They rejected the concepts of purgatory, transubstantiation, the invocation, excommunication, confession, absolution, penance and the purchase of indulgences. They only celebrated baptism, marriage and the Eucharist – once a year on the Thursday before Easter. They translated the Bible into French and – heresy of heresies – allowed women into the ministry. The Waldensian heresy proved popular. To counter it, Pope Innocent III formed the Poor Catholics, which aped the Waldensian asceticism while staying within the edicts of the Church. When that did not work, the Church resorted to persecution. Waldensians were imprisoned and burnt as heretics. St Augustine of Hippo had already ruled that it was perfectly acceptable to use force to save people from heresy. You might burn their body, but you would save their immortal soul. Waldensian cells survived in remote settlements in the Alps, however, and by the sixteenth century there were still enough to them to form an alliance with their natural heirs, the Calvinists.

The Albigensian Crusade

The persecution of the Waldensians largely came about because a more heretical cult had sprung up. During the twelfth century, the Crusades were in full swing. Travel between east and west increased enormously and ideas long suppressed in Europe began to surface again, among them Manichaeanism.

This flourished in and around the city of Albi in south-west France, before spreading to Italy, Spain and Flanders. The cult's followers were called *Cathari*, which means 'pure ones', or Cathars. They believed in both God and the Devil who struggled to rule the world and took Zoroastrian dualism to its extremes. As the material world existed on the dark, evil side of the universe, Jesus Christ, who exists on the good side, could not have been born into it. Consequently, he could not have been crucified, so the cross had no significance. The trappings of the Church also existed in the material world: these too were rejected by the Cathars.

The human soul belonged on the good side of the universe, but it was trapped on the bad side with the body. Hence the Cathars were against sex, eating meat, drinking wine and anything else that brought material comfort or pleasure. They mortified the flesh, practised savage flagellation and were vegetarians on the grounds that animals were produced by sexual intercourse and were, therefore, sinful. They did eat fish though, in the mistaken belief that fish did not copulate. The Cathars discouraged marriage on the same grounds, although they did practise sodomy, apparently permissible as it did not risk the sin of pro-creation. The laity, or 'Believers', were not required to hold too fast to this. But complete abstinence was required of the *Perfecti* who formed the inner circle of the Church.

Fearing persecution, the Cathars kept their faith secret. They knew they could not take on the power of the Catholic Church and win so, rather than opposing the church directly, they sought to undermine it by infiltrating its ranks. And in subverting it, they developed what later became the Black Mass.

However, when the Pope's attention was drawn to the sect, he sent Cistercian monks to convert them. The Cistercians met with little success and were mocked in the streets of Toulouse. Count Raymond VI of Toulouse who controlled the Cathar regions of southern France was himself a Cathar. Pope Innocent III sent an envoy to him, who was assassinated. The Pope responded by ordering a crusade, the first in Europe.

In 1208, he denounced the Cathars as satanist and began a purge. Twenty thousand knights under Simon de Monfort attacked the town of Béziers. When soldiers asked the papal legate Arnaud, Abbot of Cîteaux, how he could distinguish between a Cathar and a good Catholic, Arnaud replied, 'Kill them all: God will know his own.' And that is what they did.

But the slaughter of the entire population of Béziers only sharp-ened the Cathars' resolve. They fought on for another forty years. In 1231, Pope Gregory IX set up the Inquisition as a counter to widespread heresy. Church inquisitors employed torture and summary execution to achieve these ends and witnesses began to tell stories that became the basis of the charges laid against witches later. But for those who believe that the world is such an evil place, death holds little fear. Many Cathars performed the rite of Endura, a sanctified form of suicide through fasting. *Perfecti* given the choice between converting to Catholicism or burning chose martyrdom.

The Cathars' last stronghold was the fortress of Montségur in the Pyrenees. Thought to harbour treasure including the Holy Grail, it came under repeated attack. In March 1244, after a ten-month siege, the Cathars surrendered. Two hundred men and women walked out of the fortress singing, straight into the massive funeral pyres the crusaders had prepared for them, in the field today known as the 'Field of the Burned'. No treasure was found. Secret cells of Cathars continued for another fifty years. Some fled to the Balkans, where they continued until the fifteenth century when they were finally absorbed into Islam. But in 1320, Pope John XXII started a witch hunt in that area.

With the Inquisition already in place, Pope Innocent VIII issued the papal bull *Summis desiderantes affectibus* [Desiring with the most profound anxiety] on 5 December 1484, which marked the beginning of the official persecution of witches. It reversed the Canon Episcopi and the Inquisition was given the power to persecute witches as well as heretics. The bull read:

> *It has come to our attention, not without bitter sorrow, that in some parts of northern Germany, as well as the provinces, cities, territories, regions and dioceses of Mainz, Cologne, Trier, Salzburg and Bremen, many persons of both sexes, unmindful of their own salvation and deviating from the Catholic faith, have abused themselves with devils, incubi and succubi, and by incantations, spells, conjurations and other accursed superstitions and horrid charms, enormities and offences, destroy the offspring of women and the young of cattle, blast and eradicate the fruits of the earth, the grapes of the vine and the fruits of trees. Nay, men and women, beasts of burden, herd beasts, as well as animals of other kinds; also vineyards, orchards, meadows, pastures, corn, wheat and other cereals of the earth.*

Furthermore, these wretched afflict and torment men and women, beasts of burden, herd beasts, as well as cattle of all other kinds, with pain and disease, both internal and external. They hinder men from generating and women from conceiving, whence neither husbands with their wives nor wives with their husbands can perform the sexual act.

Above and beyond this, they blasphemously renounce that faith which they received by the sacrament of baptism and, at the instigation of the enemy of the human race they do not shrink from committing and perpetrating the foulest abominations and excesses to the peril of their souls, whereby they offend the divine majesty and are a cause of scandal and dangerous example to many others.

The bull went on to decree that:

the aforesaid inquisitors be empowered to proceed to the correction, imprisonment and punishment of any persons for the said abominations and enormities, without let or hindrance, in every way as if the provinces, townships, dioceses, districts, territories, yea, even the persons and their crimes in this kind were named and specifically designated in our letters.

As this bull made witchcraft a heresy in the eyes of the church, with it came the terrible punishment of being burnt alive.

The author of this bull, Pope Innocent VIII, was ill-named. He kept a mistress and fathered two children by her. For the last months of his life, he was kept alive by sucking milk from a woman's breast and tried to rejuvenate himself with blood transfusions, resulting in the death of three boys. Shortly after he issued the bull *Summis Desiderantes*, he authorised two Dominicans, Jakob Sprenger, dean of the University of Cologne, and Heinrich Kramer, professor of theology at the University of Salzburg and inquisitor in the Tyrol region of Austria, to stamp out the heresy of witchcraft. Together they wrote the *Malleus Maleficarum* [*Hexenhammer* or the *Hammer of the Witches*], published around 1486.

This was regarded as the standard handbook on witchcraft and its suppression until well into the eighteenth century.

The *Malleus* took the folklore surrounding black magic and codified it within Church dogma on heresy. The work is in three parts. In Part I, the reality and the depravity of witches was emphasised, and any disbelief in demonology was condemned as heresy. Part II was a compendium of fabulous stories about the activities of witches – diabolical compacts, sexual relations with devils (*incubi* and *succubi*), transvection (night-riding) and metamorphosis. Part III was a discussion of the legal procedures to be followed in witch trials. Torture was sanctioned as a means of securing confessions. Because of the nature of the enemy, any witness, no matter how bad their credentials, may testify against an accused. And secular authorities were called upon to assist the inquisitors in the task of exterminating those whom Satan had enlisted in his cause. The *Malleus* went through twenty-eight editions between 1486 and 1600 and was accepted by Roman Catholics and Protestants alike.

Its precepts soon found their way into the civil code. In 1532, the states of the Holy Roman Empire – which included what is now Germany, Austria, the Czech Republic, Switzerland, eastern France, the Low Countries, and parts of northern and central Italy – adopted the Carolina Code, which imposed torture and death as punishments for witchcraft. However, with its early crackdown on heretics, the witch hunt in France was already underway.

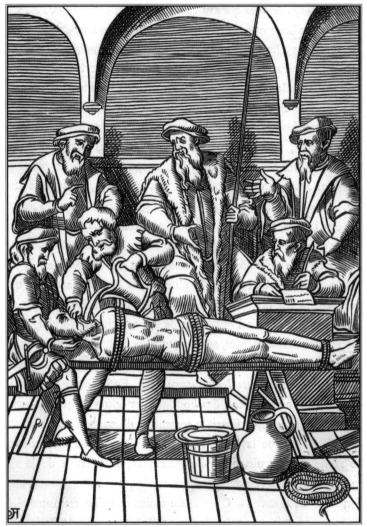

Inquisitors extract a confession using water torture. Woodcut by Joost De Damhoudere from his work *Praxis Rerum Criminalium*, published in Antwerp in 1556.

4

The Flames of France

WITCH TRIALS BEGAN as early as 1245 in the Cathar centre of Toulouse. In 1275, the inquisitor there, Hugues de Baniols, heard the confession of a 60-year-old woman, Angela de la Barthe. She was accused of having sexual intercourse with the Devil. The resulting child, she said, was a demon with a wolf's head and a snake's tail. It lived off the flesh of dead babies, and she murdered children and dug up the corpses to feed it. Angela de la Barthe was probably the first woman in France to be burned for witchcraft.

The Destruction of the Templars

At the time, the accusation of witchcraft was used as a political weapon. In 1278, Bishop Peter of Bayeux and his nephew were accused of using sorcery against King Philip II – the bishop was acquitted, but his nephew was executed. The next to suffer were the Knights Templar. An ascetic sect, the Poor Knights of the Temple had been founded in 1118 by French nobleman Hugues de Payns and eight other veteran crusaders to protect Christians travelling from Jaffa to Jerusalem, which the crusaders had captured from the Muslims nineteen years before. Since then Christian pilgrims had been harried by hostile Arabs. Payns named the outfit for Jerusalem's Temple of Solomon, where they were first quartered.

In 1128, Pope Honorius I officially recognised the order, which had become known as the Knights Templar. The Church encouraged the Templars to curb the excesses of the crusaders, who had been described by St Bernard of Clairvaux, the head of the Cistercians, as 'unbelieving scoundrels, sacrilegious plunderers, homicides, perjurers and adulterers'. Many of those recruited into the Templars had previously been excommunicated.

Knights Templar had to swear an oath of fraternity, poverty and chastity. Kissing their mothers was forbidden and, to ensure their continuing chastity, they had to sleep fully clothed in lighted dormitories. St Bernard absolved them from the sin of killing, provided they killed the enemies of the Church. He called them 'Christ's legal executioners'.

The Templars took a vow never to retreat whatever the odds and gained a reputation for being ferocious in battle. Like many modern day cults, they were told to cut themselves off from their families and members handed over all their worldly goods to the order when they joined. This made the Knights Templar immensely rich.

As the order was founded to aid travellers, it set up a banking system so that funds could be transferred from place to place safely. They also invested in real estate. Soon the Templars' distinctive circular churches and their strongly defended fortresses spread across the Mediterranean and Europe.

By the end of the thirteenth century, the crusades were over and the Knights Templar lost their original purpose. They were, however, freed from the massive cost of maintaining an army in the Middle East. Impoverished European kings, noting this, began to eye the huge wealth of the Templars and to consider ways of relieving them of it. The secrecy surrounding the order brought rumours of idolatry, homosexuality and devil worship. They were accused of witchcraft. In 1307, Philip IV of France, heavily in debt to the Templars' bank, ordered the arrest of the Templars on the grounds of heresy. He then forced Pope Clement V, the first of the popes to be exiled to Avignon, to give him permission to seize the Templars' property. The following year, Edward II seized Templar property in the British Isles and the London Temple, the order's English headquarters, was closed.

The Inquisition then moved in to torture confessions out of the Templars. Soon they were compiling a lurid dossier on the activities of the order which included homosexuality, urinating on the cross and worshipping Satan in the form of a black cat which they kissed under the tail. According to Templars' confessions, they also worshipped a pagan idol called Baphomet, which was a goat endowed with women's breasts and an erect penis. It wore a five-pointed star or pentagram around its neck and oil, said to be rendered from the flesh of dead infants, was massaged into its skin.

Baphomet was, in fact, a simple corruption of the name Muhammad. Indeed, two hundred years of presence in the Middle East had rubbed off. Many Knights Templar spoke Arabic and at least one had converted to Islam. The English Templar Robert of St Albans had even commanded a Muslim army.

In France, thirty-six Templars died under torture and, in 1310, fifty-four were burnt at the stake. In 1312, Clement admitted that there was no evidence of heresy in the order. Nevertheless, Philip of France insisted that he close it down. The remaining Templars were allowed to join other orders or go free, but the Grand Master Jacques de Molay was imprisoned for life on the strength of his confession which had been extracted under torture. On 18 March de Molay was taken before a crowd, to publicly confess his sins. Instead, he recanted his earlier confessions, insisting that his order was blameless. Burnt at the stake, according to some sources de Molay died cursing Philip and Clement, and summoning them both to 'meet him in a tribunal before God within the year'. Both died within the year.

*

In 1314, King Louis X heard that the wife of d'Enguerrand de Marigny, Alips de Mons, and her sister were trying to kill him using a wax doll. They implicated a magician called Jaques Dulot and his wife. Madame Dulot was burned alive. Dulot himself died in prison and the d'Enguerrands executed. At the time, the Church's ruling was still that witchcraft was not a crime in itself and should not be punished unless it was a manifestation of heresy. However, Pope John XXII, one of the more superstitious popes, believed that his enemies were trying to kill him using sorcery. In 1317, he tortured those he suspected into confessing. On 22 August 1320, he ordered the inquisitor at Carcassonne, near Toulouse, to take action against sorcerers, magicians and those who invoked demons or made waxen images or abused the sacrament. They were to be punished as heretics and have their property confiscated. There were sorcery trials in 1330 and 1335, when seventy-four people were accused. Trials continued there for the next seventy years.

Meanwhile Pope John XXII wrote to the inquisitors of nearby Toulouse and Narbonne telling them too to treat witchcraft as heresy. And a flurry of Papal bulls followed that spurred on the witch hunts.

In Toulouse in 1335, sixty-three men and women were tried for witchcraft and sorcery. One of the defendants, an elderly woman named Catherine Delort, admitted to killing two of her aunts and said that, at the group's sabbats, children were killed and eaten. Another of the accused defended these actions by saying that although God was King of the Heavens, Satan was Master of the World. The sabbats were devilish rites that took place on a large piece of flat, high ground with a wood or grove at one end. An altar was built out of stones. On it stood an image of Satan – a goat-like creature, but with a human body, horns and an erect penis. The worshippers carried torches, lit from a flame burning between the horns of the idol. The priestess was usually a young girl. She prayed to the Lord Satan to save her from the treacherous and violent, then planted a kiss on the idol. In some accounts, she kissed the rump; in others, the erect phallus.

Hallucinogenic herbs mixed with alcohol were then taken and the priestess would lie naked across the altar. A male worshipper would take over, playing the part of the devil. A version of the Christian creed, substituting the word Satan for Christ, was recited. Then the body of the priestess was mutilated and burned. An orgy followed, often involving children and generally employing sodomy rather than vaginal intercourse.

Some of these ceremonies were presided over by rogue priests in the Cathar tradition. Black turnip was substituted for bread in the communions and water replaced wine, while urine was sprinkled over the congregation instead of holy water. Sometimes children were sacrificed.

Catherine Delort and another woman named Anne Marie de Georgel confessed that they had been members of the numberless hosts of Satan for some twenty years, and they had given themselves to him in this life and the next. They frequently attended sabbats on Friday nights which where held in various places. There in the company of other men and women who were equally sacrilegious, they 'committed all manner of excesses, whose details are horrible to tell,' said the inquisitors. 'Each of them has been interrogated separately and they have given explanations that had entirely convinced us of their guilt.' Anne Marie de Georgel explained how she had become involved. One morning when she was washing clothes near Pech-David above the town she said she saw a man of huge statue coming towards her across the water. He was dark-skinned. His eyes burned like living coals and he was dressed in the hides of beasts. This monster asked her if she would give herself to him and she said yes. Then he blew into her mouth and 'from the Saturday following she was borne to the sabbat, simply because it was his will'. There she found a huge he-goat and after greeting him she submitted to his pleasure. In return, the he-goat taught her all kinds of secret spells.

'He explained poisonous plants to her and she learned from him words of incantations and how to cast spells on the night of the vigil of St John's day, Christmas Eve, and the first Friday every month,' said the inquisition. 'He advised her to make sacrilegious communion if she could, offending God and honouring the Devil. And she carried out those impious suggestions.'

Anne Marie de Georgel then also admitted that practising all manner of filthiness during the years that passed between her initiation and her imprisonment. She boiled together in a cauldron, over an 'accursed fire', poisonous herbs and substances taken from the bodies of animals or humans which she had sacrilegiously taken from the consecrated ground of cemeteries to use for her spells. She frequented the gallows-tree by night, stealing shreds of clothing from the hanging, or taking the rope by which they were hanging, or laying hold of their hair, their nails or their flesh.

'Like a true daughter of Satan, in answer to questions about the symbols of the Apostles and the faith which true believers have in our Holy Religion, she averred that God and the Devil were completely equal, the former reigning over the sky and the latter the earth; all souls which the Devil managed to seduce were lost to the Most High God and lived perpetually on earth or in the air, going every night to visit the houses in which they had lived and trying to inspire in their children and relatives a desire to serve the Devil rather than God,' the inquisitors reported. 'She also told us that the struggle between God and the Devil had gone on since eternity and would have no end. Sometimes one is victorious, sometimes the other, and at this time the situation was such that Satan was sure to triumph.'

The inquisition went on to say that she had been taken prisoner after having been denounced by respectable people who had good reason to complain of her spells. At first, she 'denied the abominable pact she had made and would not confess in spite of the requests of others as well as ourselves. But when she had been justly forced to give an account of herself, she finally admitted a series of crimes that deserved the most horrible punishment. She has sworn she repents, and has asked for reconciliation with the Church which has been granted to her. Nevertheless, she will be handed over to the secular arm which will realise the penalties she must pay.'

Catherine, the wife of Pierre Delort of Toulouse, also 'stands convicted on her own declarations and on the evidence of trustworthy persons, of meeting a shepherd in the field of the parish of Quint and having a relationship with him contrary to law. He, abusing his power over her, obliged her to make a pact with the Devil. This loathsome ceremony took place at midnight at the edge of a wood at a place where two roads met. She let some blood from her arm and allowed it to flow on to a fire made of human bones which had been stolen from the parish cemetery. She pronounced strange words which she no longer remembers and the devil Berit [probably the Canaanite god Ba'al-Berit] appeared to her in the form of a violet flame. Since then she has made certain harmful concoctions and potions which cause men and beasts to die.'

She fell into a strange sleep every Friday night and was carried to the Sabbat. When she was asked where this took place, she said on the slopes of Pech-David in the wood at Bouconne, in the middle of the open country between Toulouse and Montauban. Sometimes the sabbat took place further away 'on the top of the Black Mountains of the Pyrenees and in countries quite unknown to her'. At the ceremonies, she worshipped the he-goat and 'served his pleasure and that of all those who were present at that loathsome feast'. They ate the corpses of newborn children who had been stolen from their nurses at night. This was washed down with 'all manner of revolting liquids' and there was 'no savour in any of the food'.

Asked whether she had seen recognised those she had seen at the sabbat, she replied that she had often seen people she knew there. She did not give their names, but the inquisition knew who they were – 'some of them have died in their wickedness, others have been taken into custody thanks to our vigilance; a few have escaped, but the vengeance of the Lord will be upon them.'

Catherine had been 'forced to confess by means we have power to use to make people speak the truth'. She was convicted of all the crimes they suspected her of committing, although 'she protested her innocence for a long time and made several false declarations'.

The list of her crimes was long:

> She made hail fall on the fields of her enemies, caused their wheat to rot by means of a pestilential fog, and damaged the vineyards with frost. She caused the oxen and sheep of her neighbour to sicken and die for the advantages this might bring her. For the same motive she caused her aunts, whose heir she was, to die, by heating waxen figures dressed in one of their blouses over a slow fire, so that their unfortunate lives wasted away as the waxen figures melted on the brazier.

However, what is key to these accounts are the description of the sabbats. These are the earliest written accounts and are the forerunners of thousands of confessions taken by ecclesiastical and civil courts between the fourteenth and eighteenth centuries.

Only eight of the sixty-three people tried at Toulouse in 1335 were burnt. But by 1350 the inquisitions in Toulouse and Carcassonne had prosecuted a thousand people and burnt six hundred of them. The heat, quite literally, was on.

The first secular trials for witchcraft took place in Paris in 1390, after the Parlement of Paris ruled that witchcraft was a civil as well as an ecclesiastical offence. Unlike ecclesiastical courts – and later secular ones – the Grand Châlet, the central criminal court of Paris, required that specific charges of *maleficia*, that is the harm done by magic, were made and tried to ascertain the degree of guilt of the accused. Simply asserting that they were witches was not enough. The hearings were to be held in public and nearly two dozen judges and lawyers were engaged. However, torture could be used to extract confessions.

Two cases were brought. The second one lasted almost a year. On 29 October 1390, Jehan de Ruilly accused 34-year-old Jehenne de Brigue, also known as La Cordière, of being a witch because she had used sorcery to heal him. Ruilly had been given one week to live and Brigue told him that he had been hexed by Gilette, the mother of his two children. Brigue helped Ruilly make a wax doll of Gilette and suckle two toads. Ruilly then recovered after Brigue had 'unhexed' him.

In response, Brigue claimed that he had no knowledge of witchcraft. However, she did admit knowing a woman named Marion from Rozay-en-Brie, who had taught her to cast spells. This was done by avoiding washing and saying the paternoster on Sundays. She also admitted that once, with Marion, she had used magic to help a man who had lost his purse.

When Brigue appeared in court again on 9 February 1391, she admitted that she had learned how to summon up a demon named Haussibut from her aunt. She also admitted that she had been jailed for sorcery two years before in Meaux, but had been released when she promised to give it up. But she had taken pity on Ruilly when she discovered that he was ill and had summoned Haussibut who told her of Gilette's bewitchment. He had undone the hex for the standard payment of a finger or an arm at death, some cinders from her hearth and a handful of hemp seeds.

Brigue was found guilty and sentenced to death by burning. But the sentence was postponed as she appeared to be five months pregnant. However in April, the midwife decided that she was not pregnant at all but 'bad humours had accumulated in her body, where by she had become swollen'.

On 13 June she admitted that, although she had slept with a man eight days before being arrested, she had known she was not pregnant. Three days later, the provost confirmed the original sentence. However, on 1 August, Parlement ordered the provost to re-examine the trial reports with the help of two court lawyers. The following day the trial was reopened before three members of Parlement and nine other high officials.

This time Brigue admitted that she used witchcraft two years before when Haussibut had helped her discover hidden silver at a tavern in Villeneuve-Saint-Denis. However, the court decided that she was holding something back and order that she be 'put to the question' – that is, tortured. Protesting that she had nothing more to tell, she was stripped naked and tied to a trestle. But before the torture began she confessed.

She said that she had been approached by Macette, Ruilly's wife, who had asked her to bewitch her husband so that she could be free to carry on an affair with the curate at Guerat. Macette had stopped loving her husband because he beat her. Together the two women had prepared poison from a recipe provided by Macette and made a wax doll while reciting Christian prayers.

Macette was arrested. She denied Brigue's accusations but, after being stretched on the rack, confessed. However, the court then ran into legal difficulties. Did a civil court have the jurisdiction to judge such a case? All the lawyers except one agreed that it did. The dissenter said that, as no actual harm had been done, the only offence was that of heresy, so the case should be handed over to an ecclesiastical court. One lawyer also argued that the punishment should be six months on bread and water and the pillory. The rest favoured burning.

The Parlement than stepped in and, once again, examined the question of jurisdiction. They, too, decided that the case did fall within the remit of the secular courts.

On 11 August 1391, the two defendants appeared before the court again. They repeated their confessions and the provost pronounced sentence. They were to be taken to Châtelet aux Halles were they were to be mitred as sorcerers and put in the pillory. Then they were to be led to the Pig Market where they were to be burnt alive.

But the sentence was still in doubt. The provost had to consult three lawyers of the Parlement. One ruled that, as no murder had taken place, a lengthy imprisonment was enough of a punishment. As this was a 'serious and weighty' consideration, the provost consulted five other superior lawyers, including the President of Appeals. All favoured execution.

On 17 August 1391, there was yet another hearing. Ruilly stated that he never actually saw his wife trying to poison him. However, the advocate presented in evidence a piece of a communion wafer, a splinter of wood, three leaves of periwinkle, two shoots of mustard, a piece of charcoal, hair and wax. These were shown to the prisoners. Macette explained their use in magic, but denied using them in witchcraft. The two women were burnt that same day. Seven years later, in 1398, the University of Paris declared that the witches' pact with the devil was not merely superstition but an act of heresy.

In 1428, just over the border in Switzerland, the inquisition began to investigate heresy in the cantons. Those they interrogated under brutal torture began to talk of devil-worshipping witches who flew from village to village at night. As those who did not confess under torture frequently died, in order to survive the interrogation, defendants began admitting making pacts with the devil and using the powers Satan gave them to make men impotent and women barren, devastate crops and drain cows of their milk. The devil usually appeared in the form of a black animal. His followers had nocturnal sabbats where they killed and ate children, both their own and other people's. As a result between one and two hundred people were burnt.

People on the French side of the Alps also began confessing to conjuring up the devil. He would appear as a black animal or a black man, dressed in black – though he could change his sex when having sexual intercourse with devotees. Sabbats began to include a certain amount of dancing about naked, kissing the backside or penis of the devil and saying the Nicene Creed backwards. The devil also began to leave a mark on the flesh of his victims, which the inquisitors hunted for. Between 1428 and 1450, at Briançon alone, 110 women and 57 men were burnt alive as witches.

Joan of Arc was charged with witchcraft and burnt at the stake in 1431, though again this was political. Afterwards one of her followers, the legendary French knight Gilles de Rais – the original upon which the folk-tale character Bluebeard was based – retired to his estates in Brittany. There, he squandered his fortune on art and lavish court life. When his family obtained a decree from the king to prevent him from selling off or mortgaging any more of his inheritance, he turned to witchcraft. He gathered around him a group of devil worshippers and started practising ritual magic in the cellars of his chateau at Tiffauges. His servant, Poitou, was sent out to procure children usually boys between six and twelve. The children were tortured and sexually abused. Then they were killed, often at the point of orgasm. Once they were dead, their mutilated bodies would be sexually assaulted again, then ritually burnt. De Rais was arrested and charged with witchcraft. Under threat of torture, he confessed that he and his followers murdered over 800 children in the name of Satan. Sentenced to be hanged, his repentance and the resignation with which he went to the gallows were acclaimed at the time as an example of Christian penitence.

Around that time in Bern a judge named Peter burned many witches of both sexes and drove others out of the diocese of Lausanne. A young man and his wife were arrested. When they refused to confess, the judge let them go, only have them arrested again. This time they were taken to separate prisons. The youth then declared, 'If I can obtain absolution for my sins, I will freely lay bear all I know about witchcraft, for I see that I have death to expect.'

When he was assured by the inquisitors that, if he truly repented, he would be given absolution for his sins, he 'gladly offered himself to death and disclosed the methods of primeval infection'. He then explained the 'ceremony of his seduction':

First, on a Sunday, before the holy water was consecrated, the future disciple with his masters must go into the church, and there in their presence must renounce Christ and his faith, baptism, and the church universal. Then he must do homage to the magisterulus, that is, to the little master (for so, and not otherwise, they call the devil). Afterwards he drinks from a flask filled with the blood of murdered infants; and, this done, he forthwith feels himself to conceive and hold within himself an image of our art and the chief rites of this sect. After this fashion was I seduced; and my wife also, whom I believe of so great pertinacity that she will endure the flames rather than confess the least whit of the truth; but, alas, we are both guilty.

The young man was believed because, after confession, he was seen to die in great contrition. But his wife, though convicted by the testimony of witnesses, would not confess even under torture. When the fire was prepared for her by her executioner, she 'uttered in most evil words a curse upon him, and so was burned'.

Normandy

The action then moved to Normandy. In 1453, the inquisition at Evreux sentenced Guillaume Edeline, the prior of Saint-Germain-en-Laye, to imprisonment for life and beyond for intercourse with a *succubus*, flying on a broomstick and kissing a goat under its tail. And Robert Olive was burnt at Falaise in 1456 for flying to sabbats.

In 1459, the inquisition organised a full-scale witch hunt at Arras. However, witchcraft had still not been clearly defined and the accusations were founded on the charges brought against the Waldensians – or the *Vaudois* in French – that is, worshipping the devil and eating human flesh. '*Aller en vaudois*' became the expression used for going to a sabbat.

A condemned prisoner named Robinet de Vaulx denounced a feeble-minded woman named Deniselle Grensières. She was seized by the inquisitor Pierre le Broussart, who tortured her several times. Eventually, she confessed, naming four other woman and the painter

Jehan la Vitte, who was also known as *Abbé-de-peu-de-sens* – 'Father Little-Sense'. To avoid naming names under torture, Vitte tried to cut his tongue out, but only succeeded in lacerating his month. And as he could still write, he was forced to answer questions. According to the contemporary chronicler Jacques du Clercq, he revealed that the men and women involved found themselves suddenly transported to a meeting place where they found the devil in human form, though his face was never revealed. He told them that they must serve him, then made them all kiss his backside. He gave them a few coins and laid on a lavish banquet. Afterwards, the lights went out – 'each one took a partner and knew each other carnally'. Then they were all transported home again. Another contemporary tract, written in Latin in May 1460, includes a detailed description of the witches' orgies.

The evidence was reported to Canon Grégoire Nicoli and Dr Gilles Cartier, two theological experts in Cambrai, for review. They recommended leniency as neither murder or desecration of the host was involved. Broussart ignored this advice.

On 9 May 1460, Jehan la Vitte, Deniselle Grenières and three of the women she had named – the fourth had committed suicide in prison – were arraigned on a rostrum in front of the bishop's palace, where they were declared to be heretics and force to wear the heretic's mitre decorated with devils. Broussart went on to detail their crimes – excluding the charges of copulating with the devil 'lest innocent ears should be pricked by such heinous offences'. They had trampled on the cross, worshipped the devil and flown on sticks. Protesting their innocence, they were handed over to the secular authorities and burnt.

Broussart now had a list of names that he had forced from these condemned witches and began rounding them up. According to Clercq, 'Many notable people were imprisoned, as well as lesser folk, mad women and others, who were so horribly tortured and terribly tormented that some admitted they had done exactly what they were accused of. They also said that, at their night-time meetings, they had seen many gentlefolk, prelates, judges and other adminstraters of counties and towns.'

The poor were burnt. Some of the wealthy and influential managed to buy their way out of trouble. Others were promised that, if they confessed, they would be able to keep both their life and their property. This promise was not kept. The bishopric seized their goods, while their feudal overlord took over their estates.

Public opinion, however, began to turn against Broussart. When a number of clergymen urged him to declare an amnesty, he refused. But by the end of the year, the merchants of the town found that, with all the goods that were being seized, it was impossible to honour business contracts and the economy of Arras was suffering. Broussart appealed to the Duke of Burgundy, Philip the Good, for help. But then the Bishops of Paris and Amiens, along with the Archbishop of Rheims began dismissing charges of witchcraft brought before them on the grounds that sabbats were a figment of the imagination.

The Parlement of Paris demanded that some of those Broussart had imprisoned be freed. In 1461, the Bishop of Arras, Jean Jouffrey, who had been away in Rome, returned home and freed the rest. On 10 July 1461, the Parlement of Paris declared that Broussart had acted 'in error and against the order and dignity of justice'. The Inquisition of Arras had conducted 'a false trial and one without due process'. It also condemned the 'inhuman and cruel interrogation and tortures of the Inquisition, such as squeezing the limbs, putting the soles of the feet in the fire and making the accused swallow oil and vinegar'. And the Parlement recommended that prayers be said for those who had been put to death.

This did not stop the witch hunt though. In 1479, a priest in Mâcon was put to death for sorcery and dabbling in the diabolic arts. And in 1490, King Charles VIII issued an edict condemning fortune tellers, enchanters and necromancers. Their property would be forfeit.

The Inquisitor General of Besançon, a Dominican friar named Jean Boin, was then on a roll. In 1529, he secretly visited the village of Anjeux in the bailiwick of Luxeil, Franche-Comté, and noted down the gossip of the villagers. They centred on twenty-seven-year-old Desle la Mansenée, the wife of Jean de la Tour. Although none of the villagers could bring evidence to prove their charges, there were sufficient number for Jean Boin to act. A typical accusation read:

Antoine Godin, of Anjeux, aged about forty, remembering back some thirty years, as he says from a clear distant recollection, sworn and questioned like the preceding on what was formerly said, says and deposes on his oath to have knowledge that Desle la Mansenée is held and reputed in the said neighbourhood to be a witch, a wicked common woman and a sorcerer... He says furthermore to have heard that Mazelin, son of the said Desle, had said in the fields that his mother went backwards on a twisted willow stick to the meeting. He also testified that he had heard people say Desle had taken three threads from the spinning staff of a woman called Prince, while she was in labour, and said that she was going to use them for sorcery and witchcraft in Anjeux... In May his testimony was read back to him and he persisted and does persist in his disposition.

Some two dozen villagers made similar allegations and, in March 1529, Desle was interrogated in front of a six-man commission, which included the Governor of Luxeuil, the local Lieutenant and the parish priest. Throughout long sessions of question, Desle maintained her innocence. But Boin was not convinced. He had her jailed, then turned over to the civil authorities to be tortured by squassation.

Desle was stripped, then her arms were tied behind her with a rope attached to a pulley. Then she was hoisted in the air and kept there for a considerable period. This was the so-called 'strappado' and was used as a second degree of torture. It was first used in witch trials in Piedmont in 1474. The strappado was banned in England, but was used in Scotland.

However, squassation – the third and final degree of torture – was even worse. In the strappado the victim was dropped, then jerked to a halt a few feet from the ground. In France, stones or weights were attached to the feet – usually between 40 and 220 pounds in weight, though in Mâcon 660-pound weights were used. Philip Limboch left a detailed description of the effects of this torture in his *History of the Inquistion* published in 1692:

The prisoner has his hands bound behind his back, and weights tied to his feet, and then he is drawn up on high, until his head reaches the pulley. He is kept hanging in this manner for some time so that all his joints and limbs may be dreadfully stretched by the great weights hanging on his feet. Then suddenly he is let down with a jerk, by slacking the rope, but kept from coming quite to the ground, by which terrible shake his arms and legs are all disjointed, whereby he is put to the most exquisite pain – the shock which he receives by the sudden stop of his fall and the weight at his feet stretching this whole body more intensely and cruelly.

Any more than three applications was thought to result in certain death.

Desle la Mansenée soon confessed. She said that the devil had promised her wealth, but had failed to deliver. She had denied the Catholic faith, danced at a sabbat – naming others who had been there – and copulated with the devil, who was as cold as ice. She had also flown on an anointed stick, made hailstorms and poisoned cattle using a black powder.

When the authorities were consulted, they decided that she should be sentenced only for homicide, heresy and renouncing her Catholic faith – not for witchcraft. So on 18 December 1529, she was hanged. But her body was burned just to be on the safe side.

In 1556, a woman accused of witchcraft was burnt alive by mistake at Bièvres, near Laon – the executioner had forgotten to strangle her first. But this did not matter. According to Jean Bodin, whose great work *Démonomania* was published in Paris in 1580, the mistake revealed the secret judgement of God. Bodin believed that in witchcraft trials 'one must not adhere to the ordinary rules of prosecution, proof of such evil is so obscure and difficult that not one out of a million witches would be accused or punished if regular legal procedures were followed'. As in the case of Desle la Mansenée, the names of accusers should be kept secret. Children should be forced to testify against their parents and a person once accused should never be acquitted – 'unless the falsity of the accuser or informer is clearer than the sun'. And judges who refused to execute convicted witches should themselves be put to death. As a trial judge Bodin tortured children and invalids. No punishment was too cruel for witches. He advocated branding and the use of hot irons. His only real disappointment was the end came too quickly for them – burning a witch only took half an hour or so.

In 1557, another forty witches were burnt at Toulouse. Three men and a woman were burnt for witchcraft at Poiters in 1564 for kissing a goat and dancing back to back. Then in 1571, the magician Trois-Echelles, who announced that there were a hundred thousand witches in France alone, was executed in Paris.

Between 1572 and 1620, 152 witches were burnt in Thann in Alsace – though Alsace was not formally part of France until 1681. Over 200 witches had been burnt at St. Amarin by 1596. And the Attorney General of Lorrraine, Nicholas Remy personally condemned 900 witches between 1581 and 1591.

In 1579, the Church Council at Melun announced: 'Every charlatan and diviner, and other who practise necromany, pyromancy, chiromancy, hydromancy will be published by death.' And two years later, the Church Council and Rouen banned books of sorcery on pain of excommunication.

In 1582, the Dominican Inquisitor Sebastian Michaëlis pronounced sentence on eighteen men and women at Avignon in Latin, a language it is unlikely they understood. His verdict is worth quoting in full:

> We... having considered the counts wherewith you stand charged and accused before us, and having examined both the statements of yourselves and your accomplices, and your own confessions made before us and often sworn according to law, as well as depositions and accusations of the witnesses and other legitimate proof, basing our judgement on what has been said and done during this trial.
>
> We lawfully agree that you and your accomplices have denied the one and triune God, the creator and maker of all things, and that you have worshipped the devil, the ancient and implacable enemy of mankind.

You have vowed yourselves to him forever, and have renounced your most holy baptism and those who were your sponsors therein, together with your part of paradise and the eternal heritage which out Lord Jesus Christ bought for you and the whole human race by his death.

All these you renounced before the said devil existing in the species of a man, and that raging devil baptised you anew with water, which you accepted, and you did change the name give you in the baptism at the holy font, and so took and received another false name in the guise of baptism.

And as a pledge of your fealty to the devil gave him a fragment and particle of your clothing; and that the father of lies should take care to delete and obliterate you from the book of life, at his order and behest you with your own hands wrote your names in the black book there prepared, the roll of those damned to eternal death.

And that he might bind you with stouter bonds to so great perfidy and impiety, he branded each of you with his mark or stigmata as belonging to him, and you did swear homage and obedience to his orders within a circle (which is a symbol of divinity) traced upon the earth (which is God's footstool); and you and your accomplices bound yourselves to tread under foot the image of the Lord and the cross.

And in obedience to Satan, with the help of a staff, smeared with some nefarious ointment given you by the devil himself, and placed between your legs you were enabled to fly through the air at dead of night to the place ordained, at an hour fit for vilest criminals, and on stated days you were so carried and transported by the devil himself.

And there in the common synagogue of all the witches, sorcerers, heretics, conjurers and devil worshipers, you did kindle a foul fire, and after many rejoicings, lively dancings, eating and drinking, and games in honour of your president Beelzebub, the prince of devils, in the shape and appearance of a deformed and hideous black goat, you adored him in deed and word as God and did approach him on bended knees as suppliants and offered him lighted candles of pitch; and (fie, for shame!) with the greatest reverence you did kiss with sacrilegious mouth his most foul and beastly backside; and did call upon him by the name of the true God, and invoke his aid to avenge you on all who had offended you or denied your requests.

And, taught by him, you did wreak your spite in *maleficia* and charms against both men and beasts, and did murder many new-born children, and with the help of the said serpent Satan you did afflict mankind with curses, loss of milk, the wasting sickness, and other most grave diseases.

And your own children, many of them with your own knowledge and consent, you did by the said *maleficia* suffocate, pierce and kill, and finally you dug them up secretly by night in the cemetery, and so carried them to the aforesaid synagogue and college of witches.

Then you did offer them to the prince of devils sitting on his throne, and did draw off their fat to keep for your use, and cut off their heads, hands and feet, and did cook and stew them in a trunk, and roast them and at the bidding and hest of your aforesaid evil father did eat and damnably devour them.

Then, adding sin to sin, you the men did copulate with *succubi*, and you the women did fornicate with *incubi*; by most icy coitus with demons you did commit the unspeakable crime of sodomy.

And, most hateful of all, at the bidding of the aforesaid serpent thrust forth from paradise, you did keep in your mouths the most holy sacrament of the Eucharist received by you in the sacred church of God with the greatest contumely, impiety and contempt; you did dishonour our true and holy God, and promote the glory, honour, triumph and kingdom of the devil himself, and worship, honour and glorify him with all honour, praise, majesty, dignity, authority and adoration.

All of which most grave, abhorred and unspeakable crimes

are directly contumacious and contemptuous of Almighty God, the creator of all.

Wherefore we, Brother Florus, provincial of the order of Friars Preachers, Doctor of Sacred Theology and Inquisitor General for the holy faith within the jurisdiction of Avignon, having fear of God before our eyes, sitting in tribunal, have caused to be written this our definitive sentence according to the lawful precept of revered theologians and jurists, piously having invoked the names of out Lord Jesus Christ and the Blessed Virgin Mary, we say, declare, pronounce and formally sentence all you above named and your accomplices who have been or are truly apostates, idolaters, rebels from the most holy faith, deniers and mockers of Almighty God, sodomites, and perpetrators of the foulest crimes, adulterers, fornicators, sorcerers, witches, profaners, heretics, workers of the evil eye, murderers, infanticides, worshipers of the devil, satanists, adherents of diabolical and infernal law and damnable and reprobate faith, blasphemers, perjurers, infamous livers and those convicted of all the evil crimes and offences.

Wherefore by this sentence we relax you and your accomplices as limbs of Satan to the secular court, actually and effectually, for most worthy and legitimate punishment according to its own secular provisions.

Relaxing or remitting a convicted witch to a secular court was standard procedure. The Inquisition never executed those it found guilty. They were handed over to the civil authorities with a technical recommendation for clemency and the practical advice that clemency by a secular judge would be taken as an indication of his own heresy.

In 1584, the Church Council at Bourges decided that the death penalty should be passed on anyone consulting the devil. But fourteen witches at Tours appealed to King Henry III, who sent his doctor to examine them. He found no devil's marks on them.

Henry III's doctor concluded that the witches of Tours were 'poor stupid people'.

'Our advice was to purge them with hellebore rather than to punish them,' he wrote, 'and the Parlement [of Paris] discharged them as we recommended.'

As a result the king was accused of protecting witches.

Being arrested for witchcraft could be an expensive business. In most cases, in France, the cost of the arrest, torture and trial were not born by the state. Everything, including a banquet for the officials after the execution, was charged to the victim and deducted from their estate, which was usually forfeit anyway. If the accused was too poor, the local council had to pay up. After Cathin Joyeuse was arrested in Toul, near Nancy, on 14 November 1597, she was presented with an itemised bill for 104 francs for less than one month's imprisonment. This included thirteen francs for wine for her and the guards, six gros for straw to sleep on and two gros for carrying her belongings. The women who shaved her ready for the torture charged one franc. The torturer charged twenty. The guards who guarded her until she was tortured charged 3 francs 6 gros. And the man who had to go to Nancy to fetch the torturer charged 4 francs 4 gros. She later received a second bill covering the remainder of her stay in prison – and her execution.

Trials in Franche-Comté – then still part of the Roman Empire – rarely came in at under five hundred francs. After the execution of Adrienne d'Heur on 11 September 1646, for example, the local innkeeper David Morlot charged twenty-five francs for providing breakfast for the major, the provost, the scribe, the jailer and four sergeants. Another 15 francs 9 gros had to be paid for the breakfast and dinner of the burghers and other notables who watched the execution and twenty-six francs were distributed as honorariums among other minor officials.

Lycanthropy

There were mass witch trials in Béarn in 1508. Then in 1521, three werewolves stood trial in Poligny. A traveller had been attacked by a wolf, which he managed to fight off. He followed the wounded animal to a hut, where he found the wife of Michel Verdung bathing her husband's wounds. The Inquisitor General of Besançon, a Dominican friar named

Jean Boin, was called in and Verdung confessed, naming the shepherd Pierre Bourget, who also confessed. Bourget said that, in 1502, his flocks had been scattered by a terrible storm. While searching for them, he came upon three black horsemen. One of them, named Moyset, promised to help him if Bourget agreed to serve his lord and master. Soon after Bourgot found his sheep. A week later he again met the horseman, who revealed that he was a follower of the devil. Bourget was forced to renounce Christianity and swear fealty to the devil by kissing him on the back of the left hand, which was black and cold as ice.

Two years later Bourget drifted back to Christianity when Michel Verdung, another servant of the devil, turned up. He promised Bourget gold if he would returned to the devil's fold. Together they attended a sabbat where everyone carried a green taper. Verdung then ordered Bourget to strip and applied an ointment that turned him into a wolf. Two hours later, he applied another balm which turned him back into a human again. Under torture, Bourget said that he had made several attacks while he was a wolf. A seven-year-old boy he attacked had screamed so loudly that he had had to return to human form to escape detection. He had eaten the flesh of a four-year-old girl, which he found delicious. He had also eaten the flesh of a nine-year-old girl whose neck he had broken.

Another man, Philibert Mentot, was also named. All three reported that they had mated with real wolves and that they had 'had as much pleasure in the act as if they had copulated with their wives'. The three were burnt.

There was also an epidemic of lycanthropy at the end of the sixteenth century, with a number of werewolves being tried at Orleans in 1583. In the Auvergne mountains in 1588 a hunter wounded a wolf which turned out to be the wife of a nobleman. She was burned at Riom, where two men were burned in 1597 for making ligatures. A ligature was a spell made by tying a knot in a cord of a strip of leather which rendered a man impotent or prevented a women making love. Sometimes herbs were also administered. According to the *Malleus Maleficarum*, German witches could hide a man's penis in their belly, while in Scotland in 1590, Janet Clark and Janet Grant were convicted of taking away the genitals from some men and giving them to others. Such beliefs were widespread as Gratian, the Italian monk who wrote the Church's Canon Laws around 1140, had said that God had given the devil power over the genitals.

In 1598, the feeble-minded, epileptic beggar Jacques Roulet was accused of killed a boy named Cornier after he was found half-naked and covered in blood in the bushes near the fifteen-year-old's mutilated body. Under questioning, he admitted the crime and said that he had turned into a wolf. He was sentenced to death, but appealed to the Parlement of Paris, who commuted the sentence to two years in the insane asylum at St.-German-des-Près and religious instruction 'which he had forgotten in his utter poverty'. However, Jacques d'Autun was burned at Rennes for lycanthropy that year and, on 14 December, the Parlement of Paris sentenced a tailor from Châlons to death as a were-wolf. He lured children into his shop or murdered them in the woods and ate their flesh. A cask of bones was found in his cellar, but the details of the case were so terrible that the judges ordered the court records to be burnt. Judge Henri Boguet, however, preserved the record when he condemned three members of the Gandillon family for lycan-throphy and witchcraft in St.-Claude in the Jura.

Sixteen year-old Benoît Bidel of Naizan was climbing a tree to pick fruit when a tailless wolf attacked his young sister who he had left sitting by the trunk. He climbed down to defend her but, in the strug-gle, the wolf grabbed his knife and stabbed him in the neck. Before he died of his wounds he said that he had noticed that instead of front paws, the wolf had hands. Perrenette Gandillon, who confessed she was a wolf, was found nearby and was torn to pieces by an angry mob. Her sister Antoinette was also accused of being a werewolf, making hail, attending a sabbat and sleeping with the devil who appeared in the form of a goat.

Her brother was accused of witchcraft, making hail, enticing chil-dren to a sabbat and, as a werewolf, killing and eating animals and men. Under torture he explained, 'Satan clothed them in a wolf's skin, and that they went on all fours, and ran about the country, chasing now a person and now an animals, according to the guidance of their appetite.'

On the Thursday before Easter, a second brother, Pierre, was found lying in bed in a cataleptic state. When he was awoken he confessed to going to a sabbat of werewolves. His son Georges admitted covering himself with ointment to turn himself into a wolf. In the company of his aunts, he had killed two goats.

Judge Bouget visited them in jail. He wrote:

> *In company with the Lord Claude Meynier, our recorder, I have seen those I have named go on all fours in a room just as they did when they were in the fields, but they said it was impossible for them to turn themselves into wolves as they had not oint- ment and they had lost the power to do so by being in prison. I have further noticed that they were all scratched on the face and hands and legs; and that Pierre Gandillon was so much dis- figured in this way that he bore hardly any resemblance to a man and struck all those who looked at him with horror.*

Bouget was convinced. All three were burnt.

In a village in Bordeaux in 1603 three girls were tending their sheep when they were surprised by a boy named Jean Grenier who told them he was a werewolf. He told the eldest of them, Jeanne Gaboriant, that a man 'gave me a wolf-skin cape; he wraps it around me and every Monday, Friday and Sunday, and for about an hour at dusk every other day, I am a wolf, a werewolf. I have killed dogs and drunk their blood; but little girls taste better and their flesh is tender and sweet, their blood rich and warm.'

Several children had been killed in the St-Sever district of Gascony so the district attorney of Roche Chalès brought the boy up before a local judge. Jean admitted being a werewolf and accused others of lycan- thropy too. The case was referred to a higher court who had Jean's house searched for the ointment that turned men into wolves. None was found. Nevertheless Jean's father and a neighbour named del Thillaire were arrested. Even though Jean's father protested that his son was an idiot who had claimed to have slept with all the women in the village, Jean was sentenced to be hanged and have his body burnt.

Under torture, Jean's father and Monsieur del Thillare admitted seeking out little girls – but only to 'play with not to eat'.

The Parlement of Bordeaux then stepped in and the case was reviewed by Judge de Lancre. He deposed Jean who said, 'When I was ten or eleven years old, my neighbour, del Thillaire, introduced me in the depths of the forest to the master of the forest, a black man, who signed me with his nail and then gave me and del Thillaire an ointment and a wolf skin. From that time I have run about the country as a wolf.'

De Lancre went on:

> When questioned about the children who he said he had killed and eaten as a wolf, he said that once, on the way between St.-Coutras and St.-Anlaye, he had entered an empty house in a small village, the name of which he did not remember. There he had found a child asleep in a cradle. As there was no one there to stop him, he dragged the baby out of the cradle, took it out into the garden, leapt over the hedge, then devoured as much of it as satisfied his hunger. He gave the rest to a wolf. In the parish of St.-Antoine-de-Pizon he had attacked a little girl as she was keeping sheep. She was dressed in black frock; he did not know her name. He tore her flesh with his nails and teeth and ate her. Six weeks before his arrest, he had fallen on another child near the stone bridge in the same parish. In Eparon, he had attacked the dog of a Monsieur Millon and would have killed it, if the owner had not come out with his sword in his hand.
>
> Jean said that he had the wolf skin in his possession, and that he went out hunting for children at the command of his lord, the master of the forest. Before the transformation he smeared himself with the ointment, which he kept in a small pot, and hid his clothes in the bushes.

The Parlement decided that Jean was suffering from an illness brought on by evil spirits and he was sentenced to life imprisonment in a local monastery. In his judgement De Lancre said:

*In conclusion, the court takes into account the young age and
the imbecility of this boy, who is so stupid and idiotic that children of seven and eight years old normally show more
intelligence, who had been ill fed in every respect and who is
so dwarfed that he is not a tall as a ten-year-old... Here is a tall
young lad abandoned and driven out by his father, who has a
cruel stepmother instead of a real mother, who wanders over
the field without a counsellor and without anyone to take an
interest in him, begging his bread, who has never had any religious training, whose real nature was corrupted by evil
promptings, need and despair, and whom the devil made his
prey.*

Seven years later, de Lancre visited the monastery of the Franciscan
Cordeliers at Bordeaux where Jean had been confined. He found Jean
still to be small in stature, very shy and unwilling to look anyone in the
face. His eyes were deep-set and restless, his teeth long and protruding,
his nails black and worn away in places, and his mind completely blank.
He seemed unable to understand even the simplest things. He still
maintained he was a werewolf and that would like to eat children if he
could. He also liked looking at wolves. Later that year, in November
1610, Jean Grenier died, it is said, 'a good Christian'.

'A Penitent Woman'

The following year there was an outbreak of the possession of nuns in
Aix-en-Provence which attracted attention right across western Europe.
Reports were immediately translated and distributed and the Grand
Inquisitor Sebastian Michaëlis published his own self-serving account.
The English edition, published in London in 1613, was called, somewhat long-windedly, *The Admirable History of a Penitent Woman who
was seduced by a Magician in the Country of Provence in France, and
the End of the said Magician*. Fortunately a thousand-page account of
the trial survived in the Bibliothèque Nationale in Paris, which sets the
record straight.

The story began in 1605 when 12-year-old Madeleine de Demandolx de la Palud, the nervous and deeply religious daughter of a wealthy, aristocratic Provençal family, entered the newly formed Ursuline convent in Aix-en-Provençe. There was a tiny group of just six nuns there, all of noble birth. The founder of the convent and their spiritual director was Father Jean-Bapiste Romillon, a Jesuit who was also super-intendent of the convent in Marseilles.

After two years in the convent, Madeleine became depressed and was sent back to her parents in Marseilles. There under the guidance of Louis Gaufridi, the parish priest of Accoules in Marseilles and a friend of the family, her spirits improved. Although he was of humble birth, Gaufridi was popular with the wealthy families of the area. He was playful, even boisterous and had been known, on occasion, to toss soft cheeses at other guests across the dinner table. Some two dozen women, married and single, chose him as their confessor and six of them, it was thought, were in love with him.

Even so, although Gaufridi was popular with the ladies, he does not seem to have been as lecherous as most priests of that time. It was a tra-dition, for example, for a monk to have a party after his first mass. This was paid for by a local family whose daughter acted as a 'Maraine' – that is, a partner for the new priest during the festivities whose duties included dancing, kissing and 'other liberties'. However, Father Gaufridi refused to hold such a party and his fellow monks waylaid him on the road and beat him with clubs they had concealed under their habits.

Madeleine, now 14, fell for the 34-year-old Gaufridi and he visited her often. One day, he stayed with Madeleine for an hour and a half in the house while everyone else was out. During that time, she said, he had 'stolen her most beautiful rose'. News of this came to the ears of Catherine de Gaumer, the mother superior of the Ursuline convent at Marseilles. She warned Gaufridi and Madeleine's mother of the danger of this liaison.

When Madeleine entered the convent at Marseilles as a novice the following year, she confessed Father Gaufridi's intimacies with her. So Mother Catherine sent her back to Aix, where Gaufridi could not visit her. After a year or two, the 16-year-old Madeleine began to suffer from convulsive cramps and severe shaking fits, and saw visions of the devil. Just before Christmas 1609 she smashed a crucifix during confession.

Father Romillon tried exorcism, but it failed and the symptoms began to spread. Three other nuns went into convulsions. In June 1610, Father Romillon and another priest questioned Gaufridi about Madeleine. He denied having sex with her. But as Romillon's exorcisms continued, Madeleine began accusing Father Gaufridi of denying god, giving her a 'green devil' as a familiar and having sex with her since she was 13 – later, since she was 9. She said he had told her, 'Since I would enjoy your favours, I will give you a drink made of a special powder to make sure that any babies you may get by me will not look like me at all, so no one will suspect me of immorality.'

Soon the hysteria spread to five other nuns. Jealous of the richer and more notorious Madelaine, Sister Louise Capeau did her best to outdo Madelaine's symptoms of possession. Father Romillon took the two of them to see Sebastian Michaëlis, the aged inquisitor who was still famous for burning eighteen witches at Avignon. Michaëlis tried public exorcism at the celebrated shrine of St. Mary Magdalene in the grotto at Ste-Baume, but had no more success than Romillon. So the two girls were taken to the Royal Convent of St. Maximin to see the celebrated exorcist François Domptius, a Flemish Dominican. In front of a crowd of spectators, Louise suddenly developed a deep bass voice and revealed that three devils – Vérin, Grésil and Sonnillon – possessed her. She also said that Madeleine was possessed by Asmodeus, Astoroth, Baalberith, Beelzebub, Leviathan and 6,661 other devils. This was a godsend for Michaëlis, who set about creating a system of ranks for devils.

Since devils are all ex-angels, they fall into the three hierarchies of the angelic court worked out in the fourth century. This comes in three hierarchies: the first comprises Seraphim, Cherubim and Thrones; the second Dominions, Principalities and Powers; and the third Virtues, Archangels and Angels. And one demon possessing Madeleine was also kind enough to tell Michaëlis which angels in heaven were assigned to oppose each devil.

Michaëlis' first hierarchy of devils comprised:

1. Beelzebub, the Prince of Seraphim and next to Lucifer. He, Lucifer and Leviathan were the first three of the choir of Seraphim to fall. The fourth, Michael, resisted and many good angels followed him, so he is now the chief angel. While Lucifer, when Christ descended into Hell, was chained up there, but commands all...Beelzebub tempts man with pride. And as John the Baptist holds Lucifer's place in heaven...by his singular humility, Francis is Beelzebub's adversary in paradise.

2. Leviathan is also a Prince of Seraphim and is the ringleader of heretics, tempting men with sins that are directly repugnant to the faith. His adversary is Peter the Apostle.

3. Asmodeus is of the same order. He continues a Seraphim to this day – that is, he burns with the desire to tempt men with his swine of luxuriousness, and is prisoner of wantons. His adversary is also John the Baptist.

4. Baalberith is a Prince of Cherubim. He tempts men to commit homicide, and be quarrelsome, contentious and blasphemous. His adversary is Barnabas.

5. Astaroth, Prince of Thrones, is always desirous to sit idle and be at ease. He tempts men with idleness and sloth. His adversary is Bartholemew.

6. Verrine is also one of the Thrones, and next in place to Astaroth, and tempts men with impatience. His adversary is Dominic.

7. Gressil is the third in the order of Thrones, and tempts men with impurity and uncleanness. His adversary is Bernard.

8. Sonneillon is the fourth in the order of Thrones, and tempts men with hatred against their enemies. His adversary is Stephen.

The second hierarchy of devils comprised:

9. Carreau, Prince of Powers, tempts men with hardness of heart. His adversaries are Vincent and Vince Ferrer.

10. Carnivean is also a Prince of Powers, and does tempt men to obscenity and shamelessness. His adversary is John the Evangelist.

11. Oeillet is a Prince of Dominions. He tempts men to break the vow of poverty. His adversary is Martin.

12. Rosier is the second in the order of Dominions, and by his sweet and sugared words, he tempts men to fall in love. His adversary in heaven is Basil, who would not listen to amorous and enchanting language.

The third hierarchy of devils comprised:

13. Verrier is the Prince of Principalities, and tempts men against the vow of obedience, and makes the neck stiff and hard as iron, and incapable of stooping under the yoke of obedience. His adversary is Bernard.

14. Belias, Prince of the order of Virtues, tempts men with arrogance. His adversary is Francis de Paul for his great and dove-like humility. He also tempts gentle women to dress up in the latest fashions, to make wantons of their children and to prattle to them while mass is being said and so divert them from the service of God.

15. Olivier, Prince of Archangels, tempts men with cruelty and mercilessness towards the poor. His adversary is Lawrence.

16. Iuvart is Prince of Angels, but according to Michaëls he was not present in the body of Madeleine but was in another body of another nun at Louviers.

These were the principal devils, according to Michaëlis's *Admirable History*. But just how many devils there are in total is a tricky theological question. St Macarius of Alexandria prayed to God to let him see the hosts of evil. When his eyes were opened, he saw a multitude of devils 'as numerous as bees'. In 1459, Alphonsus de Spina calculated that one-third of the original angels had become devils – making 133,306,668 in all. In 1567 another demonologist worked out that there were sixty-six princes of hell commanding 6,660,000 devils. Another said seventy-nine princes commanding 7,409,127 devils; another 72 princes and 7,405,926 devils. But before the end of the sixteenth century that number had increased to more than half the population of the world. However, Madeleine seems to have been possessed by the main ones and Beelzebub, speaking through her during exorcism, said, 'It is true, Madeleine, you are a witch and have performed whatsoever belongs thereunto in great solemnity. You have renounced God at three masses, one at midnight, another at dawn, and the third at high mass.'

The devil Vérin, speaking through Louise, identified the cause of the possession, 'You [Madeleine] were deceived by a priest who was your confession. He is from Marseilles and is called Louis...'

Louis Gaufridi was summoned to try exorcising the girls as well. He knew nothing of exorcism and when he arrived at Ste-Baume on 30 December 1610 the girls mocked him for his ignorance. Louise then accused him of being a magician. He responded hastily, 'If I were a witch, I would certainly give my soul to a thousand devils.'

This was enough to get thrown into jail. Meanwhile Madeleine accused him of all the vilest offences known to demonologists including 'praying with an unclean heart'. His house was searched, but nothing was found – perhaps because he had enough friends among the Capuchin friars to stop anything being planted. Reluctantly, Michaëlis had to let him go.

Gaufridi was a popular priest and most of his colleagues thought that he was entirely innocent. However, he was determined to clear his name. He appealed to the Bishop of Marseilles and the Pope. He also petitioned to have the Ursuline convents closed down, particularly the one at Ste-Baume where Madeleine was being held.

Meanwhile Madeleine's condition was deteriorating. She sang love songs, laughed, danced, had visions, neighed like a horse, disrupted services by snatching birettas and tearing a chasuble – and she told tales of sabbats, where the participants practised sodomy and ate little children. Beelzebub caused 'her bones to crack and grate one against the other'. She brought up a frothy substance that looked like a mixture of 'honey and pitch' and her bowels 'turned topsy-turvey... so that the sounds of these unnatural motions were easily heard. When these tortures were ended, then did [the devils] cast her into a dead sleep or lethargy, so that she seemed stark dead'.

While Gaufridi attempted to clear himself, Michaëlis put pressure on to have the accused sorcerer punished. The ecclesiastical authorities seemed loath to take the matter any further, but the president of Parlement of Aix, Guillaume de Vait was a superstitious man and, in February 1611, opened hearings.

Louise and Madeleine spoke in Provençal, which had to be translated into French. But they obliged by going into fits in the courtroom. Madeleine cheekily insisted that the priests present show their tonsure, so that she could be sure they were ordained. In a quiet moment, she admitted that her allegations were 'all imaginings, illusions and had not a word of truth to them'. She also admitted to being in love with Gaufridi.

'Oh, if his tongue could carry to her ears a friendly word, what happiness,' she said.

Then suddenly she was seized with lascivious tremblings 'representing the sexual act with violent movements of the lower part of her belly'.

Devil's marks were found on her feet and under her left breast, which the doctors could stick pins without bleeding or pain. But these marks would disappear without warning. Every day she would contradict herself, first accusing Gaufridi, then retracting what she had said. Then she grew depressed and tried to kill herself twice.

Meanwhile Father Gaufridi had been kept in heavy fetters in an underground dungeon infested with rats and other vermin. His health was failing. After his body had been shaved, three devil's marks were found and his interrogation began. At the end of March he confessed to being a 'Prince of the Synagogue'. He admitted signing a pact with the devil in his own blood when the devil had promised him that all women would 'affect and follow' him. And he gave a detailed account of an orgiastic sabbat. A jubilant Michaëlis published a list of fifty-two diabolic offences Gaufridi had admitted to.

By this time Gaufridi had regained a little strength. He denied everything in the 'confession' published by Michaëlis.

'All are false, by him composed and invented to give more colour and belief to what he says,' said Gaufridi.

This, of course, was ignored and on 18 April 1611 the court found him guilty, by his own confession, of magic, sorcery, idolatry and fornication – doctors had testified that Sister Madeleine was not a virgin. He was sentenced to be burnt alive on a pyre of bushes, which burnt more slowly than the wood that was usually used.

Appearing in court yet again on 28 April, he denied having intercourse with Madeleine, but as no one believed anything he said he would confess anything they wanted him too – yes, he had eaten roasted babies at a sabbat. The truth no longer mattered.

The death warrant was signed the following day. Then he was handed over to the church to be defrocked and degraded. Afterwards they handed him back to the Parlement of Aix so that he could be tortured to extract the names of his accomplices. Hoist in the strappado, he said, 'Oh God, I know of no accomplices. Ah, leave me I am dying.' He was hoisted in the strappado twice more, eventually admitting, 'I tell you, messieurs, no, I am not a Christian. If I said I did not know Madeleine at the sabbat, it was because I had known her before.'

Then he was subjected to squassation. Monsieur Olivier, the executioner, attached heavy weights to his feet, hoisted him to the ceiling and dropped him within inches of the floor four times. His limbs were entirely dislocated, but still he had no names to give.

Flanked by ten archers, Gaufridi publicly asked for God's pardon and that of the court. Then he was strapped to a hurdle and dragged through the crowded streets of Aix. After five hours the parade reached the Place des Prêcheurs. There, by special dispensation – probably by the Bishop of Marseilles – he was strangled before being burnt. The next day, the Chronicle of the Order of the Ursulines, announced that Madeleine de Demandolx de la Palud was cured of her diabolical possession.

But Louise Capeau was not cured. She continued naming witches and was responsible for the burning of a blind girl named Honorée on 19 July 1911. Nuns at St. Claire's in Aix became possessed. One of them, Sister Marie de Sains, had been sent to St. Bridget's in Lille. Michaëlis and Domptius set out after her, but the Archbishop of Malines intervened. Finding Sister Marie mad, she was confined to the prison of Tournai.

Madeleine herself was accused of witchcraft in 1642, when she was 49. Her family disowned her but she managed to clear herself with the aid of a small inheritance. Ten years later, she was accused again. Numerous witnesses came forward to testify against her and the devil's marks were found. On 12 December 1652, she fined heavily and sentenced to life imprisonment. Ten years later, she was released into the custody of a relative and went to live in Chateauvieux, near Fréjus, where she died on 20 December 1670, aged 77.

*

In 1631 Father Dominic Gordel, a parish priest in northeast France, was accused of witchcraft by four children and several other people who had already been convicted of witchcraft. Their evidence had been extracted by torture that stopped just short of causing death. Under Continental law, the prosecution was not required to prove that Gordel was guilty. Rather he had to prove that he was innocent, as he protested. Guilt was assumed and his refusal to confess merely demonstrated the devil's hold over him. So there was only one course open to the inquisitions. The following was read out to the court by Bishop G. de Gournay of Sitie:

> We, the Bishop of Sitie, Vicar General of Monsignor the Cardinal of Lorraine at his bishopric in Toul, having seen the trial with torture made at the request of the promoter-general of the said bishopric against Master Dominic Gordel, parish priest at Vomécourt, accused and indicted for witchcraft and other crimes and the black arts, to wit:
>
> – Preliminary testimony charged against the said priest, the oral hearings on the resultant charges, confessions, contradictions, and denials;
>
> – Verification and comparison of the evidence of the foregoing preliminary testimony with the accusations especially of Claude Cathelinotte and Hanry, wife of Didier Gaubart of Béthencourt, burned for the crime of witchcraft, who supported the charge of sorcery against the said Gordel and maintained it to the end; other accusations of Bastin Claude and Mengeotte, children of Claudon Pelletier of Hymont, also of Toussaine and Jeane, children of Jean Noël of Mataincourt, both convicted of witchcraft by their own confessions and for this reason held prisoners at Mirecourt, all of whom sustained

the charges against the said Gordel, upon confronting him, that several times they had seen him at the satanic gatherings and that he had committed acts of devilry there;

– Interrogations made of the said accused on the impieties and exorcisms committed by him, along with his replies thereto, the documentary evidence alleged by the accused, our inquiry concerning its validity, with other pieces of evidence presented for his vindication; the report of the legal proceedings and torture of the accused made today, in the presence of the doctor and the surgeon who examined his body for the devil's mark, for the judgement of the said promoter-general on the said trial, and all other relevant matters;

– After deliberation, having established full jurisdiction in the aforementioned proceedings, without prejudice to the charges established by them, we have condemned and do condemn the said Gordel, accused, to be subjected to torture, ordinary and extraordinary, by the thumbscrews, strappado and vice, in order to coerce from him information and answers about all the charges resulting from these preliminary proceedings and the naming of his accomplices and other secret charges. The whole report to be drawn up and transmitted to the said promoter-general, as required by him, for whatever judgement he shall determine.

So the hapless priest was taken away to be tortured. Afterwards a report of the torture was read into the record:

In the tower called La Joliette in the episcopal palace of Tour, 26 April 1631, at one o'clock in the afternoon, in the presence of the Reverend Master Jean Midot, Grand Archdeacon and Canon of the said church of Toul, Master Antoine d'Antan, priest-almoner of the squire of Sitie, and also Charles Mathiot, doctor of medicine, and Jean Marson, surgeon of Toul, who we asked to assist in conducting the trial and to see that no unreasonable violence by inflicted on the said Gordel. Declared to the said Gordel, after being seriously admonished about the gravity of the charges laid against him, that he should freely confess his crime without forcing us to resort to the tortures which were being prepared for him, and, after we had made him swear on the Holy Gospels of Our Lord, laying his hands on the book, speak the truth. He replied that he was no sorcerer and that he never had any pact, implicit or professed with the devil.

Upon which, we ordered Master Poirson, hangman of the town of Toul, to apply the thumbscrews to the left hand (except to the fingers used in benediction). The accused called on 'Jesus, Maria' and said that he had never been a sorcerer. Then we had the thumbscrews applied to the same fingers of the right hand, whereupon he said, 'St. Nicholas!'

Questioned if he had any kind of pact with the devil, he said no, and that he wished only to die in the arms of God. Then we caused the aforesaid screws to be applied to his big toes, at which he said he had never seen nor been at a sabbat, and cried out, 'Jesus, Maria! St. Nicholas!' and 'St. Mary, Mother of God! Sweet Jesus!'

Questioned if he had not conducted Claude Cathelinotte to a sabbat, he replied he had not and that he had never been to one. After this we had him put the ladder and stretched out, and we ordered him hoisted to the first rung.

Questioned if he had ever been to a sabbat and made a pact with the devil, he said only 'Jesus, Maria!' adding 'I am dying!' Admonished to tell if he had ever committed any act of sorcery or pretended to act as a priest joining persons in matrimony at a sabbat, he said no. We observed, however, that all the time he had said nothing but 'Jesus, Maria!' and that he had never made any compact, implicit or professed, with the devil and that he had not been to a sabbat. Then we ordered him to be loosened and then again for the second time drawn to the aforesaid ladder; all the time he kept on saying, 'Jesus, Maria! St. Nicholas! Mother of God, help me!'

This continued in the same vein at length, with the torture becoming ever more severe, but Gordel continued to deny all accusations, and to call upon various saints to aid him. None did, however; when the Bishop asked the promoter-general of Lorraine to read the report and either to reach a final decision or to 'summon further evidence as he believes necessary for justice', it seems he took the latter course: it is thought that Gordel died under further torture.

Father Grandier in Loudun

In 1633, the small Ursuline convent at Loudun became a famous when the nuns there accused a Father Urbain Grandier of witchcraft. This had not been his real crime. Appointed parish priest of St.-Pierre-du-Marché in Loudun in 1617, Father Grandier had an eye for the ladies. He made no secret of the fact that one of this young penitents, Madeleine de Brou, was his mistress. It was also rumoured that he was the father of the child of Philippa Trincant, daughter of the public prosecutor of Loudun. However, his real crime was making a joke at the expense of the powerful Cardinal Richelieu, who was temporarily out of favour with King Louis XIII. On 2 June 1630, Father Grandier was charged with immorality, tried before the Bishop of Poitiers – an enemy – found guilty and suspended from duty as a priest. But Grandier had political connections of his own and managed to get his suspension lifted by Archbishop Sourdis of Bordeaux.

Grandier's other enemies included Father Mignon, the confessor at the Ursuline convent. Mignon persuaded the mother superior, Sister Jeanne de Anges – also known as Madame de Béclier – and another nun to pretend they were possessed. They went into convulsions, held their breath, altered their appearances and changed their voices. Under exorcism they revealed that they had been possessed by two demons, Asmodeus and Zabulon, who had been sent by Father Grandier. But the plot failed. Archbishop Sourdis merely prohibited Father Mignon – and his cohort Father Pierre Barré – making any further exorcisms. By this time Richelieu was back in favour and one of his cronies, Jean de Laubardemont, a friend of the mother superior, came to Loudun to supervise the demolition of a fortified keep there. He discovered that

Grandier had published a satire attacking Richelieu – and that one of the nuns, Sister Claire de Sanzilly, was related to the Cardinal. To ingratiate himself to his patron, he set up a commission under two magistrates, the seneschal and a civil lieutenant to arrest Father Grandier as a witch.

The nuns started their play-acting again and this time the Jesuit Father Surin, the Franciscan Father Lactance and the Capuchin Father Tranquille were brought in to do the exorcism. Other mistresses whom Grandier had seduced and rejected also spoke out against him. According to a contemporary accoun, 'Sixty witnesses deposed to the adulteries, incests, sacrileges and other crimes committed by the accused, even in the most secret places of his church, as in the vestry, where the holy host was kept, on all days and at all hours.'

As the nuns claimed that he was responsible for their possession, Father Grandier decided to exorcise them himself. One of the signs of demonic possession was the ability to speak in tongues, so to catch them out Grandier spoke to one of the nuns in Greek. But they had been coached. 'Ah, you are subtle,' she said. 'You know full well that one of the first conditions of the pact between us was never to speak Greek.'

After that he did not dare question the other nuns in Greek, though they dared him to do so. Instead, the nuns accused him of witchcraft with the mother superior swearing that Father Grandier had bewitched them by throwing a bouquet of roses over the convent wall.

On 30 November 1633, Father Grandier was jailed in the castle of Angers and soon discovered to have the devil's mark on him. One account says that this was done by cutting him on one part of the body with a sharp lance, then touching him lightly elsewhere. The first contact caused him to cry out in considerable pain; the second drew no response. The official record reveals that there were four such devil's marks on his testicles and buttocks. However, an apothecary from Poitiers who had witnessed the hoax grabbed the lance and deftly demonstrated the sensitivity of Father Grandier's flesh. And Dr Fourneau, the surgeon who prepared him for torture, also testified that he had no devil's marks.

Legally, Father Grandier should have been tried by a secular court.

This would have given him the right to appeal to the Parlement of Paris which was traditionally sceptical when it came to accusations of witch-craft – banning the 'swimming' of witches as early as 1601. Instead, Cardinal Richelieu set up an investigating committee which neatly side-stepped all recognised legal procedures.

Seeing that Grandier's life was now in peril, several of the nuns had a change of heart. They tried to retract their accusations, saying that their statements had be dictated by friars who hated the priest. The mother superior even turned up in court with a noose around her neck, saying that she was going to hang herself to atone for breaking the ninth commandment and bearing false witness. She was ignored. Other supporters of Grandier who wanted to testify on his behalf were intim-idated by Laubardemont, who threatened to charge them with witchcraft. When Dr Claude Quillet, a local physician from Chinon who claimed the exorcisms were fraudulent, came forward, Laubardemont ordered his arrest and he fled to Italy. Laubardemont also issued arrest warrants for Grandier's three brothers – two of whom were parish priests – and all three were forced to flee.

A public meeting was organised by the Bailli of Loudun to support Grandier and complain of the arbitrary nature of the committee. Laubardemont accused those who attended it of treason, saying that they were attacking the authority of the king. What is more, the com-mittee already had clinching documentary evidence of Grandier's guilt. They had the pact signed between Father Grandier and the devil, which had been stolen from Satan's filing cabinet by the demon Asmodeus. It was in two parts. Both were in Latin but the first half was in mirror writing, as the devil always did things backward. It read:

> *We, the all-powerful Lucifer, seconded by Satan, Beelzebub, Leviathan, Elimi, Astaroth and others, have today accepted the pact of alliance with Urbainer Grandier, who is on our side. And we promise him the love of women, the flower of virgins, the chastity of nuns, worldly honours, pleasures and riches. He will fornicate every three days; intoxication will be dear to him. He will offer to us once a year a tribute marked with his*

blood; he will trample under foot the sacraments of the church,
and he will say his prayers to us. By virtue of this pact, he will
live happily for twenty years on earth among men, and finally
will come among us to curse God. Done in hell, in the council
of the devils.

It was clearly signed by Astaroth, Beelzebub, Elimi, Leviathan, Lucifer and Satan, notarised by the chief devil and my lords the princes of hell, and countersigned by Baalberith, the recorder.

The second part was in Grandier's own hand. It read:

My lord and master Lucifer, I acknowledge thee as my God
and prince, and promise to serve and obey thee as long as I
shall live. And I renounce the other God, as well as Jesus Christ,
all the saints, the apostolic and Roman church, all the sacra-
ments, and all the prayers and petitions by which the faithful
might intercede for me. And promise thee that I will do as
much evil as I can, and that I will draw everyone else to evil. I
renounced chrism [the consecrated oil used in baptism, con-
firmation and ordination], baptism, all the merits of Jesus
Christ and his saints. And if I fail to serve and adore thee, and
if I do not pay thee homage thrice every day, I give you my life
as your own. Made this year and day.

It was signed 'Urbain Grandier, extracted from hell'.

In light of this, there could only be one sentence – burning alive. However, first he would have to be tortured. On 18 August 1634, the judgment was handed down:

We have ordered and do order the said Father Urbain Grandier
duly tried and convicted of the crime of magic, maleficia, and
of causing the demonic possession of several Ursuline nuns of
this town of Loudun, as well as of other secular women, together
with other charges and crimes resulting therefrom. For atone-
ment of which, we have condemned and do condemn the said

*Grandier to make amends publicly, his head bare, a rope
around his neck, holding in his hand a burning candle weigh-
ing two pounds, before the main door of the church of
St.-Pierre-du-Marché, and before that of St. Ursula of this town.
There on his knees to ask pardon of God, the king and the law.
This done, he is to be taken to the public square of St. Croix,
and fastened to a stake on a scaffold, which shall be erected on
the said place for this purpose, and there to be burned alive,
together with all the compacts and magical apparatus used by
him, as well as a manuscript of a book composed by him
against the celibacy of priests and his ashes scattered to the
wind. We have ordered and do order that each and every article
of his moveable property be acquired and confiscated by the
king; the sum of 500 livres first being taken for buying a bronze
plaque on which will be engraved the abstract of this present
trial, to be set up in a prominent spot in the said church of the
Ursulines, to remain there for all eternity. And before proceed-
ing to the execution of the present sentence, we order the said
Grandier to be submitted to the first and last degrees of torture,
concerning his accomplices. Given at Loudun against the said
Grandier, and executed this day 18 August 1634.*

Grandier's torture was so severe that the marrow of his bones oozed out
of his broken limbs. But throughout he maintained his innocence and
would name no accomplices. Father Tranquille and other Capuchins
assisted in the torture and, enraged by his fortitude, smashed his legs.
His silence, they said, proved his guilt. When he prayed to God, they
said, he was actually invoking the devil, who was his god.

The civil authorities took pity on Grandier. He was given permission to make a statement from the scaffold and they ordered that he be
strangled before being burnt. But the friars who accompanied him to
his execution prevented him speaking by deluging him with holy water.
In one disputed account they ensured his silence by smashing him in
the face with a heavy crucifix, on the pretext of making him kiss it.
They fixed the garrotte so that it could not be drawn tight enough to

strangle him. Father Lactance himself lit the bonfire and, with Madame de Laubardemont, gloated over Grandier's agonies as he was burnt alive. The man who had supplied the stake and the wood for burning Father Grandier received 19 livres 16 sous for this pains. He signed a receipt of his fee on 24 August 1634.

Not everyone did so well out of the death of Grandier. Within a month Father Lactance had gone insane and died with in the words 'Grandier, I was not responsible for your death' on his lips. Father Tranquille also went insane and died within five years. Even the witch-pricker, Dr. Mannouri, who claimed to have found the devil's marks, died in a horrible delirium.

Father Barré moved onto Chinon where, in 1640, he uncovered another case of demonic possession. But the Archbishop of Lyons was suspicious, saying the girls in question 'believe themselves to be really possessed on your word alone, so that the reason for their affliction is the confidence they place in your opinion'. Later Father Barré connived with a Mademoiselle Beloquin in accusing a priest of raping her on the altar. But the stains on the altar cloth turned out to be chicken's blood and Barré was banished.

The town of Loudun profited from the notoriety the burning of Grandier brought and the convent became a tourist attraction. Even though Grandier was now dead, the nuns put on displays of possession for visitors. Young Sister Claire was a star performer:

> She fell on the ground, blaspheming, in convulsions, lifting up her petticoats and chemise, displaying her privy parts without any shame and uttering filthy words. Her gestures became so indecent that the audience averted its eyes. She cried out again and again, abusing herself with her hands, 'Allez, allez, foutez-moi!'

Then she called the prior, who she was said not to have seen before, by name, and begged him to be her lover. In all the display went on for an hour.

Another contemporary account said that the nuns struck their chests and backs with their heads, as if they had their necks broken, and with inconceivable rapidity. They twisted their arms at the joints of the shoulder, the elbow, or the wrist, two or three times round. Lying on their stomachs, the joined the palms of their hands to the soles of their feet; their faces became so frightful one could not bear to look at them; their eyes remained open without winking. Their tongues issued suddenly from their mouths, horribly swollen, black, hard and covered with pimples, and yet while in this state they spoke distinctly. They threw themselves back till their heads touched their feet, and walked in this position with wonderful speed, and for a long time. They uttered cries so horrible and so loud that nothing like it had ever been heard before. They made use of expressions so indecent as to shame the most debauched of men, while their acts, both in exposing themselves and inviting lewd behaviour from those present, would have astonished the inmates of the lowest brothel in the country.

The visiting English nobleman Lord Montagu was so impressed that he became a Roman Catholic.

However, the balloon was burst when Cardinal Richelieu's niece, the Duchess d'Aiguillon, visited Loudun. She decided that these displays were a fraud and told her uncle. He had lost interest in the affair and cut off the 'pension' he had bestowed on those who had testified against Grandier. After that, the possessions ceased.

Louviers

More nuns were possessed in Louviers, Normandy, in 1647. One of them, Sister Madeleine Bavent, left a vivid account. An orphan, Madeleine had been brought up by her uncle and aunt in Rouen. At the age of 13 in 1620, she was apprenticed to a dressmaker named Dame Anne and was set to work with half-a-dozen teenage girls in an upstairs room. There they were visited by priests who came to inspect their work. At the age of 18, Madeleine was seduced by a Franciscan named Father Bontemps, who had previous seduced three of the other girls.

Soon after, she entered the convent of Franciscan Tertiaries at Louvier, which had been founded in 1616 as a charitable home for the poor. It was run by Father Pierre David. A contemporary account says,

'Under the appearance of a saintly life, he sowed the seed of the perni-cious doctrine professed by the Illuminati.' This was a mystical and heretical sect who, like the Adamites and Quietists, believed that a person filled or 'illuminated' by the Holy Spirit could do no sin, that they should worship God naked like Adam and that, when practising inward 'quietness' or devotion, was irreproachable.

As a symbol of poverty and humility, the nuns at Louviers were to receive the holy communion naked. Madeleine, who was a novice for three years under Father David, was only required to 'strip to the waist and communicate with breasts exposed'. The other nuns prevented her from covering herself with the altar cloth and forced her to stretch her arms up.

'The most holy, virtuous and faithful nuns were held to be those who stripped themselves completely naked and danced before him in that state,' wrote Madeleine, 'those who appeared naked in the choir and sauntered naked in the gardens. Nor was that all. He habituated us to fondle one another with lustful embraces, and, what I dare not whisper, to give ourselves up to the most foul and sinful infamies... I have witnessed a mock act of circumcision performed upon a huge phallus, which seemed to be made of paste, which afterwards some nuns seized upon to gratify their fancies.'

However, Father David did not have sexual intercourse with her. Instead he contented himself with 'certain indecent caresses and mutual masturbation'.

When Father David died in 1628, his heretical books were burned by the bishop and Father Mathurin Picard took over as chaplain, with his assistant Father Thomas Boullé. However, 'the obscene practices continued and were held in great repute'. Madeleine maintained that she resisted, but at Easter confession Father Picard told her that he was attracted to her and started toying with her.

'After that, I never had any other kind of confession from him,' she wrote. 'Generally, all the time he handled the most private parts of my body, although I was always respectably covered, never, as the nuns maliciously report, undressed.'

Madeleine said that she continued to resist but, finally, she became pregnant. And she was not the only one. Father Picard made love philtres using 'several clots of menstrual blood' soaked into a sacramental wafer. Under the influence of these charms, the nuns 'committed the most filthy acts'. Other charms were made with the entrails of slain babies, their broken limbs and 'blood which trickled from the holy wafer'.

Once or twice a week, Madeleine went to a sabbat. At 11pm, she fell into 'a kind of trance or ecstasy'. At the sabbat, she would see Father Picard and Father Boullé, three or four nuns from the convent, some lay people and a few demons who were half-human half-beast. The priests then recited a Black Mass from a 'paper of blasphemy'. Human flesh was roasted and, after the feast, nuns would copulate with the ghost of Father David or one of the living priests. On one occasion Father Picard 'held my hands tightly while Father Boullé lay on top of me,' reported Madeleine.

The priests would take one of the large communion wafers they had used in the Black Mass and 'cut out a round piece of about the size of a half-sou in the centre and attach it to a piece of vellum or parchment cut and trimmed in the same way, securing it in position with some kind of greasy adhesive similar to shoemaker's wax. They would then put this gadget over their genitals, reaching to their stomachs, and thus arrayed gave themselves to the women present.' Madeleine had sex with Father Picard five or six times at the sabbat 'but only once or twice in the manner I have just described'.

The devil also visited Madeleine in the form of a large black cat.

'On no fewer than two occasions, having entered my cell, I found that damned incubus of a cat on my bed in the most indecent postures it is possible to imagine, exhibiting a huge penis just like a man's. I was terrified and tried to flee, but in an instant it leapt towards me, dragged me forcibly on the bed and then violently ravished me, causing me to experience a most peculiar sensation.'

These orgies continued from 1628 to 1642, when Father Picard died. No word about them ever got out, even though visiting priests regularly took the nuns' confession, and Madeleine herself was the convent's gatekeeper and went into town several times a week. It was only after Father Picard had died that they came to light. Father Esprit de Bosroger, a Capuchin, came to investigate and found that the nuns 'suffered the most frightful convulsions night and day during four years, and have for three or more hours daily been subjected to exorcisms during a terms of two years, although they have been subsisting in these paroxysms of constantly recurring frenzy, contortions, animal howlings, clamours and outcries. And besides these excessive torments, they have experienced the peculiar motions of their own demon, their special tormentor, three or four times a day.'

Of the fifty-two nuns at Louviers, fourteen were possessed with their own particular demon – Dagon, Grongade, Putiphar and so on – while another four were tormented. They all blamed Madeleine Bavent. Crowds thronged the churches for the public exorcisms and the nuns put on a good show. Father Esprit de Bosroger would preach a sermon saying that the devil's malice was like the buzzing of a fly.

'Say you so?' came a strange voice from one of the demented nuns. 'Flies! Flies! You shall soon see what power this fly the devil has!'

At this point, the nuns would scream and go into convulsions. However, Dr. Yvelin, a royal physician, was not convinced. He thought it was all just play-acting. But the Bishop of Evreux, Monseigneur Péricaud, examined the convent for signs of witchcraft and, in March 1643, he charged Madeleine Bavent with sorcery, signing a pact with the devil, attending a sabbat, stealing the host and fornicating with the devil. Under duress, Madeleine admitted being a witch and was expelled from the order. She was sentenced to life imprisonment in an underground dungeon with bread and water three days a week. The body of Father Picard was exhumed and excommunicated.

Picard's brother and nephew found Picard's body flung on a tip and complained to the authorities. On the advice of a royal investigating committee, the Parlement of Rouen stepped in and for the next four years the matter made its way through civil and ecclesiastical courts.

Held at the Ursuline convent at Rouen, Madeleine found herself cruelly mistreated. The Grand Penitentiary of Evreux – the local inquisitor – personally searched her for devil's marks 'roughly and indecently' twice and came along to watch on other occasions. She tried to commit suicide, bribing a boy to bring her arsenic, swallowing spiders and stopping the flow of her menstrual blood with bandages. In August 1647, the court postponed making a formal sentence, but left her in solitary confinement. She died later that year at the age of forty.

Before being burnt as a heretic, one of the Louiver witnesses confessed that he had prompted Madeleine Bavent with the sabbat stories. Everything he told was 'merely gossips' twaddle'. However, the story of the 'paper of blasphemy' used in the Black Mass 'had been suggested to him by his interrogator, the Grand Penitentiary of Evreux, who bribed him with six sous to give evidence against Madeleine and besmirch her name. Being utterly destitute, he agreed to bear false witness for the sake of money.'

Father Thomas Boullé who had taken over as chaplain after the death of Father Picard was arrested on suspicion of witchcraft on 2 July 1644. After three years in jail, he was condemned on similar evidence – though another two priests charged with him were cleared as the only evidence against them came from convicted criminals.

Father Boullé was then tortured to reveal his accomplices, made his public apology with 'his head and feet being bare, clad only in a shirt, having a cord around his neck, and holding in his hands a lighted taper of two pounds weight'. Then, on 21 August 1647, he was dragged on a hurdle to the Old Market Square where he was burnt alive and his ashes scattered to the wind.

Although the Parlement of Rouen had found the exhumation of Father Picard illegal, he was found guilty of witchcraft and his body was burnt alongside Boullé. Joining them was a Father Duvall, whom Madeleine Bevant had also accused. The remaining nuns of Louviers were dispersed to other convents to moisten the 'dryness' of their souls.

Auxonne

Ursuline nuns seemed particularly prone to possession and the devil was a frequent visitor to their convent at Auxonne from 1658 to 1663. However, they blamed not their father confessor, but their mother superior, Sister St. Colombe, née Barbara Buvée. Rumours of lesbianism at the convent had been circulated for five years, when eight nuns claimed to have been sexually stimulated by one of the convent's two confessors, Father Nouvelent, who was ugly but young. One, Marie Borthon, 'on his account suffered great temptations of the flesh'. Others had erotic fantasies, especially during menstruation. Witchcraft was obviously the cause. As Father Nouvelent was the link between the women's temptation, he suggested that he too was bewitched. Two local peasants were seized and charged with witchcraft but, as no evidence could be produced, they were merely sentenced to banishment. Unfortunately, as they left court, they were grabbed by a mob and lynched.

Father Nouvelent then began a course of exorcism in the convent's chapel with spectacular results. Sister Denise found that she could lift a heavy vase, which two strong men could hardly move, with two fingers. Other nuns lay on their bellies with their arms and legs arced upwards while they adored the sacraments.

The dedicated Father Nouvelent then took to exorcising the nuns by lying in bed with them, so close that 'only the sister's veil separated her face from that of the priest'. He paid special attention to Sister Claudine Bourgeot. They travelled together and slept in the same bedroom.

Sister St. Colombe, who had been mother superior, opposed the exorcism. However, she had fallen out with the previous confessor, Father Borthon, whose three sisters were nuns at the convent. As punishment she had been subjected to a series of fasts and floggings. It was decided that she was to blame and on 28 October 1660 she was formally charged with witchcraft. On 13 November, she was put in solitary confinement with heavy shackles on her legs. Then on 5 January 1661, she appeared before the Parlement at Dijon.

The nuns were unanimous in their condemnation of Sister St. Colombe. Sister Henriette Cousin told the court that the mother superior had put her hand on her breasts and kissed her passionately. When she protested the mother superior said that she thought she was kissing a holy statue. Sister Humberte Borthon testified that she had had a vision of hell, where the mother superior had put a serpent in her private parts, embraced her and 'lay down on her like a man on a woman'. Sister Françoise Borthon, who was regularly violated by the devil, swore that the mother superior had 'once made her sit across her knees and put her finger in her private parts just like a man would have done'. Further more, the mother superior had claimed that the sister was pregnant and 'put her hand in her and pried open her secret place, causing a lot of blood, both cleared and clotted, to flow out'. Sister Charlotte Joy had seen the mother superior kissing Sister Gabrielle de Malo and place a hand under her petticoat. Sister Joy, it seems, made 'reciprocal touchings'. Another sister had a vision in which the mother superior appeared holding a stolen host with a man's penis on it in one hand. In the other hand she had an artificial penis made out of linen with which 'she committed on herself impure acts'.

On 18 March 1661, the Parlement ordered further investigations to take place. A number of doctors were sent to the convent to examine the nuns. On one occasion, one doctor found them all to be frauds, though he conceded that some might be ill. A second found that they were genuinely possessed, while a third thought that nothing had been proved either way. On 15 June 1662, a Dr. Bachet wrote an official report to the chancellor, in which he stated: 'I can assure your honour that in all their acts, whether bodily or mental, the nuns have never displayed any legitimate or convincing signs of true demonic possession, neither in understanding foreign tongues, knowledge of hidden secrets, revelations, levitation of their bodies in the air, movement from one spot to another, nor in their extraordinary contortions which exceed those normally found.'

In August 1662, Sister St. Colombe was released after nearly two years in prison. She moved to another convent and the nuns' symptoms at Auxonne gradually disappeared. But not everyone got off so lightly.

In 21 September 1659, 60-year-old Thomas Looten surrendered himself to the Jacques Vanderwalle, bailiff of Meteren and official prosecutor in the 'sovereign court of the town and lordship of Bailleul'. The old man had been hounded by neighbours who accused him of causing the death of a child by giving him a bewitched plum. Looten asked for a trial so that he could clear himself. He was imprisoned.

Two days later, Vanderwalle reported that he had found twelve witness against Looten and the local citizens sitting as judges in the case ordered him to search Looten's house for ointment and magic powder.

On 25 September, three witnesses were examined. Then, on 27 September, eleven judges – the numbers sitting varied from four to twenty one – began the public examination of the prisoner. They asked him when and where he was born, who his parents were and were he now lived.

'I was born at Zuberquin and am about sixty years old,' he said. 'My father was called Maillard and my mother Nanette Heyeman, and I have lived in the parish of Meteren since my marriage.'
Asked why he had given himself up as a prisoner, Looten replied,
'Because a child of Adam Wycaert, a neighbour in the parish, died about a month ago, and folk suspected me of having killed it by sorcery, so I wished to clear myself.'

Over the next three weeks, the witnesses were examined and on 28 October Vanderwalle announced that he had enough evidence to prove sorcery. Three days later, two of the judges, Pierre Boddaert and François Hysenbrant, visit Looten in jail and outlined the case against him. They asked whether he had any counter-evidence that would vindicate him. He said he hadn't. They also asked whether he wanted to hire a lawyer. He declined, saying only that he was 'not guilty either in word or deed of any of the enormities attributed to him and that he would accept whatever verdict the judges choose to render in this action, but they should strive to reach a judgement so scrupulously that afterwards they will not themselves be condemned in the life to come'.

Looten was out of luck. On 1 November the official torturer of Dunkirk happened to be passing through Meteren and the eight judges who were sitting asked him to examine the prisoner for the devil's mark. Sure enough, the torturer found a mark 'in which the aforementioned torturer has several times thrust a pin as far as its head without the same prisoner feeling it or shedding a single drop of blood, although the aforesaid torturer squeezed the spot from underneath to make it bleed. And the aforesaid torturer declared under oath that the prisoner had the aforesaid devil's mark, and that he himself had examined and executed between five hundred and six hundred witches, so that he was very certain that this was a real devil's mark.' The torturer's affidavit to this effect was signed with a cross.

In light of this discovery, the judges ordered the prisoner to be 'put to torture to obtain by this means his sworn oath on the deeds charged against him'. On 2 November, Looten was 'seated on a wooden chair with his arms stretched out, his feet twisted under another chair and tightly bound', while an iron collar was put around his neck and tightened with screws. Under torture, he affirmed that Robert Beicqué had told him in Jean Boone's tavern that Jean Merlinck had said he was a witch and that he had given plums to many children, including Adam Wycaert's. He had heard that this child had become sick and died a few days later. Asked why he had not complained to the judges about this slander, he replied that was why he was in prison.

Two days later, the torturer testified that the prisoner had a strong constitution and could stand a more rigorous torture. This time Looten was placed 'on another chair previously blessed, his shirt is removed and burnt in his presence, and another blessed one put on, while his whole body is sprinkled with holy water by Father Martin, a Capuchin friar, who had exorcised him; finally, the judges stay close by the side of the prisoner, so that, when it appears necessary, they can call a doctor to survey the case and determine the capacity of the victim'. He was tortured with the garrotte again.

At 8pm, Looten broke down and confessed. He admitted that he had been a sorcerer for eight years, signed a pact with the devil in blood drawn from his right thumb and had been marked on the shoulder. The devil, who he called Harlakyn, appeared to him dressed in green. He had a deformed foot. Looten provided a list of local places where he had attended sabbats in the company of three or four beautiful women. He always had intercourse with at least one of them. And he had drunk beer and cider and feasted on unsalted veal. The devil had given him large sums of money to buy cows and houses, and green ointment so that he could fly wherever he wished. Looten also admitted giving Wycaert's child 'three plums which he had previously spat on, for which he received five coins from the devil'.

The following day, about twenty hours after he had been released from the garrotte, Looten was found dead. His neck was broken and he had been 'suffocated by the devil himself'. The judges ordered then that his body should be taken to the scaffold to be burnt, then the charred remains taken on a cart to a nearby gibbet to be displayed on a wheel. The sentence was carried out as ordered the following day.

Bailiff Vandewalle keep a scrupulous record of the proceedings. He also noted that the judges received an honorarium of 2 livres 10 pattars, each time they sat. This was probably spent on a meal and on one day – 1 November – they sat four times. Another 10 pattars were spent on court expenses at each meeting. Vandewalle himself received 22 pattars for examining each of the sixteen witness. The prisoner's three guards were each paid 8 pattars a day – a grand total of 68 livres 8 pattars including expenses. In fact, though they worked for forty-seven days, they were paid for fifty-seven. Looten was also charged for the search of his house, his transportation from Bailleul to Meteren, paper used in the trial, travel expenses for two judges to accompany his burnt body to the gibbet and even the wood burnt during his torture. Looten would also have had to pay for his food while a prisoner, but Vandewalle left a blank space in the manuscript for this amount. The fees of the tor-turer and the scaffold-makers were paid separately by the bailiff.

The cost of itemised items alone totalled 197 livres 10 pattars – or 3,950 pattars. The judges ordered the confiscation of Looten's goods to cover the expenses of his trial, torture and execution. His cows fetched 10, 16 or 20 pattars (1 livre), while his heifers fetched just 5 pattars. Vandewalle also noted that the nearby lordship of Cassel had written asking from the names of any of its residents named by Looten under torture. He sent six, but it is not known what became of them.

In 1669, there was an outbreak of nervous maladies in the districts of Coutances, Caretan and Le Haye de Puits in Basse-Normandie. Unable to find any cure, the local doctors claimed that the epidemic was caused by sorcery. Normandy had already suffered two severe witch epidemics in 1589–94 and 1600–45. Hearings were held, and a number of people recollected seeing their neighbours at sabbats. In May 1669, James le Boulenger had seen a flight of naked people in the air lasting half an hour. Michael Marais had seen over two hundred people dancing naked near La Haye de Puits. When sleeping in a cabin in the woods, Isaac Marais was awoken by naked people holding candles surrounding a goat. In other nude gatherings priests had been seen celebrating the Black Mass while standing on their heads. A curé, impressed by the quality of this evidence, wrote:

> This sabbat was just like those described in books, at all time and in all places. The witches anointed themselves, and a tall man with horns carried them up the chimney. Their activities followed the established pattern: dancing, what they call their 'pleasure', cutting infants to bits, boiling them with snakes over the fire, taking devil's powder to work maleficia, singing the pact with their master in their own blood, the huge goat, right down to the black candles. The only thing peculiar to this sabbat at La Haye de Puits was that the devil, for greater protection, frequently put his mark on his vassals. It was also most unusual that more than a hundred priests were identified. For my part, I am convinced of the truth of everything that was said at the trial, and I believe that [the devil in the shape of] a rat really spoke to one of the accused, a boy of ten.

In all 525 people were indicted for witchcraft. They were named by just nine people. Jean le Coustelier named 154, Marguérite Marguérie named ninety, Jacques le Gastolois eight-five, Siméon Marguérie seventy-eight, Jean le Marchand forty-three, Charles Champel thirty-five, Anne Noël twenty, René le Marchand fifteen and Catherine Roberbe just five.

Torture ensured that most of those arrested confessed and forty-six were condemned to death. However, when the death sentence on the first twelve was confirmed, their families appealed to the king for clemency. On the advice of his influential minister Charles Colbert, Marquis de Croissy, Louis XIV remitted their sentences to banishment from the province and restored their property. The Parlement of Normandy insisted that this violated their traditional rights – they had been burning witches since Joan of Arc – and demanded that he rescinded his pardon. Louis refused and forced Normandy to toe the line.

The Affair of the Chambre Ardente

However, witchcraft trials only came to an end in France when they began to come rather too close to the court of Louis XIV, in what was known as the Affair of the Chambre Ardente. In 1673, two priests told Paris Police Commissioner Nicholas de la Reynie that they had heard a string of disturbing confessions from wealthy men and women. A number of them had told the priests that they had murdered their wives and husbands. Although the priests would not breach the sanctity of the confessional and refused to give their names, Reynie, a meticulous detective, decided to investigate the matter.

The middle of the seventeenth century is known in France as the Age of Arsenic. Arsenic was used in the facial cosmetics that were the rage then, but murder by poison was also fashionable, especially among the upper classes. At first, Reynie thought he was after a gang of crooks who were selling so-called 'succession powders' to aristocrats. These were poisons that would dispose of an unwanted spouse or parent, allowing the poisoner to succeed to their property and titles.

Suspicion fell on a fortune-teller named Marie Bosse. Reynie sent an undercover policewoman to consult Bosse on the best way of getting rid of her troublesome husband. Bosse sold her some poison and was arrested. Bosse's husband, two sons and another fortune-teller called La Vigourex, who had slept with all the members of the Bosse family as well as La Bosse's previous husband, were also arrested. And when the Bosses' home was searched, a huge cache of poisons was found. Facing torture, La Vigourex and the Bosse family eagerly provided the police with a list of their clients. Many of them turned out to be members of the court of Louis XIV.

In 1679 Reynie persuaded Louis XIV to set up a committee of enquiry, known as the *Commission de l'arsenal*. But as the investigation was conducted in secret in a room draped in black, lit solely by candle-light, it became known as *la Chambre ardente*. For his interrogations de la Reynie used the *sellette* – a spiked torture chair heated from underneath – and *brodequins*, otherwise known as Spanish boots which crush the legs when wedges are hammered into them.

In *la Chambre ardente*, Marie Bosse and La Vigourex claimed that they were part of a devil-worshipping ring led by Catherine Deshayes. She was the wife of a failed haberdasher who set up in business making skin-cleansing treatments using arsenic compounds. Her experiments led her to learn a good deal about chemistry and she subsequently developed a number of potions which promoted what she claimed was inner cleanliness. As a sideline, Madame Deshayes took up astrology. Her clients were the rich and fashionable. To lend weight to her readings, she developed a network of female informers throughout Parisian society, which included Marie Bosse and La Vigourex. Most of them adopted pseudonyms to disguise their identities. Madame Deshayes became La Voisin.

In her astrological business, Deshayes would predict that a woman's husband was going to die mysteriously. If the woman seemed pleased at the prospect, Deshayes could help the process along a bit by selling the woman some poisons. The business proved so lucrative that Madame Deshayes could soon afford to pay 30,000 livres for a secluded house in a run-down area of Paris. It was protected by a high wall and hidden behind tall trees. Madame Deshayes lived there with her husband, a successful jeweller, her 21-year-old daughter, Marie-Marguerite Montvoisin, and a lodger, Nicholas Levasseur – an executioner by trade.

Reynie put the house under surveillance. An undercover police officer overheard one of Deshayes' assistants in a bar drunkenly describing acts of devil worship. The police picked up two of the people who had attended meetings there. Under interrogation, they said that Deshayes and a sixty-six-year-old priest, L'Abbe Guibourg, regularly conducted Black Masses. During the ceremony, a naked woman would lie in front of the altar with her legs open. Guibourg, wearing an alb with black phalluses embroidered on it, would rest a chalice and wafers stolen from the local church on her stomach. Intoning words from the Catholic mass, with 'the Infernal Lord Satan' substituted for the words 'God' and 'Christ', he would press the wafer against the breasts and vulva of the woman. A child would urinate in the chalice and the contents would be sprinkled over the worshippers. The wafer was then inserted into the woman's vagina, while Guibourg chanted 'Lord Satan sayeth, "In rioting and drunkenness I rise again. You shall fulfil the lusts of the flesh. The works of the flesh are manifest – they are drunkenness, revelling, immodesty, fornication, luxury and witchcraft. My flesh is meat indeed."'

An orgy of indiscriminate sex followed.

The police raided Deshayes' home. In a pavilion in the garden, they found a room completely draped in black with a white cross at one end. There was an altar, covered in black, with black candles made from the fat from human flesh placed upon it. Under interrogation, Deshayes' daughter Marie said that animals had been sacrificed and their blood drunk. Then she admitted that there had been human sacrifices too. During one ceremony, she said, Guibourg had intoned 'Astaroth, Asmodeus, prince of friendship, I beg you to accept the sacrifice of this child which we now offer you.'

Guibourg then held an infant up by its feet and slit its throat, so that the blood drained into the chalice on the belly of the naked woman. Guibourg then smeared the blood on his penis and on the woman's vagina and had sex with her.

The children used in these sacrifices belonged to Deshayes' inner circle and included the child of Deshayes' own goddaughter, Françoise Filastre. Others were provided by a midwife. Occasionally living foetuses were taken from unsuspecting women by Deshayes, who had another sideline as an abortionist. Foetuses' and babies' entrails were also distilled for occult use, while the rest of the bodies were burned in a stove.

La Filastre admitted sacrificing a child to the devil in a circle of black candles and renouncing the sacraments. At one Black Mass, celebrated by Abbé Deshayes and Abbé Cotton, she said she sacrificed her own newborn baby and the priest said mass over the placenta. Father Davot was supposed to have said a 'love mass' over the body of a naked girl, kissing her throughout the ceremony on her private parts. Madame de Lusignan and her priest practised other 'abominations' with an

Easter candle, naked in the woods, while Father Tourent said three amatory masses, during which he publicly lay on the girl on the altar.

The situation was potentially explosive as the worshippers included the Marquise de Montespan, Françoise Arthenais de Mortmart, who had been the king's mistress for twelve years. Fearing that she was losing the king's favour she attended three 'love masses' where she tried to secure his affections by acting as the naked altar. Another account of a love mass celebrated for the king's mistress reads:

> *Robed in his aube, stole and manciple, Guibourg read a conjuration in the presence of Mademoiselles des Oeillets, who was making a charm for the king. She was accompanied by a man who gave him the words of conjuration. For this rite it was necessary to have the sperm of both sexes, but Mademoiselle de Oeillets, since she was having her period, was incapacitated, so instead she put some menstrual blood into the chalice. The gentlemen who was with her went into the space between the bed and the wall and Guibourg directed his semen into the chalice. Into this mixture, each put a powder made from the blood of bats, and added some flour to give it a firm consistency. The Father Guibourg recited the conjuration and poured what was in the chalice into a little bottle at Mademoiselle des Oeillets and the gentleman took away with them.*

Louis XIV found this a little too close for comfort and the Chambre Ardente investigation was suspended in August 1680. But as the evidence pointed to the fact that Madame de Montespan had attempted to procure arsenic to poison the king and his new mistress, Mademoiselle de Fontanges, Reynie continued his work in secret. Catherine Deshayes was tortured three times, but said nothing. The Attorney General demanded that her tongue be cut out and her hands chopped off, but the court was satisfied with burning alive. On 22 February 1680, she was taken to the stake 'tied and bound with iron. Cursing all the time, she was covered with straw, which five or six times she threw off her, but at last the flames grew fiercer and she was lost to sight.'

During the investigation, 319 people were arrested and 104 sentenced: thirty-six to death, thirty-four to banishment and four to slavery in the galleys. However, the Marquisse de Montespan returned, briefly, to favour, only to be replaced by Madame de Maintenon, the middle-aged governess the King had employed to bring up de Montespan's children. At the age of 70, Louis XIV decided to destroy the records of the Chambre Ardente investigation and on 13 July 1709 they were burnt. However some copies of the official transcript and Reynie's notes survived.

After the Affair of the Chambre Ardente, legislation was introduced which controlled the sale of poisons and banned fortune-telling. Then in an edict of 1682, Louis XIV declared witchcraft a superstition and ended all witchcraft trials. It was ratified by Parlement on 31 August. In the main, the provincial Parlements obeyed it. However, three shepherds were burnt at Brie in 1691 for spreading epidemics among sheep – though to augment their spells they used arsenic.

In 1718 – three years after the death of Louis XIV in 1715 – Bordeaux burnt its last witch, a man accused of making a ligature. In 1728 at Lorient, several men, including a priest, were banished or sent to the galleys for making a pact with the devil. A woman involved was merely reprimanded.

The Case of Mary Catherine Cadière

However, witch trials continued and, in 1731, a particularly salacious case appeared before the Parlement of Aix-en-Provence. Indeed it was only brought because the alleged sorcery resulted in fornication. The case involved Marie-Catherine Cadière, the daughter of a very religious family. As girl she demonstrated 'extraordinary gifts of prayer' and would swoon in church. As a ravishing 18-year-old, she joined a prayer group which was under the spiritual guidance of the 50-year-old Jesuit Father Jean-Bapiste Girard. She was eager to become a saint and told him that she had sought him out because God had recommended him in a vision.

Girard took her on as his special protégée. She liked him too and testified later that she felt 'something like finger moving about my entrails and making me feel quite wet; and this happened every time Father Girard came to the house'. Unfortunately, Girard did not see this as evidence of her holiness. But Catherine was well schooled in the lives of the mystics such as St. Theresa and St. Catherine of Sienna. In June 1729, she claimed an 'intimate communion with God'. In November that year, God told her that she would suffer in the place of a soul in mortal sin and went into convulsions and lost the power of speech. The following February she regained it miraculously, through the prayers of a recently deceased nun.

Her brother, Father Thomas Cadière, a Dominican friar, seemed equally eager for her beatitude and kept a detailed record of her stigmata and visions – which included seeing a bleeding heart and naked men and women. She also had regular 'transfigurations' or death trances in the honour of Christ's passion, which left her face covered with blood. While all this was going on, Father Girard obtained a dispensation from the Abbess to visit her privately and to write to her in confidence.

After a year, Father Girard was still not convinced of Catherine's saintliness and advised her to go on a retreat to the convent of Ste-Claire-d'Olioules. There she suffered fits, hallucinations and hysteria, and developed symptoms of insanity. The Bishop of Toulon sent her home. Her new confessor, 38-year-old Father Nicholas of St. Joseph, Prior of the Barefooted Carmelites at Toulon, tried exorcism. Catherine then claimed to have been bewitched by Father Girard. Her brother persuaded two of Father Girard's other devotees – a 65-year-old woman and 23-year-old La Baratille – to testify that they had been seduced by the Jesuit. Cadière's lawyers then produced four other devotees and four nuns who all said that they had been intimate with Father Girard.

Girard appealed to the Bishop, but the friends of La Baratille went to the police and the matter came up in the civil courts. The scandal came to the ears of the king who ordered the Parlement at Aix to hear the case and hearings began on 10 January 1731. To bolster their case, Catherine and her brother held midnight exorcisms which attracted huge crowds. She stood 'senseless and motionless, with her neck swollen and the swelling rising to her mouth', while he performed the exorcism 'standing naked to his shirt, with a violet stole about his neck, in one hand the holy water, and in the other the *rituale* [order of service], which Father Nicholas had taken care to bring with him'. Other priests, who arrived later, denied the possession and Catherine recovered before a doctor could examine her. However, at four in the morning the next night, Catherine 'rolled about the room, and screamed out, so as to be heard in the middle of the street'.

Catherine outlined her case in *Justification de demoiselle Catherine Cadière* published in 1731, which appeared in English as the *Case of Mistress Mary Catherine Cadiere* in 1732. This was written 'to teach persons of my sex that they must be on guard against the appearance of piety'. In it, she outlines, all too clearly, the dangers, stating that Girard, '...stooping down and putting his mouth close to hers, he breathed upon her, which had such a powerful effect upon the young lady's mind that she was immediately transported in love and consented to give herself up to him. Thus did he bewitch the mind and inclinations of his unhappy penitent.'

Being bewitched saved 'the young woman's honour'. Catherine told the court, 'You see here before you a young girl of twenty years, plunged into the abyss of evils, but whose heart is still unsullied.'
Catherine described step by step how Father Girard had seduced her, all the time claiming it was God's will. A witness testified that she had seen Girard kissing Catherine and placing her hands under his cassock. 'My dear child,' he said, 'I want to lead you to perfection. Do not be disturbed by what happens to your body. Banish your scruples, your fears and doubts. By this means, your soul will become stronger, purer, more illuminated. It will acquire a holy freedom.'

Catherine wrote, 'One day I remember among others, as I was coming out of a severe fainting spell, I found myself stretched out on the floor with Father Girard behind me, running his hands over my breasts, which he had uncovered.' When she asked what he was doing, he told her that it was the will of God that she experience humiliation in order to achieve perfection: 'He told me that one day God would wish him to put his belly to hers.'

One another occasion she said, 'Father Girard found me in bed, and having locked the door he lay down beside me. Drawing me to the edge of the bed, he put one hand under my buttocks, and the other in front; then he undressed me and without warning kissed me. Often he made me expose myself, while his hands explored every nook of my body. As I was subject to fainting spells, I could not answer for what he did when I was in that state. I can only recall when I came to, I found myself in such a condition that I knew only too well that Father Girard had not been content just to look at me.'

He visited her almost every day and made love to her for two or three hours on end. Being an older gentleman, he often required a little added stimulation:

Sometimes he would give me strokes with a cane, and then immediately afterwards kiss the spot where he had beaten me. One day, coming to see me to punish me for refusing God's grace, having locked the door, he ordered me to kneel before him. He held in his hand a cane and told me I deserved the whole world should see what he was doing to me, but nevertheless he made me swear faithfully and promised him never to speak about it. I promised him, not knowing what he was going to do. Evidently reassured by my promise, he told me that it was the will of God, that divine justice, seeing I had refused God's grace, demanded that I should take off my clothes and stand naked before him. At these words I was revolted, my mind went blank, and I fell senseless to the floor. He lifted me up. To my surprise I found myself so dazed that afterwards I obeyed him without questions and allowed him to do whatever he wished. He ordered me first to remove my veil, then my coif, my belt and finally my dress; to put it bluntly, he left me nude except for a chemise. In this undressed condition, I felt him kiss my buttocks. I am not sure what he did next, but I felt a kind of sadness which I had not known before. After this he helped me get dressed. More than once, he made me lie on the bed, and in this position he whipped me and then kissed me without the least inhibition or decorum, always telling me that this was the new way to reach the highest stages of perfection.

Another day, she said, Father Girard made her take off even her chemise and place it on the bed. He told her that she must be punished for the sin she had committed by not freeing herself of her scruples – 'at which she felt moist and ticklish in her private parts'. Again he whipped her on both buttocks, then kissed them gently. It was then that 'he gently scratched her until she was all moist'.

Elsewhere she described the position she was to take for this. She said he 'ordered her to climb on the bed and put a hassock under her elbows in order to raise her up,' adding: 'It is not proper to express what followed, but 'tis easily imagined.' It was also alleged that he impregnated her and gave her a potion to make her miscarry. His letters were also introduced into evidence. In one of them, he told her, 'Do everything I tell you, like a good girl who finds nothing difficult where her father asks for it.'

Father Girard defended himself against the charges as best he could. He was a little deaf, he said. That was why he had to put his head close to hers – he was not kissing her. He had locked the door because he wished to conceal her angelic possession. Her brother was already broadcasting her 'miracles' and Girard has sent her to the convent to prevent news of his sainted state being revealed prematurely. The abortion 'potion' he had given her was merely water he had brought when she was thirsty. And his letters, he said, must be interpreted in the light of heavenly love – not the earthly kind.

He then sought to show that Catherine had suborned three witnesses. One, a maid, had testified that she had caught them in *flagrante*, but, curiously, had only asked what colour vestments Father Girard wanted for his next service.

Her 'transfigurations' he pointed out had occurred miraculously on 7 May, 6 June and 7 July – and he maintained that she had smeared her face with her own menstrual blood. Catherine's lawyer argued that she had had another transfiguration on 20 July and that no woman had two 'incommodities' in one month. Catherine's diary was then produced in evidence. It showed regular periods on 8 March, 4 April, 8 May, 11 June, 4 July, 8 August. This meant that he had not procured an abortion, as she had not been pregnant. Then he sprang another surprise, producing the 'Holy Cross' that had been sent to Catherine direct from heaven. Somehow she had miraculously obtained a duplicate.

There was other evidence that Catherine was economical with the truth. While in the convent, Catherine had claimed to have fasted for days on end. But one night the nuns found her out in the garden gorging herself on peaches. She said that God had sent her the sin of gluttony to humble her and, by thinning out the fruit, the trees would produced a better crop. Girard's lawyer dismissed Catherine as a 'cunning, artful girl'. He also sought to discredit the prosecution by calling a prostitute who claimed to have had sex with Prior Nicholas.

The case concluded with an argument about the running sores that had appeared all over her body that Catherine claimed with stigmata. Father Girard admitted lifting her veil and sucking the sore on her throat. He did this every day for three months. He also admitted kissing an ulcer near left breast. Catherine's lawyer seized on this.

'Here is an angel of purity,' he said, indicating Girard, 'who teaches us the art of gazing upon the naked body of the girl or woman he loves passionately, and even flagellating her, without any trace of erotic emotion and without peril to his soul. What a prodigy of chastity!'
But Girard's lawyer simply retorted, 'Can anyone believed that such things as ulcers should provide fuel for a lewd flame?'

The case ran for nine months. On 11 October 1731, the Parlement at Aix returned its verdict. It was split down the middle. Twelve judges said Father Girard should be burnt and twelve said that Catherine should be hanged. The casting vote fell to President Lebret. He decided that Father Girard should be handed over the ecclesiastical authorities for his irregular conduct as a priest and Catherine be sent back to her mother. The mob were not pleased. Girard was manhandled, while Catherine's lawyer was carried shoulder high in triumph. Father Girard was cleared by the church and died in his native Dôle two years later.

*

One Father Bertrand Guillaudot was not so lucky, however. He was burnt alive in Dijon in 1742 for the divination of treasure. He named twenty-nine accomplices. Five were sentenced to death in Lyons in 1745, the rest banished or sent to the galleys. Father Louis Debaraz, who had said the sacrilegious masses to locate the treasure, was burnt alive, the last man to be executed for witchcraft in France.

The Hexen of Germany

ERMANY TOOK ITS WITCHCRAFT SERIOUSLY. At least a hundred thousand people were executed, with burning alive the prescribed punishment and torture the tool to extract a confession. So many witches were burnt that in 1590, according to a chronicler in Wolfenbüttel, Brunswick, 'The place of execution looked like a small wood from the number of stakes.'

Visiting Cologne in 1636, Cardinal Albizzi wrote, 'A horrible spectacle met our eyes. Outside the walls of many towns and villages, we saw numerous stakes to which poor, wretched women were bound and burnt as witches.'

Chillingly in Neisse in Silesia, in the interests of efficiency, the executioner built an oven where, in 1651 alone, he roasted to death forty-two women and girls for witchcraft. Over nine years, he roasted over a thousand people, including children as young as two.

Germany then consisted of about 300 autonomous states, forming part of the Holy Roman Empire. Although from 1532 they all officially recognised the Carolina Code which specified that witches were to be tortured and executed, whether these laws were enforced or not was up to each individual ruler. In 1582, the General Synod of Protestant Hesse-Kessel declared that the devil only had power if people were afraid of witchcraft and some states freed witches if no injury had been done.

Witches hold commune in this German engraving of a woodland landscape. One of them flies through the air, riding backwards on the back of a goat.

Not all the aristocracy were convinced by the witch-burners. In 1700 Frederick I took action against one of his barons for executing a 15-year-old girl who had confessed to having intercourse with the devil. The Protestant Duke of Juliers-Berg, William III was influenced by his personal physician Johann Weyer, who was a sceptic: tragically, in his old age the Duke had an apoplectic fit and dismissed Weyer, and in 1581 he sanctioned the torture of witches.

Much of the witch persecution took place during the Counter Reformation from about 1570 and the Thirty Years War, between 1618 and 1648, when towns could change from Protestant to Catholic or Catholic to Protestant virtually overnight. One woman accused of witchcraft in Hagenau, Alsace, but freed by Protestant judges was re-arrested several years later. Her trial by Catholic judges lasted a year. She was tortured seven times, finally confessed and was burnt, along with an accomplice. Six other women were also implicated.

One of the authors of the *Malleus Maleficarum*, Heinrich Kramer, a Dominican, started the witch hunt in the Tyrol in the 1480s. He was not supported by the local people so he persuaded a dissolute woman to hide in an oven and pretend that the devil lived there. From inside, she denounced numerous people, who Kramer then had cruelly tortured. The Bishop of Bixel finally managed to expel Kramer, but by that time he had interested the Archduke Sigismund in the whole topic of witch-burning.

The Jesuits took over the witch hunt under the leadership of such men as Martin Del Rio, who published *Disquisitionum Magicaum Libri Sex* in 1599. Del Rio insisted 'Judges are bound under pain of mortal sin to condemn witches to death who have confessed their crimes. Anyone who pronounces against the death sentence is reasonably suspected of secret complicity. No one is to urge the judges to desist from prosecution. Nay, it is evidence of witchcraft to defend witches, or to affirm that witch stories which are told as certain are mere deceptions or illusion.' And del Rio found it perfectly acceptable to kill children, saying 'In this, God is neither cruel or unjust, since, by the mere fact of original sin, the children had already merited death.'

The Lutheran 'lawgiver of Saxony' Carpzov, who claimed to have read the Bible fifty-three times, is said to have burnt 20,000 witches. The Prince-Abbot Balthasar von Dernbach of Fulda appointed the savage Balthasar Ross as witch-finder in the hope of terrifying Protestants into submission. Ross delighted in thrusting hot skewers into women while they hung on the strappado. Between 1603 and 1606, he executed 300 witches, until a new abbot, Johann Friedrich von Schwalbach, stopped the trials and arrested Ross. Held in jail until for twelve years, he was eventually executed in 1618 – not for burning innocent people, but because he had 'deducted exorbitant expenses which he appropriated for his own use'.

Even the universities were equivocal about witchcraft. When Duke Maximilian I of Bavaria wanted to introduce torture to witchcraft trials, he was opposed by three of his councillors, so he appealed to the universities for a ruling. Cologne university was against, but both Freiburg and Ingolstadt pronounced in favour of torture.

Large scale witch trials began in the archbishopric of Treves or Trier. These spread over the border from Alsace, Lorraine and Luxembourg. Theologians blamed the Protestant Albert of Brandenburg for bringing witchcraft with his raids in 1552. Five women were burnt in 1572 by the Abbey of St. Maximin.

The persecution proper began in 1582 under the Prince-Archbishop Johann von Schönenburg, the governor Johann Zandt and the Suffragan Bishop Peter Binsfeld. However, the civil courts in Treves, under Dietrich Flade, were not as enthusiastic about persecuting witches as the ecclesiastical authorities, so Zandt had Flade arrested for witchcraft and Binsfeld wrote a *Treatise on Confessions by Evildoers and Witches* in 1589 condemning him. Three years after Flade's execution the celebrated Catholic theologian Cornelius Loos also spoke out against the Treves witch hunt. He wrote a tract called *True and False Sorcery* exposing the witch hunters' methods, but the Papal Nuncio had the book destroyed and Loos banished to Brussels. Binsfeld published a new edition of his *Treatise*, specifically condemning Loos.

One of the remaining relics of the persecution is the witch register of the Benedictine Abbey of St. Maximin. It covers the period 1587 to 1594 and details the court proceedings against 306 witches, who denounced another 1,500 people. Two villages outside Treves were wiped from the map when 368 witches were burnt. In another two, in 1586, only two women were left alive.

In his *History of Treves* the canon of Treves Cathedral describes how vested interests and big business profited from the witch hunts:

Inasmuch as it was popularly believed that the continued sterility of many years was caused by witches through the malice of the Devil, the whole country rose to exterminate the witches. This movement was promoted by many in office, who looked for wealth in the ashes of victims. And so, from court to court throughout the towns and villages of all the diocese, scurried special accusers, inquisitors, notaries, jurors, judges, constables, dragging to trial and torture human beings of both sexes and burning them in great numbers. Scarcely any of those who were accused escaped punishment. Nor were the leading men of the city of Treves spared. For the judge [Flade], two burgomasters, several councillors and associate judges were burnt. Canons of sundry collegiate churches, parish priests and rural deans were swept away in this ruin. So far, at length, did this insanity of the enraged people and of the courts go in this thirst for blood and booty that there was scarcely anyone who was not besmirched by some suspicion of this crime. Meanwhile notaries, copyists and innkeepers grew rich. The executioner rode a blooded horse, like the noble of the court, and went clad in gold and silver. His wife vied with noble dames in the richness of her attire. The children of those convicted and punished were sent into exile, their goods confiscated. Ploughman and vintner failed – hence came sterility. A direr pestilence or a more ruthless invader could hardly have ravaged the territory of Treves in worse manner than this inquisition and persecution which knew no bounds. There were many reasons for doubting that everyone was guilty. This persecution lasted for several years and some of those who presided over the administration of justice gloried in the mul-

titude of the stakes, at each of which a human being had been given to the flames.

At last though, the flames were still unsated. The people grew impoverished, the cost of examinations and the profits of the inquisitors were restricted, and suddenly, as in war when funds fail, the zeal of the persecutors died out.

However, Catholics did not have a monopoly on witch-burning. At Quedlinburg in Protestant Saxony, with a population of 12,000, 133 were burnt as witches in one day in 1589. Four other beautiful girls were spared by the executioner, who claimed that the devil had spirited them away.

Swabia

In 1590, there was a witch hunt in Nördlingen, Swabia, led by the local burgomaster Georg Pheringer and two local lawyers Conrad Graf and Sebastien Roettinger. Despite the favourable testimony of their neighbours, thirty-two women were burnt, including the wives of the town clerk, a former burgomaster and other local officials. On of them was Rebecca Lemp, the wife of Peter Lemp, a well-educated accountant. He was away on business in April 1590 when she was arrested. Confused by what was happening, their six children wrote to their mother in jail:

Our dutiful greeting, dearly beloved Mother. We let you know that we are well. You have informed us that you are well too. We expect that father will come home today, God willing. So we will let you know as soon as he gets home. Almighty God grant you his grace and the Holy Spirit that, if it please God, you may come back to us hearty and well. God grant it! Amen.

Dearly beloved Mother, let beer be brought for you, bread for soup and a little fish. I have just killed two chicken. The Reverend Rummel had dined with us. If you need money, send for it. You have some in your purse. Fare thee well, my beloved Mother. Do not be worried about the housekeeping until you come back to us.

The letter was signed 'Rebecca Lempin, your loving daughter; Anna Maria Lempin, your loving daughter; Joannes Condradus Lempius, *tuus amantissimus filius*' – young John showing off his Latin here – 'Samuel Lemp, your loving son' and 'X', the mark of Peter Lemp Jr. They signed off, 'For the thousandth time, God grant you a good night.'

Rebecca then wrote to her husband, fearing that he might believe some of the accusations made against her:

> *My dearly beloved husband, do not be troubled. Were I charged with a thousand accusations, I tell you I am innocent – or else let a thousand demons from hell come and tear me to pieces. Were they to pulverise me and cut me into a thousand pieces, I could not confess anything. So don't be alarmed. Before my conscience and before my soul, I am innocent. Will I be tortured? I do not believe it, as I am not guilty of anything. My husband, if I am guilty of anything, may God reject me forever far from his sight. If they do not believe me, Almighty God, who knows everything, will work a miracle so that they will believe me. Otherwise, if I have to stay in this state of anxiety, there is no God in heaven. Don't hide your face from me, you know that I am innocent. In God's name, do not leave me in this anguish which is choking me.*

But she was tortured – five times – and she eventually confessed. Afterwards she wrote another note. It read:

> *O thou, the chosen of my heart, must I be parted from you, though I am entirely innocent? If so, may God be followed throughout eternity by my reproaches. They force you and make you confess. They have tortured me so, but I am as innocent as God in heaven. If I know the least thing about such matters, may God shut the door of heaven against me. O thou, dearly beloved husband, my heart is nearly broken. Alas, alas, my poor children are orphans. Husband, send me something*

that I may die, or I must expire under torture. If you can't do
it today, do it tomorrow. Write to me directly, – R.L.

On the back, she wrote: 'Oh husband of your innocent Rebecca, they take me from you by force. How can God suffer this? If I am a witch, may God show no pity on me. Oh, what wrong is done to me. Why will God not hear me? Send me something, or else even my soul will perish.'

He sent her some poison, but it was intercepted. The court then forced Rebecca to write another letter to her husband, confessing that she was a witch. He wrote back:

Honourable and esteemed lords, most wise and magnanimous,
Recently, on 1 June, I addressed a humble petition to the
court concerning my dear wife, where I requested that she be
set free, but my request was turned down. This time may my
petition have a different result. Since then, I have received
from my wife a true report, in which she tells me she is closely
confined in prison for something for which she is not guilty
and asks me to come to her help – me, her closest, dearest and
best friend, her husband, spouse – and to succour her in her
tribulations and suffering. In truth, I would not be a Christian
if I did not seek to comfort and help her.

He then asked to be allowed to confront the witnesses because he believed that his wife's confession had been secured by torture.

I hope, I believe, I know that during all our life, my wife has
never even thought about what she is accused of, let alone
having done it. I swear this by my soul. Very many well
respected people who know me and my wife testify, as I do,
that she has always been a pious, chaste, honest housewife,
the enemy of any evil; that she had always cherished me faith-
fully as her dear spouse. She has, moreover, as a good mother
to her family carefully raised our dear little ones, taught them
– together with me – not only their catechism, but furthermore

*the Holy Bible, especially the beautiful psalms of David.
Indeed, thanks to God – and I say this without boasting – all
the children with which God has blessed us, without exception,
know and can recite several psalms.*

*No one in this world – I say this to the best of my belief –
can maintain that my wife ever worked the least ill, no matter
what, or that anyone had the slightest suspicion about her...
This is why, in my name and in the name of my dear little children, who now number six – God be forever praised – I humbly
pray you, for the love of God and the prospect of the last judgement at which Jesus Christ will himself appear as judge, and I
beg you, who manifest in yourselves wisdom and duly consti-
tuted authority, to show a favourable regard for my dear wife
and to set her free.*

After the court received this petition from Peter Lemp, they tortured his
wife again. Then, on 9 September 1590, she was publicly burnt. After
that, the witch hunt in Nördlingen intensified and the jails were soon
overflowing. In 1594, Maria Hollin, the landlady of the Crown tavern in
Nördlingen was arrested. For eleven months she maintained her innocence in the stinking dungeon. During that time she was tortured fifty-six
times – the highest number recorded by someone who had survived.
This was done for her own good as those who are possessed by the devil
can only save their immortal souls by confessing. She was eventually
rescued by her home town of Ulm, who claimed jurisdiction over her,
and her fortitude gave the local pastor Wilhelm Lutz the courage to speak
up against the persecution in the name of the Protestant church.

'The proceedings will never end,' he said. 'For there are people who
have informed on their mothers-in-law, their wives or husbands,
denouncing them as witches. What can come of all this?'

Public opinion turned abruptly against the witch trials, forcing an
end to them in Nördlingen.

Bavaria

In Bavaria, however, they were just beginning. In Schöngau, the public executioner Jörg Abriel grew wealthy discovering witches. He charged two florins for searching a woman's body for the devil's mark, regardless of outcome. On one occasion he could find no mark, but burnt the woman anyway because, he claimed, she looked like a witch. An execution brought him eight florins.

However, Duke Ferdinand suspended witch trials in Schöngau from 1587 to 1589, so that all the accused could be brought before one grand inquisition. As a result sixty-three women were beheaded or burnt in one go. The *Hofrat* at nearby Munich supervised the procedure, ordering one woman to be tortured continuously until she confessed.

After a hailstorm at nearby Freising, one woman remarked that worse weather was to be expected. She was arrested and tortured into confessing and named others who, in turn, were arrested and executed. And in the small alpine town of Werdenfels, forty-nine women were burnt in twenty months in 1590-91. The villagers were charged four thousand florins for this holocaust. Finally a special judge petitioned the bishopric at Freising to stop the witch trials on the grounds that, if they continued how they had started, there would soon be no women left.

In 1597, William V of Bavaria abdicated in favour of his son Maximilian I. Brought up by Jesuits, Maximilian had watched witches being tortured at Ingolstadt when he was just seventeen. During his fifty-four year reign, Maximilian introduced numerous edicts against witchcraft – urging repeated torture, burning and confiscation of property – perhaps because he believed that ligature was responsible for his wife's barrenness. He maintained that those who did not believe in the burning of witches were not fit to call themselves Christians. Under his edicts, denunciation under torture was sufficient grounds for arrest and showing fear after arrest was proof of guilt. Court proceedings were further speeded by disallowing the recantation of a confession extracted under torture. This body of law was codified in his vicious *Instructions on Witchcraft* of 1622. He personally intervened three years earlier when a woman and her three children were acquitted in Ingolstadt. Thanks to Maximilian it is estimated that between one thousand and two thousand witches were burned in the small town of

Riezler alone, with a similarly number in each of the two other episcopal enclaves at Augsburg and Freising.

Baden

Offenburg, an imperial city or *Reichsstadt* of the Holy Roman Empire
in what is now Baden, was rigidly Catholic with its schools controlled
by the Jesuits. If any of its two to three thousand inhabitants did not
attend Easter confession, they were automatically jailed for three days.
If they then did not fulfil their obligation in the next two weeks, they
faced further imprisonment. At the turn of the seventeenth century a
witch-hunting councillor named Rupprecht Silberrad was determined
to crush those opposing the persecution who were led by councilman
George Laubbach, whose wife had already been burnt as a witch in
1597. On 7 September 1601, Silberrad accused two of Laubbach's
daughters, Helene and Adelheid, of the murder of his son by witchcraft. Then on 31 October, a third witch named Else, the wife of Martin
Gwinner, a baker, was added to the indictment on the evidence of two
beggars caught stealing grapes. Instead of going to the pillory as
thieves, the beggars were tortured as witches until they admitted that
their accomplices in *maleficia* were Laubbach's daugthers. They also
denounced Silberrad's sister-in-law and other prominent townswomen,
but these accusations were ignored.

Immediately after her arrest Else was tortured, but would say
nothing. She screamed fearfully when she was put in the strappado,
but all she would say was 'Father, forgive them, for they know not what
they do.'

Her young daughter Agathe was then arrested, but she refused to
implicate her mother. Else was tortured again on 7 November. Hanging
by the wrists, heavy weights were attached to her feet, but still she said
nothing. A week later, the judges, determined to make progress, had
young Agathe brutally flogged until she confirmed the judge's accusations against her mother. On 22 November, the two beggars were
executed, and mother and daughter were brought face to face.

'Why did I not drown my unfortunate child in her first bath?' asked
Else.

'Oh, that you had done so!' sobbed Agathe.

Else was then tortured with thumbscrews until, at last, she admitted copulating with the devil. But more was required of her and she was thrown into a freezing dungeon. The torture was resumed for a fourth time on 11 December. During the process the exhausted woman fell into a dead faint and had to be revived by being doused with cold water. She then admitted flying to the sabbat where she had had intercourse with the devil and denounced two other women. Two days later she rescinded her confession and protested her innocence despite the priest who urged her to confess her guilt. On 15 December the judges resumed torturing her mercilessly with the aim of making her break down. However, she courageously maintained her innocence until, in frustration, on 19 December 1601, the judges summarily sentenced her to death. Two days later, she was burnt.

Alone, in chains in a tiny cell, Agathe was disowned by her father and the rest of the family for denouncing her mother, even though she had been flogged. However, the town council now had a problems as, legally, Agathe was too young to burn. Three weeks after her mother died, her father relented and petitioned for her release. She was freed on condition that she was exiled to another Catholic town in Germany. Silberrad protested against the show of mercy, but the rest of the councillors rounded on him and he was arrested. On this occasion, however, the Church urged leniency, and he was merely kept under house arrest. Soon he was released, successfully sued the council for damages and resumed his former position. The persecution then intensified, largely because they were immensely profitable to the judges and everyone else involved. The iron witch's chair was introduced as a method of torture. The suspect was tied to it and slowly roasted until they confessed.

A new wave of persecution began in Offenburg in 1627. Condemned witches from nearby Artenberg said that a number of witches from Offenburg had been present at a sabbat on the Blocksberg so the local *Rat* or town council began to look into it. Being short of funds, they arrested a number of wealthy witches, burning five of them on 12 January 1628 and confiscating their property. There was a lull for the next six months, while the Protestant Swedish army occupied the town, but on 27 June the *Rat* renewed its efforts, offering a reward of two shillings for every witch apprehended. By 7 July, four rich women had been burnt. However, Austria owned much of the town and claimed the witches' property in the name of the Emperor, so witch-burning was stopped until the matter was settled. After litigation, Austria withdrew its claims and the witch-burning continued. Four rich women were burnt on 23 October, another four on 13 December and three wealthy men on 22 January 1629. However, under torture they had named rather a lot of accomplices – to the point that almost everyone in the city had been accused of being a witch. Opposition grew, but it was quelled when two of its ringleaders were burnt. On 4 May, three women were burnt; on 24 May, four women and a man; on 8 June, two women and two men; on 4 July, five women and a man; 6 August, five more.

The persecution then hit another snag when the clergy claimed they were not getting their fair share of the goods confiscated. The witch-burnings were halted again until this could be sorted out. They resumed on 19 October when another four unfortunates were burnt. Another four were burnt on 23 November, but the clergy still felt they were being short-changed and secretly encouraged condemned witches to revoke their denunciations. They also protested the immorality of torture. This curbed the *Rat*'s enthusiasm, but in just two years they had burnt seventy-nine people.

There was a similar dispute occurred in Hagenau between the *Hexenschuss* or city witch commission and the Reichsschultheiss, representing the Emperor, when four wealthy people were executed on 13 January 1629. It was settled when the money was split three ways between the commissioners, the Emperor and the *Oberlandvogt* or High Sheriff Archduke Leopold. The city noted that if it did not make the payments, witches would not be burnt, which would be an affront to God.

As the persecution intensified, so did the savagery. The following is a verbatim report of the first day's torture of a woman accused to witchcraft at Prossneck in 1629:

1. The hangman bound her hands, cut her hair, and placed her on a

ladder. He threw alcohol over her head and set fire and burnt her hair to the roots.

2. He placed strips of sulphur under her arms and around her back and set fire to them.
3. He tied her hands behind her back and pulled her up to the ceiling.
4. He left her hanging there from three to four hours, while the torturer went to breakfast.
5. On his return, he threw alcohol over her back and set fire to it.
6. He attached very heavy weights on her body and drew her up again to the ceiling. After than he put her back on the ladder and placed a very rough plank full of sharp points against her body. Having thus arranged her, he jerked her up again to the ceiling.
7. Then he squeezed her thumbs and big toes in the vice, and he trussed her arms with a stick, and in this position kept her hanging about a quarter of an hour until she fainted away several times.
8. Then he squeezed the calves and the legs in a vice, always alternating the torture with questioning.
9. Then he whipped her with a rawhide whip causing the blood to flow out over her shift.
10. Once again he placed her thumbs and big toes in a vice, and left her in this agony on the torture stool from 10am to 1pm, while the hangman and the court officials went out to feed themselves. In the afternoon, an official came who disapproved of this pitiless procedure. But they whipped her again in a frightful manner. This concluded the first day of torture.

The next day they started all over again – 'but without pushing thing quite so far as the day before,' said the *Hexenmeister*.

Witch-hunting reached Bamberg later then the other German states, but Bishop Johan Gottfried von Aschausen burned some 300 witches between 1609 and 1622. In 1617 alone, 102 were killed. He was succeeded by the *Hexenbischof* Gottfried Johann Georg II Fuchs von Dornheim who, with his vicar-general Suffragan Bishop Friedrich Förner, were responsible for burning at least 600 people between 1623 and 1633. They built a special *Drudenhaus* to house thirty or forty prisoners at a time, with smaller witch prisons in the other towns in the bishopric. And in the vicious witch trials of 1626-30, one commissioner, Dr. Ernst Vasolt, burned some four hundred witches.

The vice-chancellor of Bamberg, Dr. George Haan, tried to moderate the witch trials only to find himself denounced as a witch-lover. In 1628 he was burned along with his wife and daughter – despite an imperial order for their release as 'their arrest was a violation of the law of the Empire and not to be tolerated'. During his torture, Haan denounced the chancellor of the city and five other leading citizens who were also burned alive. Among them was Johannes Junius who had served as burgomaster from 1608 up until his arrest in 1628. His wife had been burnt shortly before. According to the minutes of his trial:

> *On Wednesday, 28 June 1628, Johannes Junius, burgomaster of Bamberg, was examined without torture on charges of witchcraft: how and in what fashion he had fallen into that vice. He is fifty-five years old and was born in Niederwayisch in the Wetterau. He says he is wholly innocent, knows nothing of the crime and had never renounced God in his life. He says that he is wronged before God and the world and would like to hear of a single human being who has seen him at sabbats.*
>
> *Confrontation of Dr. George Adam Haan, who tells him to his face that he will stake his life on it that he saw him, Junius, a year and a half before at a witch gathering in the electoral council room, where they ate and drank. The accused denies the same wholly.*
>
> *Confronted with the servant Ellse, who tells him likewise that he was on Hauptsmorwald at a sabbat where the holy wafer was desecrated. Junius denies this. He was then told that his accomplices had confessed against him and was given time for thought.*
>
> *On Friday, 30 June 1628, the aforesaid Junius was again without torture exhorted to confess, but again confessed nothing. Since he would confess nothing, he was put to the torture.*

Thumbscrews were applied. He says he has never denied God his Saviour not suffered himself to be otherwise baptised. Again he will stake his life on it. He feels no pain in the thumb screws.

Leg vices. He will confess absolutely nothing, knows nothing about it. He has never renounced God, will never do such a thing, has never been guilty of this vice. Feels likewise no pain.

Is stripped and examined. On his right side is found a bluish mark, shaped like a clover leaf, is pricked three times, but feels no pain and no blood flows out.

Strappado. He has never renounced God. God will not forsake him. If he were such a wretch, he would not left himself be tortured so. He knows nothing about witchcraft.

On 5 July, the above-named Junius is without torture, but with urgent persuasions, exhorted to confess, and at last begins and confesses:

When in the year 1624 his law suit at Rottweil cost him some six hundred florins, he had gone out, in the month of August, into his orchard at Friedrichsbronnen; and, as he sat there in thought, there had come to him a woman like a grass-maid [woman of loose character], who asked him why he sat there so sorrowful. He had answered that he was not despondent, but she led him by seductive speeches to yield to her will... And thereafter this wench had changed into the form of a goat, which bleated and said: 'Now you see with whom you have had to do. You must be mine or I will forthwith break your neck.' Thereupon he had been frightened and trembled all over with fear. Then the transformed spirit had seized him by the throat and demanded that he should renounce Almighty God, whereupon Junius said 'God forbid', the spirit vanishing through the power of these words. Yet it came back straight away, brought more people with it and persistently demanded of him that he renounce God in Heaven and all the heavenly host, by which terrible threatening he was obliged to speak this formula: 'I renounce God in Heaven and his host, and will henceforth recognise the devil as my God.'

After the renunciation he was so far persuaded by those present and by the evil spirit that he suffered himself to be baptised in the evil spirit's name. The Morhauptin had given him a ducat as dower-gold, which afterwards became only a potsherd [shard of pottery].

He was then named Krix. His succubus he had to call Vixen. Those present had congratulated him in Beelzebub's name and said that they were now all alike. At this baptism of his there were among others the aforesaid Morhauptin Christiana, the young Geiserlin, Paul Glaser, Caspar Wittich and Claus Gebhard, who were both gardeners. After this they dispersed.

At this time, his paramour had promised to provide him with money, and from time to time to take him to the witch-gatherings. Whenever he wished to ride to the sabbat, a black dog would come to his bed, whereupon he would mount it and the dog would raise itself in the devil's name and so fly off.

About two years ago he was taken to the electoral council-room, on the left-hand side of the entrance. Above, at a table, were seated the chancellor, the burgomaster Neudecker, Dr. George Haan... [twenty-four others are named]. Since his eyes were not good, he could not recognise more people.

More time was now given for consideration:

On 7 July, the aforesaid Junius was again examined to know what further had occurred to him to confess. He confesses that about two months ago, on the day after an execution was held, he was at a witch-dance at the Black Cross, where Beelzebub had show himself to them all and said expressly to their faces that they must all be burned together on this spot, and ridiculed and taunted those present. He names four more witches.

The minutes of the trial then detailed his crimes:

Immediately after his seduction, his succubus demanded that he do away with his youngest son Hans Georg, and had given him for this purpose a grey powder. But this was difficult for him and he did away with his brown horse instead.

His succubus had also often urged him to kill his two daughters... and he had been beaten because he had refused. Once, at the suggestion of his succubus, he had taken the holy wafer out of his mouth and had given it to her. He was occasionally obliged to have intercourse with his succubus.

A week before his arrest, as he was going to St. Martin's church, the devil met him on the way in the form of a goat and told him that he would soon be imprisoned, but that he should not trouble himself – he would soon be set free. Besides this, by his soul's salvation, he knew nothing further, but what he had spoke was the pure truth, on that he would stake his life.

On 6 August 1628, there was read to the aforesaid Junius this his confession, which he then wholly ratified and confirmed, and was willing to stake his life upon it. And afterwards he voluntarily confirmed the same before the court.

But before he was burnt at the stake, Junius smuggled a note to his daughter, telling his side of the story. It read:

Many hundred thousand goodnights, dearly beloved daughter Veronica. Innocent I have come to prison, innocent I have been tortured, innocent I must die. For whoever comes into the witch prison must become a witch or be tortured until he invents something out of his head and – God pity him – bethinks him of something. I will tell you how it has gone with me. When I was put to the torture the first time, Dr. Braun, Dr. Kötzendörffer and two strange doctors were there. Then Dr. Braun asked me, 'Kinsman, how come you here?' I answered, 'Through falsehood and misfortune.' 'Hear you,' said he, 'you are a witch. Will you confess it voluntarily? If not, we will bring in witnesses and the executioner for you.' I said, 'I am no witch.

I have a pure conscience in the matter; if there are a thousand witnesses, I am not worried, but I'll gladly hear them.'

Then the chancellor's son was set before me, who said he had seen me. I asked that he be sworn and legally examined, but Dr. Braun refused. Then the chancellor, Dr. George Haan, was brought, who said the same as his son. Afterwards Höppfen Ellse. She had seen me dance on Haupstsmorwald, but they refused to swear her in. I said, 'I have never renounced God, and will never do it – God graciously keep me from it. I'll rather bear what I must.' And then came also – God in highest Heaven have mercy – the executioner and put the thumb-screws on me, both hands bound together, so that the blood ran out at the nails and everywhere, so that for four weeks I could not use my hands as you can see from my writing.

Thereafter they stripped me, bound my hands behind me, and drew me up in the torture. Then I thought heaven and earth were at an end; eight times did they draw me up and let me fall again, so that I suffered terrible agony. I said to Dr. Braun, 'God forgive you for thus misusing an innocent and honourable man.' He replied, 'You are a knave.'

And this happened on Friday, 30 June, and with God's help I had to bear the torture. When at last the executioner led me back into the cell, he said to me, 'Sir, I beg you, for God's sake confess something, whether it is true or not. Invent something, for you cannot endure the torture which you have been put to; and even if you bear it all, yet you will not escape, not even if you were an earl, but one torture will follow after another until you say you are a witch. Not before that,' he said, 'will they let you go, as you may see by all their trials, for one is just like another.'

Then came George Haan, who said the commissioners had said the Prince-Bishop wished to make such an example of me that everybody would be astonished. And so I begged, since I was in wretched plight, to be given a day for thought and a priest. The priest was refused me, but the time for thought was given. Now, my dear child, see in what hazard I stood and still stand. I must say that I am a witch, though I am not – must now renounce God, though I have never done it before. Day and night I was deeply troubled, but at last there came to me a new idea. I would not be anxious but, since I had been given no priest from whom I could take counsel, I would think of something to say myself. It were surely better that I just say it with mouth and words, even though I had not really done it; and afterwards I would confess it to the priest, and let those answer for it who compel me to do it... And so I made my confession, as follows; but it was all a lie...

He then repeated his confession, which is much the same as that in the minutes of this trial:

...Then I had to tell what people I had seen at the sabbat. I said that I had not recognised them. 'You old rascal, I must set the executioner on you. Say – was not the chancellor there?' So I said yes. 'Who besides?' I had not recognised anybody. So he said: 'Take one street after another. Begin at the market, got out on one street and back on the next.' I had to name several people there. Then came the long street [die lange Gasse] I knew nobody. I had to name eight persons there. Then the Zinkenwert – one person more. Then over the bridge to the Georgthor, on both sides. I knew nobody again. Did I know nobody at the castle – whoever it might be? I should speak without fear. And thus continuously they asked me on all the streets, though I could not and would not say more. So they gave me to the executioner, told him to strip me, shave me all over and put me to the torture. 'The rascal knows one on the market place, is with him daily, and yet won't name him.' By that they meant Dietmeyer, so I had to name him too.

Then I had to tell what crimes I had committed. I said nothing...'Hoist the rascal up!' So I said that I was to kill my children, but I had killed a horse instead. It did not help. I had also taken a sacred wafer and had desecrated it. When I had said this, they left me in peace.

Now, my dearest child, here you have all my acts and confession, for which I must die. And it is all sheer lies and inventions, so help me God, for all this I was forced to say through dread of torture beyond what I had already endured. For they never cease the torture until one confesses something; however pious, he must be a witch. Nobody escapes, even though he were an earl. If God send no means of bringing the truth to light, our whole kindred will be burned. God in heaven knows that I know not the slightest thing. I die innocent and as a martyr.

Dear child, keep this letter secret, so that people do not find it, else I shall be tortured most piteously and the jailers beheaded. So strictly is it forbidden... Dear child, pay this man a thaler... I have taken several days to write this, my hands are both crippled. I am in a sad plight...

Junius urged his daughter to collect together what money she could and leave town for her own safety on the pretext that she was going on a pilgrimage. He signed off 'Good night, for your father Johannes Junius will never see you more.'

In the margin of the letter he added 'Dear child, six have confessed against me at once: the chancellor, Neudecker, Zaner, Hoffmeister Ursel and Höppfen Ellse – all false, through compulsion, as they all told me, and begged for my forgiveness in God's name before they were executed... They know nothing but good of me. They were forced to say it, just as I myself was.'

*

In April 1631, when the persecution in Bamberg was dying down, the witch prison still held twenty-two inmates, including the Bishop's treasurer. Their combined property, which had already been confiscated, amounted to 222,000 florins. This money had gone to line the pockets of Prince-Bishop Gottfried, who had already collected 500,000 florins from witches he had executed. According to the episcopal records, those who contributed included:

George Neudecker – 100,000 florins
Barbara Schleuch – 2,000 florins
Christina Miltenberger – 9,000 or 10,000 florins
Caspar Cörner, Bailiff of Münchsberg – 9,000 or 10,000 florins
Wolfgang Hoffmeister, Treasurer of Bamberg – 50,000 florins

By this time many of the prominent citizens of Bamberg had fled to Bohemia, Rome or the Holy Roman Emperor's court at Regensburg. Prince-Bishop Gottfried had little time for the Emperor and his his court, and disregarded it when he intervened on behalf of Dorothea Block, the wife of a wealthy citizen. There are no records of the charges against her, but she was not allowed a lawyer and was burnt like all the rest in May 1630. Her father fled. But Bamberg was not the only place suffering from the witch-craze at the time. In Strasbourg, it is esti-mated that five thousand witches were burnt between 1615 and 1635.

Witches were usually speedily dispatched, as in the case of Anna Hansen. On 17 June 1629, she was imprisoned on suspicion of witch-craft. The following day, having refused to confess, she was scourged. On 20 June, she was tortured with the thumbscrews and confessed. On the 28th, her confession was read to her. Two days later she voluntarily confirmed her confession and was sentenced. On 4 July she was told of the date of her execution and on 7 July she was beheaded and burned.

Along with the thumbscrews, leg vices, strappado and squassation, the authorities also employed scourging on or off the strappado to extract a confession. Suspects were also put in stocks armed with long iron spikes for up to six hours. A rope was pulled around their neck until it cut down to the bone. They were force fed salted herring and denied water, or made to kneel on prayer stools that had sharp wooden pegs sticking out of them. Burning feathers, often dipped in sulphur, were held under the arms and groin. They were dunked in baths of freezing or scalding water to which lime had been added – six people were killed in nearby Zeil in 1630 while being tortured in this fashion.

After sentencing and on the way to being burned, extra punishments could be exacted, such as cutting off the right hand or tearing a woman's breasts with red-hot pincers. But such barbarity began to bring criticism.

'Some people began to feel great sympathy for the unfortunate victims,' wrote Heinrick Türck of Paderborn, a Jesuit. 'And grave doubts were raised as to whether the numerous persons who perished in the flames were really guilty and deserved so horrible a death. In fact, many people thought that this treatment of human beings, who had been bought with the precious blood of Christ, was cruel and more than barbaric.'

Councillor Dümler, who fled from Bamberg after his pregnant wife had been horribly tortured and burned, told the Emperor, 'People are protesting that it is impossible that justice had been done to all the people in Bamberg.' And he suggested halting the confiscation of the accused's property.

Another man who had escaped from the *Drudenhaus* presented a petition to the Emperor from Barbara Schwartz, who had spent three years in the dungeon and been tortured eight times without confessing. In September 1630, Emperor Ferdinand's Jesuit confessor refused him absolution unless he curb the excesses in Bamberg and warned that his inaction was causing public hostility to the election of his son to succeed him. So Ferdinand subpoenaed the court records of Bamberg for investigation. He ended the confiscation of prisoners' property, insisted that the basis of the accusation – usually a malicious defamation – should be made public at all future trials and that the accused by allowed a lawyer. Torture, however, was not abolished.

Twenty-four witches were burned in Bamberg in 1630; none the following year. This was partly because of growing opposition, partly because of the death of Bishop Förner that summer and partly because of the threat of King Gustavus of Sweden who had entered Leipzig that September. Then, in 1632, Prince-Bishop Gottfried died and the persecution in Bamberg was over.

However, his cousin Prince-Bishop Philipp Adolf von Ehrenberg had been even more savage in nearby Würzburg, where he had burnt over nine hundred witches. There had been random executions since 1600, but the persecution in Würzburg began in earnest when Johann Gottfried von Auschhausen came from Bamberg in 1617. Ehrenberg took over in 1623.

In 1626, a peasant was accused of *maleficia* on the basis of common gossip. Under torture he named seven others. All eight were burnt, one of them after being torn with red-hot pincers. The following year, there were between twenty-nine and forty-two burnings – the record is unclear.

In January 1628, three children aged between eight and thirteen confessed to having intercourse with the devil. Two were burnt. That October, a schoolboy named Johann Philipp Schuck was arrested. After forty-six lashes, he still protested his innocence. After seventy-seven more, he confessed to attending a sabbat, named his accomplices and was put to death on 9 November. The following day twelve-year-old Jacob Russ was executed. After repeated beatings he said he had seen priests at a sabbat.

In 1738 the *Bibliotheca Magica* published a list dated 16 February 1629 detailing twenty-nine mass executions at Würzburg which consumed 157 victims in all. There were nearly as many men as women. Many victims were wealthy and highly placed and thirteen were children, twelve-years-old or younger. Those executed included:

'Seventh execution, seven persons:
'A little girl, a stranger, aged twelve. A stranger. A stranger, a woman. A village mayor, a stranger. Three women, strangers. At the same time was executed in the market place a guard who had let some prisoners escape.

'Eighth execution, seven persons:
'The Senator Baunach, the fattest burgher in Würzburg. The chief provost of the cathedral. A stranger. A man named Schleipner. A woman who sold visors. Two women, strangers.

'Tenth execution, three persons:
'Steinacher, one of the wealthiest citizens. Two strangers, a man and a woman.

'Eleventh execution, four persons:

'A vicar of the cathedral named Schwerdt. The wife of the Provost of Rensacker. A woman named Stiecher. A man named Silberhans, a fiddler.

'Thirteenth execution, four persons:

'Old Hof-Schmidt. An old woman. A little girl nine or ten years old. Her younger sister.

'Nineteenth execution, six persons:

'A son of a nobleman from Rotenham was executed at six o'clock in the courtyard of the Town Hall, and his body burnt on the following day. The wife of Secretary Schellhar. Another woman. A boy, ten years old. Another boy, twelve years old. A baker's wife named Brügler is burned alive.

'Twenty-first execution, six persons:

'The Master of Dieterich hospital, a very learned man. A man named Stoffel Holtmann. A boy fourteen years old. The young son of Senator Stolzberger. Two seminarians.

'Twenty-third execution, nine persons:

'The son of David Cot, a boy aged twelve in the upper school. The two young sons of the Prince-Bishop's cook, schoolboys, the elder fourteen and the younger twelve years old. Melchior Hammelmann, parish priest of Hach. Nicodemus Hirsch, a canon of the new cathedral. Christopher Berger, a vicar of the new cathedral. A seminarian. N.B. An officer of the Court of Brembach and a seminarian were burned alive.

'Twenty-fifth execution, six persons:

'Frederick Basser, a vicar of the cathedral chapter. Stab, parish priest of Hach. Lambrecht, a canon of the new cathedral. The wife of Gallus Haus. A boy, a stranger. A woman named Schelmerey, a shopkeeper.

'Twenty-sixth execution, seven persons:

'David Hans, a canon of the new cathedral. The Senator Weydenbusch.

The wife of the innkeeper at Baumgarten. An old woman. The young daughter of Valkenberger was executed privately and the body burned in a coffin. The young son of an officer of the Council. Wagner, a vicar of the cathedral chapter, was burned alive.

'Twenty-ninth execution, nine persons:
'Viertel Beck. Klingen, an innkeeper. The steward of Mergelsheim. The wife of the baker at Oxenn Gate. A fat noblewoman. N.B. A doctor of theology, named Meyer, of Hach, and a canon of Hach were executed secretly at five o'clock in the morning; their bodies were burned. A gentleman of rank, named Squire Fischbaum. Paul Vaeker of Breit-Hüt. Since then there have been two other executions. 16 February 1629.'

And this barely scratched the surface. In August 1629, the chancellor of the Prince-Bishop of Würzburg wrote this chilling missive to an unnamed friend:

> As to this matter of witches, which Your Grace thought over some time ago, it has started up again and no words can adequately describe it. Ah, the woe and misery of it all. There are still four hundred in the city, high and low, or every rank and sex, even clergy, so strongly accused that they may be arrested at any minute. It is certain that many of the people of my gracious Prince-Bishop here, of all offices and faculties, must be executed: clerics, electoral councillors and doctors, city officials, court assessors, several of whom Your Grace knows. Law students have been arrested. My lord the Prince-Bishop has more than forty students who should soon become priests, of whom thirty or forty are said to be witches. A few days ago, a dean was arrested. Two others who were summoned have fled. A notary of our cathedral consistory, a very learned man, was arrested yesterday and put to the torture. In one word, a third of the city is surely implicated. The richest, most attractive, most prominent of the clergy are already executed. A week ago, a girl of nineteen was burned, of who it is said everywhere

that she is the fairest in the whole city, and was universally regarded as a girl of singular modesty and purity. In seven or eight days, she will be followed by others of the best and most attractive persons. Such people go in fresh mourning clothes undauntedly to their deaths, without a trace of fear of the flames. And thus many are burned for renouncing God and attending the witch-dances, against who nobody has ever else spoken a word.

'To conclude this horrible matter, there are three hundred children of three and four years, who are said to have inter-course with the devil. I have seen children of seven put to death and brave little students of ten, twelve, fourteen and fifteen years of age. Of the nobles... – but I cannot write any more about this misery. There will yet be persons of higher rank, whom you may know and admire, and would scarcely believe it true of them. Let justice be done.

Then he concluded with a postscript:

P.S. Though there are many wonderful and terrible things happening, it is beyond doubt that, at a place called Fraw-Rengberg, the devil in person, with eight thousand followers, held an assembly and celebrated mass before them all, administering to his congregation (that is, the witches) turnip rinds and parings in place of the Holy Eucharist. I shudder to write about these foul and most horrible and hideous blasphemies. It is also true that they pledged themselves not to be enrolled in the Book of Life, but all agreed that their decision should be recorded by the notary who is well known to me and my colleagues. We hope, too, that the book in which they are enrolled will yet be found, and everyone is searching diligently for it.

Similar things were going on in Bonn, the official residence of the Archbishop of Cologne. A priest named Duren from the village of Alfter just outside the city wrote to Count Werner von Salm, 'That I haven't written for so long is because nothing unusual has happened, only that they have begun burning witches in Bonn. At the present time there is imprisoned a wealthy woman, whose husband had formerly been a magistrate in Bonn, named Kurzrock, who was the sole owner of the inn *At the Sign of the Flower.* I don't know whether your Grace knew him or not. Be that as it may, she is a witch and the opinion grows day by day that she be executed, and without doubt some more of these [Lutheran] blockheads must follow her.'

Later he explained the extent of the persecution:

> *The victims of the funeral pyres are for the most part male. Half the city must be implicated for already professors, law students, pastors, canons, vicars and monks have been arrested and burnt. His Prince Grace has seventy seminarians training to become priests, one of whom, eminent as a musician, was arrested yesterday; two others were sought, but escaped. The chancellor and his wife and the private secretary's wife have already been apprehended and executed. On the Eve of our Lady's Day [7 September] there was executed here a girl of nineteen who had the reputation of being the loveliest and most virtuous in all the city, and who had been brought up by the Prince-Bishop himself. A canon of the cathedral named Rotensahe, I saw beheaded and burned. Children of three or four have devils for their paramours. Students and boys of noble birth of nine, ten, eleven, twelve, thirteen and fourteen have been burnt here. To sum up, things are in a pitiful state, that one does not know with what people one may talk and associate.*

In Cologne itself, there were fewer witch trials because the city council reserved the right to make arrests. And in 1626, Catherine Henot successfully defended a case in an ecclesiastical court where the nuns of St. Clare denounced her for bewitching them when a counsel – a rarity in itself – argued that the evidence of demoniacs was inadmissible. Archbishop Ferdinand of Cologne simply ordered a new trial before a secular court, where Catherine Henot was found guilty and burned. In 1629, Christine Plum, a woman who was believed to be possessed, accused numerous others of witchcraft. When priests denounced the testimony of what was plainly a mad women, they found themselves being accused of witchcraft. The Archbishop encouraged this, but the city council limited the number of arrests, so the persecution in Cologne did not rival those in Bamberg, Würzberg or Bonn.

Elsewhere 1629 was a particularly bad year. At Miltenburg in the archdiocese of Mainz, out of a population of three thousand, 178 were executed in the township with another fifty-six losing their lives in the village nearby. At Burgstädt, again with a population of less than three thousand, seventy-seven were burnt. Another nineteen were burnt in the tiny village of Eichenbühel.

Around this time the Prince-Bishop of Würzburg's sole heir, Ernest von Ehrenberg, was beheaded as a witch. He would have been rich if he had survived. A brilliant student with a promising future, he had suddenly quit his studies to pursue an older woman. Gradually he turned to drink and dissipation. The Jesuits investigated and found that he was engaged in all types of vice, including witchcraft. He was denounced and tried secretly, and sentenced to death without his knowledge.

The unsuspecting Ernest was woken one morning at seven and told that he was going to lead a better life. He was led to the castle and taken to the black-draped torture chamber. At the sight of the instruments of torture, he fainted. Some of the judges were moved by this and asked the Prince-Bishop for mercy. But Ehrenberg was unmoved and confirmed the sentence. Ernest resisted and in the resulting fight was hit over the head. A Jesuit who recorded the scene said, 'He fell to the ground without any sign of grief or any manifestation of piety. May God grant that he does not fall like this into the eternal fires of hell.' This may have brought about a change of heart in Ehrenberg. Soon after he stopped the trials and ordered commemorative services for all those he had burnt. The advance of the Swedish army might also have had something to do with it.

In 1631, Franz Buirmann, an itinerant witch judge in the service of the Prince-Archbishop of Cologne turned up at the little village of Rheinberg. He charged a number of prominent citizens with witchcraft and confiscated their possessions. One of them was an wealthy widow named Christine Böffgen, who was so well liked and respected that five of the seven assessors refused to take part in the proceedings. Frau Böffgen was blindfolded, exorcised, stripped, shaved and pricked. Then she was put in a leg vice until she confessed. Released from the torture stool, she retracted her confession, so she was tortured again. She refused to name her accomplices and, on the fourth day of torture, she died. Masses were said for the repose of her soul in St. George's church in Rheinbach until 1926.

Having lined his pockets with Frau Böffgen's money, Buirmann made advances to a local woman, but was spurned. So without telling to the local justices, he seized her sister, Frau Peller, the wife of a court assessor, and began torturing her. When her husband protested, Buirmann had him thrown out of the courtroom. She was exorcised, stripped, shaved and searched in the most intimate places – the torturer's assistant raping her in the process. To stifle her cries, Judge Buirmann stuffed a soiled handkerchief in the mouth. When asked to name her accomplices, she gave so many names that even the bloodthirsty Buirmann stopped writing them down. Convicted of witchcraft, she was burnt alive in a hut of dry straw, the preferred method of execution in the Rhineland. Her husband also died a few months later.

Buirmann then went after Herr Lirtzen, the burgomaster of Rheinbach and the brother-in-law of a court assessor. He was tortured with legs vices and 'crocodile jaws' but refused to confess. Then he was tied to a St. Andrew's cross with a jagged iron collar around his neck. The cross the shaken violently and the collar cut the flesh away from his neck. When this brought no confession, he was tied to a metal witch's chair and a fire was lit underneath it. After twenty-four hours of this treatment he still refused to confess. Two days later he was burnt alive with Frau Peller.

The mayor of Rheinbach, a wealthy and educated man named Dr. Schultheis Schweigel opposed Buirmann and spoke out particularly against the trial of Christine Böffgen. When the judge returned to

Rheinbach in 1636, he arrested Dr. Schweigel as a 'witch patron'. After seven hours of torture, he died. His corpse was dragged from the prison and burnt. In his will, he had left his considerable fortune to the poor. Buirmann took it. This turned the townspeople against him. Even the local priests spoke out against him, though Father Hubertus of Meckenheim, who preached against the persecution, found himself branded a witch. Buirmann was forced to move on to Siegburg, where he discovered that his own executioner was a witch and burnt him.

The outlook for the residents of Cologne was also looking bleak. After the Battle of Leipzig in 1631, the Swedish army drove a number of witch-hunting churchmen – including the Archbishop of Mainz, the Bishops of Bamberg, Würzburg, Worms and Speyer, along with the Abbot of Fulda – from their domains. They sought refuge in Cologne where they took up witch-hunting again. By 1636, the persecution had reached such a pitch that the Pope sent Cardinal Giretti and Cardinal Albizzi to put an end to it. There was a long hiatus and last execution took place in Cologne in 1655.

There had been an outbreak of witchcraft at Eichstätt in 1590, then again from 1603 to 1630. Records show that, in the twenty-four years to 1627, 113 women and nine men were burned. In 1629 alone, the judge at Eichstätt said that he sentenced 274 witches, at the behest of the Bishop of Eichstätt, Johann Christoph. There must have been some opposition because on 11 December 1627, the Bishop stopped confiscating the property of his wealthy victims to show that his sole motive was to honour God. One of the victims was Anna Käser, who was denounced as a witch in 1620, 1624, 1626 and 1627. In 1629, she was charged with attending a sabbat. After being tortured four times, she confessed, but then told her confessor that her confession had been a lie and that she, and all the other prisoners, were innocent. He told the court who simply had Anna tortured a fifth time, even more brutally. On 29 September 1629, she was beheaded and burnt.

In 1637, an unnamed peasant woman was denounced as a witch, once again, in Eichstätt. A copy of the record of her trial survives, though the names have been omitted, perhaps to protect their relatives. She was denied access to a lawyer and a priest and was not even faced by her accusers, who had probably given her name under torture. Her trial began on Monday, 15 November 1637. Present were 'the Herr Chancellor, the Herr Doctor, the Herr Secretary and the Herr Recorder':

'After serious consideration by the civil councillors of the court, the prisoner commonly known as —, having been taken into custody on suspicion of witchcraft, and on fifteen sworn depositions, meriting death, is thorough examined as follows:

Q. What is her name?
A. —, aged forty years. She does not know the names of either her father or mother, where they were born, where they were brought up, or when they died. She has lived with her husband twenty-three years, and during that time has borne eight children, five of whom are still living. Of the three deceased, one died of smallpox twenty-one years ago at the age of two. Another died eight or nine years ago at the age of six. And the third lad died six years ago, also of smallpox. Because of the suspicious circumstances of death, she was told to appear at the town hall.
Q. Does she know the reason why she was summoned to appear at the town hall?
A. She knows of no reason other than the accusation of being a witch.
Q. That is true. Otherwise she would not have been brought here. Therefore she should make a start at admitting her guilt, and not look round for any excuses.
A. She will suffer anything, but cannot admit that she is a witch.

The judges then tried to persuade her to confess in the strongest possible terms, but it did no good. The full indictment and the depositions were then read to her. While the first deposition was being read, she laughed heartily and said that she preferred death. She asked how she could admit anything when she had not been to the place mentioned. However, she admitted that she might possibly be guilty of what was said in the second deposition. Regarding depositions three, four, five and six, she said that she had never been to a sabbat. And she denied participating in what was alleged in depositions twelve, thirteen, fourteen and fifteen. She said that she was in no way answerable to or responsible for what is charged and, again, said she would prefer to die. When asked whether she wanted to die like a witch, she said whatever God wished was her wish too.

Q. Indeed. So she should start making her confession and tell how long she has been engaged in this vice, and how she was first enticed into it.

A. Yes, your worships, I will go willingly wherever you want me, but I am not a witch, as true as Christ was tortured and made to suffer on the cross.

Then she was examined for the devil's mark, which was found on the right side of her back, near the shoulder blade. It was about the size of a half-kreutzer. Then the mark was pricked and found to be insensitive. When she was pricked in other places she immediately behaved like she was crazy. Many more suspicious marks were observed and she was questioned again:

Q. Where had she received these devil's marks?

A. She does not know. She had nothing to do with the devil.

The court record continues:

As the accused does not respond to merciful treatment, she is taken to the torture chamber.

After being put on the ladder and the ropes tightened, she says, yes, she could be a witch. When released, she announces that she is no a witch. So she is put back on the ladder and drawn once, twice, three times. Finally she is released when she admits she is a witch. But immediately she become stubborn and denies she is a witch. Then again she is drawn even more tightly on the ladder. She confesses it is true that four-teen years ago when she was unmarried she had become a witch.

Q. But since she had testified that she had been married for twenty-three years, how could it be only fourteen years ago that she became a witch?

A. At this, she asked to be taken off the ladder, when she would tell the truth.

Q. No, she must first make a start at confessing. She deserves to stay on the ladder.

When she finds out she is going to be released, she says that about eighteen years before her husband had come home drunk and said he wished the devil would take her – at the time she had just given birth to another child. And she thought, oh, when would he come. Oh, soon. And at one time she had an illicit love affair with a hangman, and the devil presented himself the next day during the night in the guise of this same hangman. In fact, he arrived during the first night, but since a light was continuously burning, he could not get anywhere with her. And since she was under the impression that he was the hangman, the next night about ten o'clock she had impro-priety with him, and his penis was very cold. After having had intercourse a second time, the devil revealed who he was, talking lewdly, and demanded that she give herself to him, and deny God and our dear lady and all the holy saints. He threatened her so she had to submit to him, but now she was penitent and wanted to turn to God again.

Q. Didn't the devil demand anything more of her?

A. To do evil everywhere.

Q. What methods was she supposed to employ to do evil?

A. Eight days after her seduction, the devil gave her a green powder and a black ointment in an earthenware dish, which she was to use on both men and beasts.

Q. What did the devil call her, and what did she call him?

A. She called the devil Gokhelhaan [rooster] and he called her

Shinterin *[bone-breaker]. Three weeks after her seduction, the*
devil baptised her and poured something over her head.
Q. Is all that she is saying true?
A. Yes
   She is led out of the torture chamber.

The trial continued the following day, Tuesday 16 November 1637.

The accused went on to relate other instances of *maleficia* using the
ointment and implicated one of her victims who she said she had introduced to witchcraft. Later she denied this. Then she told how her little
daughter was taken sick after being given some of the ointment.

The next day, she said that she thought a sore on the side of her
body was a symptom, but the hangman Mathess said that it was not a
cause for concern. Then she said that our lady had appeared to her the
previous night and she was beautiful and snow white.

'Since the prisoner feigns sickness and seems to want to deny her
evidence, and since signs of piety yesterday seem to have faded, she is
ordered to be flogged in the torture chamber to induce fear and true
testimony. After three floggings she says that the devil, dressed in black,
came to her prison cell last night and this morning. Last night he
arrived between eleven and twelve o'clock and had sex with her, but it
caused her so much pain that she could hardly hold him and she
thought her back and thighs were falling apart. Moreover, she promised to surrender her body and soul to him, to reveal nothing of their
pact, to remain true only to him and to oppose the judges as long as she
can. In return, her incubus promised to help her and ordered her to
think how she could commit suicide. To this end, she continued scratch-
ing her middle veins on her right arm open with her fingernails, a half
batzen wide, where she had had a blood-letting two weeks before,
because the scars were very recent and the veins could be opened very
easily. In this way she could kill herself without attracting attention
and go to the devil in both body and soul.'

She then testified that the devil had told her to attribute the effects
of the ointment to the plague and revealed how the devil had forced
her to surrender herself to him.

Over the following days, she identified forty-five accomplices, describing what each was wearing, what they did and the nature of the *incubus* or *succubus* with them. By way of change from the traditional broomstick, she also confessed to flying on a pitchfork provided by the devil, and regular attendance at sabbats. She also admitted to storm-raising.

She was cross-examined on the subject of storm-raising on the following day, Saturday, 27 November 1637.

> *The accused said she had thought about storm-raising for a long time, and had helped cause ten tempests. She had made her first storm fifteen years, between midday and one o'clock, in her own garden, urged on by the devil, to make the fruit drop so that it would not ripen. This happened.*
> *Q. What materials did she use to make the storm, or how else did she created it.*
> *A. She does not want to divulge her secret.*
> *Since she also tried to recant, she was confronted by the hangman and was again asked:*
> *Q. Whether she wants to confess voluntarily or under torture. It was discussed.*
> *A. She will confess voluntarily.*
> *The hangman left, and she was questioned again.*
> *A. She says that the devil supplied her with powder made from children's corpses and told her to use it for raising storms. She gave the powder to —, her loyal accomplice, who buried it in the ground but it popped out. Then she herself buried it, but she pretends to be uncertain what happened.*

On Friday, 3 December 1637, she was cross-examined on the question of exhuming children's corpses, used in the storm-raising spells.

> She says that once, seven, eight or nine years ago, she helped
> — to exhume her own child from the cemetery. The child
> had lain in the grave for six years and its body had all rotted

away. They took the remains home and put them in a pot and stirred them for two days and nights, then pounded them into powder with the handle of a scythe. They gave the powder to the devil. — is not implicated, for even though the devil asked for more powder, she refused to make it and consequently the devil beat her.

She is led away and suspected of subornation.'

On Saturday, 11 December 1637, she said she had not suborned anyone. Then she was questioned on her passage into cellars:

She passed through closed into the wine cellars of [giving five names] about forty times. Also present were two witches, identified by name, who drank wine from the measuring cup or right from the bung.

She also flew into the stable of — and with the help of the devil rode the animals so that they should die. They did not die.

She also went often to the servant's room and seduced her servant —. Indeed, he had let her show it to him often.

Q. What other crimes can she think of, and are there other things she can remember?

A. No. But what she has testified is the truth, for which she is responsible before God and the world. She wishes to live and die according to this testimony and be justified by the verdict of the court. Whereupon she is led back to the torture chamber and the list of her accomplices is read to her, and she confirms it.

On Monday, 13 December; Tuesday, 14 December and Wednesday, 15 December, she again confirmed all the foregoing testimony is true. The entry for Friday, 17 December 1637, is the simple, if ominous statement: 'She died penitent.'

The trial of this unnamed woman took place during the Thirty Years' War, which lasted from 1618 to 1548. After it, the administration of Lindheim was left to the chief magistrate, a blood-thirsty veteran named Geiss. In 1661, he wrote to the High Bailiff of Brunswick-Lünberg, Baron Hermann von Oynhausen – who, along with the Dean of Würzburg Cathedral Hartmann von Rosenbach and several other noblemen formed the *Herrenschaft* – saying that Linheim was swarming with witches.

'The majority of the citizens are very much upset and offer, if his Lordship just expressed a desire to burn them, gladly to provide the wood and pay all the costs,' Geiss said. 'His Lordship might also acquire much money thereby, so that the bridge as well as the church might be brought into good repair. Furthermore, his Lordship might also have so much wealth that in future his officials might be better paid.'

As a result, the *Herrenschaft* agreed to resume the witch trials which had been held in abeyance for eight years. And in July 1661, Geiss appointed four assistant judges to help him. These were men of such vicious reputation that one woman fled at the sight of them. Captured, she was tortured until insensible, then burnt. This was done in a particularly gruesome way. Victims were suspended by chains from a wall about fifteen feet above the fire and slowly charred. The Witches' Tower, where this was occured, later belonged to the writer Leopold von Sacher-Masoch, who gave his name to masochism. These *Hexenturms* appeared in towns all over Germany.

Children as young as eight were burnt, but usually – as this was a moneymaking venture – wealthy men and women were chosen. In 1663, Geiss wanted to seize the property of a respectable miller named Johann Schüler. His wife had given birth to a stillborn child the year before and he got a confession from the midwife that she had killed the child by witchcraft. The woman also named six accomplices who were arrested. Under torture, they admitted digging up the child's body and cooking it to make witch ointment. But the Schülers insisted that no one was to blame for the death of their child and demanded that the grave be opened to disprove what was being said. The grave was opened in the presence of Johann Schüler and the corpse was found intact. Under threat of torture, Geiss insisted that Schüler hold his tongue, while the midwife and her six accomplices were burnt – on the grounds that confessions extracted under torture were always true.

Later that year an old woman named Becker-Margareth was arrested. Knowing what Geiss had in store for her, she implicated fourteen others in the death of the child, including Frau Schüler. She was arrested and an old scar, from a fall, which had been treated by the surgeon-barber of Hanau, was identified as a devil's mark. Herr Schüler fled to Würzburg in an attempt to get the Dean of the Cathedral to release his wife. While he was away, Fran Schüler was tortured, confessed and implicated her husband. When he returned, Geiss had him thrown in a freezing dungeon in the Witches' Tower with no covering or straw.

Geiss took a special delight in torturing him and finding new methods to extract pain. Schüler held out for five days. He confessed, but immediately retracted and was tortured again. He confessed again and retracted again. Geiss was just about to have him racked a third time, when the people of Lindheim rioted. In the confusion, Schüler and others – sadly, not including his wife – got free and fled to Speyer, the seat of the Imperial Supreme Court. The terrible sight of the tortured bodies of the women who had escape caused consternation and a prominent lawyer took up their case. Meanwhile on 23 February 1644, Geiss had Frau Schüler burnt alive. But in early March, the mob forced Geiss and his henchmen to flee. Oynhausen dismissed him but, despite having killed thirty innocent people, he was not punished. Indeed he had done well out of it. Geiss had amassed 188 thalers and 18 albus in cash, along with a large amount of livestock, while his men had been paid exorbitant expenses. When Geiss was questioned about this, he said that he had taken only the standard commission of one-third of the confiscated property, after deductions. Two-thirds had gone to the *Herrenschaft*.

On 10 March 1676, in Naumburg, Saxony the daughter of sixty-six-year-old widow Chatrina Blanckenstein went to a neighbour's to get some fuel. She had no money with her and gave the neighbour some of her mother's jam instead. The neighbour fed some jam to her baby who passed four curious worms and died. This was clearly a case of witchcraft. On 15 March, the town council began an investigation. A hare which was being pursed by boys with dogs had miraculously escaped near Frau Blanckenstein's house. The tax collector found the money received for her payments was unaccountably short. A nightwatchman had seen three cats with red eyes in the main square. And when a court official went to make an inventory of Frau Blanckenstein's property – in anticipation of its confiscation – his inkstand, which was perched on the top of three sacks of court, inexplicably crashed to the floor when he walked across the creaky floor.

On 25 March 1676, the council got permission from the nearest university law school to charge Frau Blanckenstein with murder by witchcraft. She was arrested, along with her daughter who had resisted the arrest. Her four grown-up sons protested that their mother was being held in prisoner when she could easily afford bail and hired a defence counsel, which was now permitted in witchcraft trials. The lawyer answered each of the flimsy charges in detail and submitted his brief to the university.

The council reconvened to hear fresh witness on 28 April. A man testified that his badly-laden cart had turned over outside Frau Blanckenstein's garden, where the road was uneven. A guard said that the prisoner had expressed concern at the disgrace she had brought on her family, which was surely a sign. Another said that Frau Blanckenstein seemed unconcerned at the prospect of torture. This evidence was also submitted to the university.

In May, the law school told the council to question the doctor who had attended the dead child, who said that the worms had big red heads and many legs – a sure sign of witchcraft. Meanwhile they should torture Frau Blanckenstein with the ladder and the boot.

Blanckenstein's sons managed to get their mother's torture delayed for a few days while they appealed to the Elector. But this did no good and at 11pm on 9 June 1676, Chatrina Blanckenstein was put to the torture. The first session lasted two hours. The ladder and boots were used. She was also tortured with thumbscrews. Coarse ropes stripped the flesh off her legs and a cord around her neck was twisted so tightly that the hangman thought she might die. She confessed nothing – proving her guilt. The torture only stopped when she fell unconscious on the ladder. It was said that she was sleeping.

Later that month, her body was shaved, but the executioner could find no devil's mark.

'You may look where you will,' she said defiantly. 'There is nothing anywhere. I trust in God my creator and Jesus Christ my saviour.'

Further reports were sent to the university who, on 23 June, ordered that the case be dismissed. However, Frau Blanckenstein had to take the *Urfeld* – an oath swearing she would not seek retribution – and pay the huge sum of seventy thalers to the court for her torture. She was eventually released on 16 July.

However, the case had blackened her name and, to escape the gossip, she left town. Fleeing was another indication of her guilty and the local magistrates sought the authority to have her arrested. But the university said that they must build a stronger case. Eventually Chatrina Blanckenstein returned, as she is buried in the churchyard in Naumburg. After her death, suspicion fell on her daughter, who on 1 May 1689 – thirteen years after the acquittal of her mother – was charged with using witchcraft to cause the death of a nine-month-old baby, whose father had borrowed thirty thalers from her.

Without waiting for permission from the university, the council began hearings. Her estranged husband refused her the money for a lawyer, but her brothers stepped in. However, when a lawyer studied the prosecution case he refused to defend her. The hearings continued anyway. Eventually the university sanctioned the trial. On 17 June 1689, the defendant was taken to the constable's house where she was to be torture. At the sight of the instruments, she said, 'What do you want me to confess?'

Asked whether she had killed the child, she said – after a long pause – yes. Then she admitted that she had been seduced by a devil named Heinrich who wore a dark plume and had sex with her regularly. She had renounced the Trinity and killed horses and cows. And she named accomplices. Two days later she tried to hang herself with her belt and was only cut down after her face had turned black. Later, when she revived, she withdrew her accusations against her accomplices.

Reviewing the evidence, the university ordered that she be burnt alive. Those she had accused were to be investigated secretly.

Elsewhere in Saxony, 10-year-old Althe Ahlers had learned a conjuring trick. She could produce a mouse from a handkerchief. When she was arrested she said that she had been taught to do this by 63-year-old Elsche Nebelings. Protesting that she knew nothing about mouse-making, she too was arrested on 25 August 1694. Five days later three children described the trick to the court and on 11 September Althe was formally charged with sorcery. The prosecutor demanded the death penalty. He also insisted thumbscrews and whips be used to extract the truth.

However, as Althe was a child, the court appointed a defence counsel. He argued that her trick was sleight of hand. And even if it were sorcery, it was entirely innocent. On 1 October 1694, the judge sent the court reports to the university and asked a number of questions. Should both the old woman and the child should be tortured using the thumbscrews and strappado? Should they be shown the instruments of torture? Should they be searched for the devil's marks? If the devil's mark was found on Althe, how should she be punished? And if Althe was not to be tortured, what should be done with her? The university ordered the release of the prisoners, saying six weeks in jail was sufficient punishment for a 10-year-old.

In 1715, at Wasserburg, near Munich, nine schoolboys accused their teacher, Caspar Schwaiger, of visiting a sabbat. Savagely tortured, he refused to confess. A second session brought a confession and he named others. He recanted but, unable to face more torture, let his statements stand. A similar case happened seven years later at Moosburg, near Freising, where boys accused Georg Pröls of witchcraft. The boys' motive could have been revenge. A year earlier, eleven adolescents, including one 13-year-old boy and three of 14, had been executed there. The torture chamber was sanctified with incense and the whips were blessed before his flogging began. Under torture, he confessed, but recanted. Nevertheless he was beheaded and burnt. But the authorities, fearing widespread hysteria, freed thirteen others, some of whom had already confessed.

Then came the case of Sister Maria Renata Sänger von Mossau, the 65-year-old sub-prioress of the convent at Unterzell, near Würzburg.

She had had doubts about taking Cecilia Pistorini, the daughter of an Italian family living in Hamburg, as a novice in 1745. She suffered from hysteria, shrieking during services, writhing and foaming at the mouth. Soon other nuns followed suit. Then, on her deathbed, one of the older nuns accused Sister Maria Renata of bewitching her. The abbot of a nearby monastery, Father Oswald Loschert – later an assessor at her trial – noted that a 'demon declared by the mouth of a possessed nun that he seized Renata in her mother's womb, that she was his slave and a cursed thing'.

Under exorcism it was discovered that six of the nuns were possessed by the devils Aatalphus, Calvo, Datas, Dusacrus, Elephatan, Nataschurus and Nabascurus. Father Loschert wondered, in all humility, how heaven could have allowed such a terrible curse to fall on a convent that day and night devoted itself to the praise of God and prayer.

'However,' he said, 'this hour has been ordained by providence to expose that foul witch who hid her sorceries beneath the holy habit, to expel her from that fair community to which in spirit and in truth she never belonged.'

A search of Sister Maria Renata's rooms turned up witch salves and noxious herbs, along with a yellow robe which she was said to wear to sabbats. She was interrogated for months on end. The Jesuits at the University of Würzburg recommended torture and after twenty lashes with a consecrated rawhide she confessed. She said she had signed a pact with Satan at the age of 8 and had sex with him at 11, and as a teenager she had learned all about Satanism. Then at 19 she had entered the convent in order to destroy it. Since then she had renounced God and the Church, desecrated the host, rubbed herself with ointment, flown on a broomstick, danced naked with others a sabbat, copulated indiscriminately with devils, recruited three others to the devil's service and caused the six nuns to be possessed.

A details transcript of the court proceedings exists in which she admits having led a 'godless life' – hard to believe as she had spent fifty years in a convent, although she had only become a nun because her parents had forced her to. In Vienna, where her family had gone during the Hungarian war, a grenadier had taught her a spell which she had used to cripple people. She had signed the devil's book in her own blood. She had variously thrown the host into the cesspit, the sea and taken at least one to a sabbat. The devil visited her every Monday in the convent for fornication, often staying two or three hours with no one knowing it. Sex with him caused her intense pain.

She was convicted on thirteen counts of sorcery, heresy and apostasy. The Bishop of Würzburg defrocked her on 28 May 1749, then handed her over to a secular court to be burnt as a witch. However, the Bishop was a compassionate man and asked that she be beheaded first 'in consideration of the extreme youth of the accused when she was first seduced to the heinous sin of witchcraft'.

On 17 June 1749, Father George Gaar and Father Maurus took Maria Renata to Marienberg. No longer entitle to wear a nun's habit, she was dressed in a long black robe with a white apron and neckerchief, and black-and-white hood. There she was beheaded – the executioner taking her head off so dexterously that the crowd cried: 'Bravo!' Her body was then burnt in a bonfire of wood and tar barrels. While she was burning, Father Gaar, a Jesuit, preached a sermon justifying execution for witchcraft and detailing Maria Renata's terrible sins. He was so proud of his sermon that he had it published in German and Italian. This was counter-productive as the German people were growing tired of witch trials. While the Bavarian Criminal Code of 1751 retained death by burning for making a pact with the devil, the penalty for *maleficia* was reduced to beheading.

The Price of Witchcraft

The costs of a witch trial in Germany, like those in France and Scotland, were usually borne by the estate of the witch or their relatives and the witch-finder and his executioners were not the only ones to benefit. Judges, clerks, torturers, guards, clergymen to attended the condemned and even the labourers who cut the wood for the bonfire all had to be paid. Local inn-keepers also made a profit from the crowds who turned up to see the burnings and the local town nobleman, bishop, king or the inquisition itself took whatever remained of the victim's estate. So the authorities had a vested interest in letting the witch persecutions continue. However, in the town of Offenberg in 1629, Councillor Philipp Beck disputed the bill he was presented with for the burning of his wife. On top of everything else, the executioner charged him ten batzen for transporting her from one jail to another. Two attendants who guarded her during the trial had to be paid a weekly wage of ten batzen and seven measures of wine. And after every court session the judges were given a banquet which cost four batzen a head, with an extra two batzen for each messenger. For questioning these charges, Councillor Beck was fined for contempt of the *Rat*.

On 22 June 1595, three women were burnt alive at Appenweier. In the three days since their sentencing, they had run up a bill of 33 florin 6 batzen and 6 pfennig for the 'maintenance of the prisoners and their guards'. They were also charged 14 florin 7 batzen and 10 pfennig for the executioner and 32 florin 6 batzen and 3 pfennig for the entertainment and banquet of the judges, priests and advocate.

And you did not even have to be guilty. On 8 October 1608, the trial of Frau Dietrich was delayed for lack of evidence. The following January her husband demanded the dismissal of the case on the grounds that he could not afford the accumulated court costs. Likewise the trial of Frau Pabst dragged on for three years, due to lack of evidence, until she died in an insane asylum in April 1611. The following February the property of the Pabst family was sold at auction to cover the costs of her imprisonment.

While in Cologne by the eighteenth century they were no longer burning witches alive, they were still torturing, hanging and beheading them – and still making them pay for the privilege! The Archbishop paid a high executioner a retainer of eighty reichsthaler and twenty albus, plus twelve malder of grain and four cords of wood. However, when one particular executioner put in what the Archbishop described as 'unsubstantiated and exaggerated claims' for expenses in 1757, the archbishopric was forced to set out a detailed price list:

Witch Hunt

		Reichsthaler	Albus
1.	For tearing apart and quartering by four horses	5	26
2.	For quartering	4	0
3.	For the necessary rope for that purpose	1	0
4.	For hanging the four quarters in four corners, the necessary rope, nails, chains and the transport included	5	26
5.	For beheading and burning, everything included	5	26
6.	For the necessary rope, and for preparing and igniting the stake	2	0
7.	For strangling and burning	4	0
8.	For rope and for preparing and igniting the stake	2	0
9.	For burning alive	4	0
10.	For rope and preparing and igniting the stake	2	0
11.	For breaking alive on the wheel	4	0
12.	For rope and chains for this procedure	2	0
13.	For setting up the body which is tied to the wheel	2	52
14.	For beheading only	2	52
15.	For the necessary rope for this purpose, and for cloth to cover the face	1	0
16.	For making a hole and disposing of the corpse	1	26
17.	For beheading and tying the body on the wheel	4	0
18.	For the necessary rope and chains, together with the cloth	2	0
19.	For cutting off a hand or several fingers and for beheading, all together	3	26
20.	The same, plus burning with a hot iron	1	26
21.	For the necessary rope and cloth	1	26
22.	For beheading and sticking the head on a pole	3	26

	Reichsthaler	Albus
23. For the necessary rope and cloth	1	26
24. For beheading and tying the body on a wheel and for sticking the head on a pole, all together	5	0
25. For the necessary rope, chains and cloth	2	0
26. For hanging	2	52
27. For the necessary rope, nails and chains needed for this purpose	1	26
28. Before the actual execution starts, for squeezing the delinquent with red-hot tongs, apart from the above-mentioned fee for hanging, for every application	0	26
29. For cutting out the tongue entirely, or part of it, and afterwards for burning the mouth with a red-hot iron	5	0
30. For this procedure, the usual rope, tongs and knife	2	0
31. For nailing to the gallows and cutting of the tongue or chopping off a hand	1	26
32. For one who has hanged himself, or drowned himself, or otherwise taken his own life: to take down, remove, and dig a hole to dispose of the corpse	2	0
33. For exiling a person from the city or country	0	52
34. For flogging in jail, including the rods	1	0
35. For thrashing	0	52
36. For putting in the pillory	0	52
37. For putting in the pillory and for whipping, including the rope and rods	1	26
38. For putting in the pillory, branding and whipping, including coals, rope and rods, also the branding ointment	2	0
39. For inspecting a prisoner after he has been branded	0	20

	Reichsthaler	Albus
40. For putting the ladder to the gallows, regardless whether one or several are hanged the same day	2	0

Concerning torture

	Reichsthaler	Albus
41. For terrorising by showing the instruments of torture	1	0
42. For the first degree of torture [stripping, scourging, racking etc]	1	26
43. For arranging and crushing the thumbs of this degree	0	26
44. For the second degree of torture [strappado], including setting the limbs afterwards, and for salve which is used	2	26
45. Should, however, a person be tortured in both degrees of torture, the executioner is to get for both degrees performed at the same time, setting the limbs afterwards and for use of the salve, for all this he should be paid	6	0
46. For travel and daily expenses for every day, exclusive, however, of the days of execution or torture, regardless whether on these days one or several criminals are punished	0	48
47. For daily food	1	26
48. For each helper	0	39
49. For hiring a horse, together with fodder and stabling, the daily fee	1	16

The price list goes on to say that, if the torture or execution takes place in Cologne, the executioner will have to make do with the set execution or torture fee without additional expenses for travel, daily expenses, food, hay and horse fodder. And if the torture or execution takes place over the river in Deutz or in nearby Melaten he will only received expenses for hay for his horse and nothing else. And, under the current rules, items 16, 32 and 40 were the duties of the weapons' master and he should receive the respective fees.

If the executioner performed a torture or an execution for a vassal or sub-vassal of the archbishopric he should received a third on top of the specified prices, as the vassals and sub-vassals did not contribute towards his annual salary. And only the executioner himself should get this; no 'stranger' was to be employed by vassals or sub-vassals.

The final items goes on to explain, 'Because there have been many complaints that at an execution where an official of the archbishopric presides, the executioner, either in addition to accepting fees, or instead of accepting them, dared to demand a certain sum of money, and since this demand is regarded as an abuse, it is once and for all forbidden. Therefore, herewith we order that every official of the archbishopric keep strictly to the above-mentioned rules and pay the executioners only the stipulated fees and nothing else, any time there is an execution; and they are asked to submit their accounts with all their vouchers afterwards to the treasury of the archbishop.' This was approved by the Archbishop of Cologne on 15 January 1757.

The last witch officially executed in Germany was Anna Maria Schwägel who died in Kempten, Bavaria in 1775. A servant girl and a Catholic, she was already in her mid-thirties and still single, when she fell prey to a coachman who said he would marry her if she became a Lutheran. She travelled to Memmingen, where she formally renounced Catholicism. But once the coachman had seduced her, he abandoned her. Turning back to her faith, she sought absolution from an Augustinian friar, only to discover after she had received it that he too had converted to Protestantism. Believing that she had been tricked by the devil, she became crazed and wandered about the countryside, ending up in a mental asylum in Laneggen, near Kempton. There the matron, Anna Maria Kuhstaller, forced her to admit having sex with the devil in the guise of the coachman. Frau Kuhstaller then denounced her to the magistrates. On 20 February 1775, Anna Maria Schwägel was arrested and thrown in jail.

Two weeks later she went on trial. It seems that torture had not been used and, in her befuddled state, Anna Maria Schwägel freely admitted having a pact with the devil and having sex with him, awake and in dreams. Even though no charges of *maleficia* were made, on 30 March, the judges handed down a death sentence, though they could not decide whether she should be burnt, hanged or beheaded. Honorius, Prince-Abbot of Kempten, then examined her and said: '*Fiat justicia*' – let justice be carried out. Anna Maria Schwägel was beheaded on 11 April 1775.

Scandinavian Sabbats

THERE WAS AN EXTRAORDINARY outbreak of witchcraft around Mora in the province of Dalarnas, central Sweden in 1668. On 5 July, the pastor of Elfdale reported that 15-year-old Eric Ericsen had accused 18-year-old Getrude Svensen of stealing children for the devil. Others were accused of the same crime. All of them said that they were innocent, except for one 70-year-old woman.

In May 1669, King Charles XI – a sceptic – appointed a commission to redeem the accused witches with prayers. Prosecutions were brought under 1608 anti-witchcraft laws of the Lutheran King Charles IX and the 1618 anti-*maleficia* laws of his son Gustav II Adolf. Under these liberal statutes, a charge of sorcery had to be supported by six witnesses and could be refuted by the accused if they could produced twelve character witnesses.

But there had been no witch hunts for thirty years, after they had been banned by Queen Christina. She believed that those who confessed to making a pact with the devil suffered from delusions or internal female disorders and freed all accused witches, except for those clearly guilty of murder. The reintroduction of witch trials sparked mass hysteria and when the commission assembled for the first time on 13 August 1669, three thousand people turned up as witnesses. The following day, after taking testimony from children, the commission

Seventeenth-century woodcut of a witch burning (anonymous).

named seventy witches. Twenty-three of them freely confessed and were burnt within a fortnight. The other forty-seven were sent to nearby Falun where they were burnt a little later.

In addition, fifteen children were burnt. Thirty-six others – between the ages of 9 and 15 – judged to be less guilty had to run the gauntlet, then were beaten with rods on their hands outside the church door every Sunday for a year. Twenty children under 9 who 'showed no great inclination' towards witchcraft were beaten this way for three weeks running.

The evidence against the condemned was that they had attended a sabbat, flying there by magical means, and had proposed *maleficia* – though no actual harm had been done. The children said that the witches had flown with them on goats or sticks or sleeping men. They had flown through windows after the devil had thoughtfully removed the glass. The children were told that if they were tempted to repent or reveal the names of the witches, they would be beaten. When it was noted that 'the judges could not perceive the marks of the lash on them' the children testified that 'the witches said they would quickly disappear'.

The sabbat was held at Blocula – 'a delicate large meadow, where you could see no end'. There was an enchanted house there with a gate painted in many colours and in a smaller field there were animals the children could ride on. However, there were dark deeds going on. Those present were made to deny God by cutting their finger and writing their name in the devil's book using their own blood. They were baptised by the devil and were forced to swear an oath of fidelity, during which the witches flung bits – or 'filings' – of clocks into water, while chanting 'As these filings of clocks do never return to the clock from which they are taken, so may my soul never return to heaven.'

A banquet was held, serving 'broth with coleworts [a kind of headless cabbage] and bacon in it, oatmeal, bread spread with butter, milk and cheese'. Then there was dancing – ending with 'fighting one another' – music and copulation. Participants were also involved in a building a stone house to preserve witches at the Day of Judgement, but the walls kept falling down.

The witches had to promise the devil to do evil, but the worst they seemed to do was spread migraine. At the trial 'The minister of Elfdale declared that one night these witches were, to his thinking, upon the crown of his head; and from there he had a long and continued pain of the head. One of the witches confessed, too, that the devil had sent her to torment that minister. She was ordered to use a nail and strike it into his head, but it would not go in very far and so became that headache.'

It seems they were not very good at performing diabolical tricks either, as 'the Lord Commissioners were indeed very earnest and took great pains to persuade them to show some of their tricks, but to no purpose. For they did all unanimously confess that since they had confessed all, they found that all their witchcraft was gone.'

Even intelligent and well-educated people were caught up in the witch scare. An assessor named Anders Stjernhök, and a professor at Uppsala university believed that the devil had appeared to them three times in one night, and a school teacher who went to become Dean of Mora claimed that the devil had transported him to the Island of Blocula.

Before the self-confessed witches were burnt en masse on 25 August – 'the day being bright and glorious, and the sun shining' – they were forced to confess the truth of the children's accusations.
'At first, most of them did very stiffly, and without shedding the least tear, deny it, though much against their will and inclination.' And when questioned individually, most continued 'steadfast in their denials.' It did not matter. They were burnt anyway.

In 1676, there was witch scare in Stockholm, but it was stopped by a young doctor named Urban Hjärne who showed that the witchcraft epidemic actually sprang from morbid imagination, malice and a desire to attract attention.

'Is it not plain?' said a sceptical bishop. 'The people had frightened their children with so many tales, that they could not sleep without dreaming of the devil, and then made the poor women of the town confess what the children had said of them.'

From Mora, the witchcraft epidemic also spread through Norrland to the two Swedish-speaking provinces of Finland. In 1670, special commissions were set up for Uppsala and Helsinki. Churches held special services to ward off witchcraft. Many were jailed, and in 1674 and 1675 seventy-one people were burned or beheaded in three parishes.

Christianity had not come to Finland from Sweden until 1157 and heathen traditions continued long after. Swedish vagabonds made a living by playing on the Finns' belief in sorcery. This was exacerbated by visiting German craftsmen and Finnish soldiers returning from the Thirty Years' War. Laplanders also continued to boast of their ability to raise storms.

In 1573, the Synod of Turku – then the capital of Finland – excommunicated witches and fortune-tellers. They were handed over to the civil authorities for punishment, usually banishment. A law of 1554 also imposed a fine of forty marks on those who housed witches without reporting then to the minister or sheriff. However, at the time Finland was a grand duchy under the Swedish crown. In 1575, King Johan III of Sweden ordered a tour of inspection, looking for witches. Those found guilty of a first or second offence were to be whipped at the church door. The punishment for a third offence was in the hands of the judges.

In Finland most superstitions were punished by a term of imprisonment on a diet bread and water, flogging and running the gauntlet. However, scholars and scientists in Finland were particularly interested in magic and a number of occult books were in circulation among clergymen and professors. This lead to Professor Martin Stodius and two of his students being tried before the university council of Turku in the later sixteenth century. The widow of Dean Alanus was also tried, after an accusation by Bishop Gezelius. However, in Finland, those in good standing in the community – and able to produce character witnesses – usually got off; only the poor and the lonely were condemned.

Finnish anti-witchcraft laws followed those in Sweden. The Articles of War of 1683 stated that a woman who caused death by witchcraft should be burned, a man hanged. In 1687 a new statute introduced the death penalty for both witchcraft and making a pact with the devil. But no special commissions were set up in Finland to try witches and there were no systematic persecutions. Rather individual acts of *maleficia* were tried by the normal courts. Torture was prohibited, though mutilation was sometimes ordered as a punishment.

The first recorded witch trial in Finland occurred on 1 August 1595, when a woman was charged after wishing misfortune on people, only for these threats to come true, and causing illnesses which she later purported to cure. She was condemned to death.

Then in 1620s there was an outbreak of witch trials in two Swedish-speaking areas Pohjanmaa and Ahvenanmaa. These reached their peak in the 1650s, when fifty cases were tried at Pohjanmaa assizes – during the same period only eleven witch trials occurred in the rest of Finland. In Finland as a whole, only fifty or sixty condemned witches received death sentences – and not all of them were carried out. Some thirty of them came from Pohjanmaa. In all, ten of the condemned were men and spoke Finnish. The rest were Swedish-speaking women.

In 1641, the Court of Appeals urged the clergy in Vehmaa and Lower Satakunta to condemn witchcraft from the pulpit. Then, following the outbreak of witchcraft in Mora, special prayers were said in Finnish churches. Theologians wrote tracts condemning witchcraft and one, Andreas Hasselqvist, advocated the destruction of the servants of the devil by fire and sword.

In Ahvenanmaa, the persecutions flared from 1666 to 1678. Trials showed a distinctly German influence, with overzealous prosecutors quoting from German demonologists. In April 1666, Karin Persdotter, the sick wife of a beggar, was sentenced to death by burning at an extraordinary session in Finström. She named thirteen other women, nine of whom followed her to the stake.

In Norway – though the belief in storm-raising and sabbats was just as common as in the rest of Scandinavia – there were less than two-dozen witch trials. In 1592, Oluf Gurdal was sentenced to death in Bergen. Two years later in Bergen, Anne Knutsdatter, the wife of Kirsten Jyde, and Johanne Jensdatter Flamske – a Jute and a Flem – were burnt, while a third witch, Ditis Røncke, was outlawed. No further witch trials were called until 1622. The accused was a woman known as Synneve, who strangled herself in prison while awaiting trial. Her body was burnt.

In 1650 Karen Thorsdatter admitted that, at the age of 26, she had entered the service of a man calling himself Lucifer. He had taught how to steal milk by magic – by sticking a knife in the wall. He also gave her spells to protect her own cattle. She had flown through the air on a cat, accompanied by the widow of the burgomaster Sidsel Mortensen, who flew a poker, and their leader Christen Klod, who rode a calf. They had once tried to kill two magistrates, but failed because they were both god-fearing men and one wore a gold cross around his neck on a chain. Bodil Kvams, another woman accused by Karen Thorsdatter, admitted riding a poker and trying to kill the magistrates. In turn, she joined Karen in accusing another woman of being a storm-raiser, who was then arrested at her wedding to a country judge. At her trial her husband successful argued that, on a charge so grave, she could not be condemned on the word of two self-confessed felons. Karen Thorsdatter and Bodil Kvams were sentenced to be burnt at Kristiansand.

In 1667, at a christening party in Leinstrand, Trondheim, Erik Kveneld slandered Ole Nypen, calling him witch. Erik blamed Ole for the rheumatism in his hands and threatened to let 'the red cock crow over him' if he did not cure him. For his part Ole Nypen claimed that Erik Kveneld was trying to turn his neighbours and the minister against him. A brawl broke out. Three years later, on 30 April 1670, the case came to court. Ole Nypen's charge of slander was countered by Erik Kveneld's accusation of sorcery against both Nypen and his wife Lisbet. Witness were called to substantiate this and Lisbet admitted using salt and charms to cure illnesses.

Kveneld claimed that he had been hexed by the Nypens – he was unable to raise his arms and his breasts had grown big like a woman's. Also his wife's eyebrows had grown so long she could not see and her ears hung down to her shoulders like a dog's. The witnesses testified seeing Lisbet rubbing salt into wounds while reciting spells. And the patient paid her a small fee when they were cured.

Lisbet said the curative power lay, not in salt, but the words she said over them in God's name. She gave a sample of the 'prayer' she used to cure grippe:

Christ walked into the church with a book in his hand. Then the Virgin Mary came walking. 'Why are you so pale, my blessed son?' 'I have caught a powerful grippe.' 'I cure you of that powerful grippe – cough grippe, stomach grippe, back grippe, chest grippe – from flesh and bone, to beach and stone, in the name of the Father, Son and Holy Ghost.'

Four months later, in August 1670, Lisbet faced criminal charges of saying sacrilegious prayers and maintaining the reputation of a witch. Four witnesses told of her use of charmed salt and how she relieved aches and pains by transferring them to other people or animals. Their local parson said that he had heard that the Nypens had been trafficking in witchcraft for years. The court itself affirmed that the local people 'could not deny there had been rumours about the Nypens for many years, and that many had fed their animals out of fear'.

The court asked Lisbet whether she had willingly served Satan using forbidden prayers. No, she replied, nor could anything she said be misconstrued in that way, then she blamed her own ignorance for any misunderstanding. The court then directed her to curse Satan and she complied.

Then she was asked by whose power she had helped or harmed men and beasts. She said that if she had helped anyone, it was by God's power, and that she had harmed no one. Did she know anyone else, in the district or outside it, who knew these prayers, except for Ane Fergstad? She said she knew only one other and that she had heard Ane read a prayer for frostbite.

The court then got down to the matter of an alleged incident of *maleficia*. Had the evil that had hit a girl really been intended for her, or for the girl's mistress, Kari Oxstad? Lisbet insisted that she was wholly innocent of the matter.

On 27 August 1670, a third hearing was held. The girl was called and she swore that she had been crippled by a spell intended for Kari Oxstad – whom Lisbet thought had slandered her daughters. The local prefect, Hans Edvardsen, then indicted both Ole and Lisbet Nypen on four counts:

1. *Their general evil reputation as testified to the pastor and the people of the district.*
2. *Curing people by transferring the devil from them to their enemies – or, having failed in this, transferring it to animals.*
3. *Harming their neighbours by driving some mad, crippling or disfiguring others, or blinding them – or helping others when it suited them.*
4. *Taking the Lord's name in vain.*

The prefect recommended to the judge that the accused be executed and burned, after having to been tortured into a fuller confession. The couple did not confess. They were condemned, particularly for taking the Lord's name in vain and having a bad reputation, and were sentenced to be burned – though Ole would be beheaded first.

That same year, 1670, another trial took place at Kristiansand. Councilman Niels Pedersen had been away in Copenhagen on business when he was racked with pain and lost the power of speech. He had been bewitched! After prolonged interrogation, Karen Snedkers confessed that she had tried into injure the councilman by sprinkling fine salt on his clothes after making herself invisible. With her accomplice Dorthe Fudevik, she flew to Copenhagen and emptied a vial into his mouth while he was sleeping. Transformed into a raven, she had buried bones, nails, hair and feathers in the garden of Johan Worm, the city clerk, so that his chickens and other domestic animals would fall ill. The hairs, she said, she had plucked from 'her boy, Whitegoose, who is shaped like a colt, and who she rides on when she wants to get somewhere in a hurry'. Many witnesses testified against her.

At a later hearing, she admitted to flying like a raven with two other witches to raise a storm to destroy Councilman Pedersen's ship. One of them had landed on the rubber, the other two on the rails, but they could not harm him as he held a prayer book in his hand. Karen Snedkers was burnt, along with six other women she had named as witches.

Another witch was executed in the district of Sondmore in 1680, and in 1684, a man named Ingebrigt confessed that he had foresworn

Christianity before the devil by walking backwards three times around a graveyard. At sabbats at Dovrefjeld, he had played the drums with two calves' tails: he had also stolen a communion wafer so he could poison cattle. At his trial at Jaederen, he named several others, then withdrew his accusations. He was burnt.

In 1687, a girl was executed for being the ghost of another girl murdered fourteen years before. She had confessed when the ghost led the court to the scene of the crime. There was another case of ghostly possession in a Bergen high school in 1701, but the principal became convinced it was a hoax, even though the accused confessed.

Other than a reported outbreak of poltergeists in Norway in the early eighteenth century, the Scandinavian witch phenomenon was over. It had been a comparatively mild experience – except for the poor unfortunates burnt alive for 'witchcraft' –, never reaching the depths of hysteria and malevolence of the German and French witch hunts. The Spanish experience, however, was of a different order entirely.

7

The Spanish Inquisition

T HE SPANISH INQUISITION is associated with the mass burnings in their *auto-da-fé*. However, their efforts to rid the Iberian Peninsula of heretics overshadowed an earlier interest in witchcraft. The earliest of all the general treaties on witchcraft was written in 1359 by the Dominican inquisitor in Aragon, and in 1370, diviners and those who consulted them were declared heretics. However, under a law of 1387, laymen would be punished by the civil authorities, while only the clergy would face ecclesiastical courts. There were various attempts to tighten up the law on witchcraft, but the debate about whether necromancy and sorcery were heresy continued.

In 1436, the theologian Alonso Tostado maintained that the idea of visiting a sabbat was a delusion brought on by drugs. However, in 1467 Alphonsus de Spina insisted that the delusion was evoked by the devil. His book *Fortalium Fidei [Fortress of the Faithful]* was the first to discuss the punishment for witchcraft. It also condemned Jews and Muslims and is full of anti-Semitic tales, despite – or perhaps because of – the fact that Spina himself was a Jew who had converted to Christianity. The final ruling on witchcraft was made by *Opus de Magica Superstitione [Book about Belief in Magic]*, which remained the classic work on sorcery in Spain for over a century. It concluded that the flight of witches was an illusion, but that illusion was caused by making a

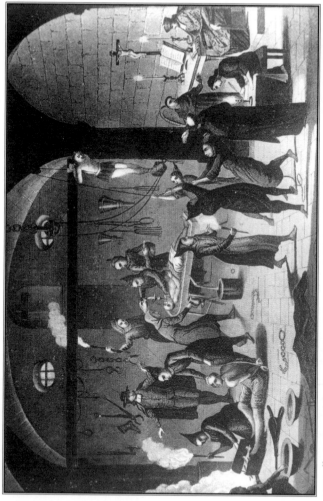

1520 illustration of the Spanish Inquisition at work. Various favourite tortures are detailed, including the strappado, the water torture, and a version of the Spanish Chair, in which the unfortunate victim's feet are basted with fat and roasted.

pact with the devil, and that while witchcraft was not a formal heresy it should be treated and punished as such.

After the Muslims were driven out of Spain in the late thirteenth century, the political authorities in Aragon and Castile began looking for a way to impose their authority on the rest of country and, in 1478, they persuaded Pope Sixtus IV to authorise a separate Spanish Inquisition. They set to work and the first *auto-da-fé* took place in Seville in 1481. Hundreds were burnt alive and the Spanish Inquisition was so savage that the Pope tried to ban it. But the civil authorities had found the Spanish Inquisition such a powerful political tool that they restored it and named their own Inquisitor-General. The man they chose was the Dominican Tomás de Torquemada who, in his fifteen-year career, was personally responsible for burning more than two thousand people at the stake.

Tomás de Torquemada was the nephew of the famous theologian Juan de Torquemada, who was made a cardinal for promoting the idea of papal infallibility. From an early age, Tomás was exceedingly pious. After a brilliant scholastic career, he joined the Dominicans. This was a disappointment to his father, a nobleman who wanted his only son to marry and continue the family line.

Torquemada withdrew to the Monastery of Santa Cruz in Segovia, where he lived an extremely austere life. He refused to eat meat and, unlike other Dominicans, he refused to wear linen under his coarse habit. If that was not chafing enough, he often resorted to wearing a hair shirt, and always went barefoot.

As his reputation for piety spread, Torquemada was made confessor to Isabella, the sister of Henry IV of Spain. He got her to promise that if she was ever made queen, she would restore the Inquisition. She did become Queen. True to her word, she re-introduced the Inquisition and made Torquemada its head.

Torquemada was not one of the many clergymen who joined the Church for the wealth and power it brought them. This made him all the more dangerous. What he wanted to do was force the austerity that he enjoyed on other people, and he did not care how he did it. He also earned the title 'the Scourge of the Jews'. Although his own grandmother was Jewish, he persecuted Jews – even those who had converted to Christianity – as heretics. One did not have to be Jewish: it was enough for a witness to testify that you were. Witches could be similarly denounced, and Dominicans such as Torquemada led the fight against witchcraft in Spain.

As soon as he was made Inquisitor-General, Torquemada produced a new set of rules for the Inquisition. These twenty-eight articles ensured that the Spanish Inquisition operated very differently from that in Germany or France. At each new place the Inquisition visited, an eloquent priest or one of the inquisitors would give a sermon. At the end of it, faithful Christians were to come forward and swear their allegiance to the Inquisition and promise to work for it. Then anyone who had lost their faith or practised heresy – which included witches, Jews and any remaining Muslims – was given thirty or forty days to come to the Inquisition and confess. They would not be dealt with harshly – that is, they would not be burnt at the stake – provided their repentance was sincere and that they confessed, not only their own sins, but also those of their neighbours.

There would, of course, be some punishment. Those who had offended against God's holy law could not expect to get off scot-free. They would have to perform penances and give up wearing jewellery and fine clothes. They were not to ride horses or bear arms, and they would be liable to forfeit some of their property to Queen Isabella and King Ferdinand to help in their Holy War against the Muslims in Granada.

Anyone guilty of heresy or apostasy – which embraced witchcraft – who did not come forward during the period of grace, but came forward voluntarily later, would again be treated mercifully. They would simply have to surrender all their property and would be sentenced to life imprisonment – but no fire. Even if you gave your property away beforehand, the Inquisition would seize if from whoever you had given it to.

The slaves of those condemned by the inquisition would be freed – giving them ample incentive to inform on their master. Children who had become heretics due to the teachings of their parents were treated especially kindly. Provided they told the Inquisition of their parents' heresies, they would be given light penances and be taught the true faith. The children of those condemned by the Inquisition would be sent to monasteries and convents. The girls were supposed to receive a small dowry so they could marry, but in practice this rarely happened.

Anyone arrested for heresy or apostasy could ask for reconciliation with the church, but they would have to prove that their confession was sincere. The only way to do that was to inform on friends. If it was judged that their confession was not sincere, they would be handed over to the civil authorities and be put to death.

If a suspect fled, his name would be posted on the doors of all the churches in the area. He would be given thirty days to present himself to the Inquisition, otherwise he would be judged guilty of heresy. Those who had successfully fled the country were burnt in effigy, which did not hurt nearly as much.

There was no hiding place from the Inquisition. If a count or a duke refused to let the Inquisition into his realm, he would be found guilty of aiding and abetting heresy. Even death was no escape. If someone was found guilty after they were dead, their body would be dug up and their corpse burnt at the stake. Their estate would naturally be forfeit. Officers of the Inquisition were not allowed to take gifts from suspects. If they did, they would have to forfeit twice the value of the gift and might suffer excommunication – putting paid to a lucrative career in the church. Torquemada also reserved the right to sack inquisitors for other misdemeanours, such as not being harsh enough.

Torquemada took a broad definition of heresy. Besides being a witch or a Jew, bigamy also counted as marriage was a sacrament. Sodomy was punished by burning. But ordinary unmarried fooling around was okay, provided that the participants did not say it was all right. That would be contradicting the word of God.

One reason this fornication was not included was that the Spanish priesthood was notoriously debauched. The Borgia pope Alexander VI, famed for his incest and his extravagant orgies in the Vatican, was Spanish. It was not until the sixteenth century that a screen was put in confessionals separating the priest and the penitent. Before that time licentious priests would lure attractive young women into the confession boxes and give them a few extra sins to confess. Torquemada would have loved to sweep this sort of behaviour from the church with his Inquisition but, by that time, Innocent VIII was pope, a proud family man, whose children lived with him in the Vatican.

One priest was brought before the Inquisition because he had been sent to a convent as confessor and promptly seduced five nuns. But, he told the Inquisition, he had been told to go the convent and take care of the nuns... and, as a good and faithful servant, he had done exactly what he was told. Another priest was caught sodomising a 14-year-old boy in his care. As a priest, he was confined to a monastery for a year. But the boy was not a priest. He made to wear a mitre full of feathers and whipped so severely that he died.

When a man or woman was suspected of heresy, they would be called to the Holy Office. All that was required to condemn a person was the testimony of two witnesses. The names of the witnesses were kept secret in case reprisals were taken against them. Theoretically, the accused could be represented by an advocate. But in practice, no one was foolhardy enough to stand up to the Inquisition.

There were no guards at the Holy Office and the accused could simply walk out. But that would invite condemnation as a heretic. Once you were accused by the Inquisition, there was very little hope of getting off. Both church and state wanted a uniformly Catholic country and the exchequer was eager to get its hands on as much confiscated property as possible.

Arrests often took place at night. *Alguazils* or familiars of the Inquisition would knock and, if there was any resistance, they would force entrance. The victim would be told to dress and they would leave immediately. The *alguazils* liked to work silently. They brought a painful gag for anyone tempted to cry out and alert their neighbours. It was shaped like a pear and was forced into the mouth. Screws then enlarged it, forcing the jaw open. Silence and secrecy made the *alguazils'* terror tactics more effective. Everyone felt vulnerable.

Inside the Holy Office, everything was designed to intimidate the suspect. The 'trial' was held in a darkened room. The inquisitors wore white habits with black hoods. They sat at a table swathed in black velvet. It had a crucifix, a Bible and six candles on it.

The trial would take place *in camera*; the public would not be allowed in. A secretary would read the charges from a pulpit. Then there would be a long pause. Torquemada instructed his inquisitors to spend time examining papers before they spoke to the suspect as a method of instilling fear.

The prisoner would then be asked for their name and address. They would be asked if they knew why they had been arrested. If the prisoner said they did not know why – which was usually the case – the inquisitor was instructed to study the papers before him once more. After a while the prisoner would be asked if they had any enemies and whether they attended confession regularly. What was his diocese? Who was his confessor? When did he last go to confession?

Torquemada instructed his inquisitors not to be moved by anything the prisoner might do or say. Any sobbing, weeping, begging or heart-rending tales should be ignored. Heretics were a crafty lot. Had they not pretended to be good Catholics while practising their heresy in secret? The inquisitors were reminded that the condemnation of one man might be the salvation of thousands. After all heretics not only practised heresy themselves, but often persuaded others to follow in their diabolical ways.

If the prisoner stubbornly refused to be intimidated into confessing, the inquisitor was instructed to soften his expression. The prisoner was told that they were an errant child and, like a father, the inquisitor was merely trying to make them recognise the error of their ways. The Church was ready to forgive them and welcome them back. But first they had to unburden their soul by confessing and show true penitence which, of course, meant revealing the names of those who shared in their sin. Many fell into this trap and willingly provided more fodder for the Inquisition.

If the prisoner still refused to confess, they would be taken back to prison to think about it. If the suspect still remained firm, the inquisitor would tell them that, although they appeared to be innocent, their jailers were not convinced. So they would have to stay in prison, but they would be moved to more comfortable quarters and be allowed visitors. Visitors would be sent by the Inquisition to encourage the prisoner to be careless in their talk. Prisoners were told that, if they confessed, they would get off with a light penance. An officer of the Inquisition was concealed so that they could overhear any conversation. They searched for any words that could be construed as an admission of heresy. Sometimes they would be made to share a cell with another prisoner who was actually an agent of the Inquisition. The agent would talk openly of their own feigned heresy in the hope of entrapping the prisoner.

If all this failed, the prisoner would be taken back before the Inquisition and cross- examined at lightning speed. It would be a long and wearisome interview. The inquisitor would try and force the suspect into contradicting themselves. For those quick-witted enough to avoid the inquisitors' snares there was but one reward – the torture chamber.

Torture was largely Torquemada's contribution to the Inquisition. He instructed that torture could be used in any case where heresy was 'half proven' – in other words, an accusation had been made, but no confession had yet been extracted. Simply being brought before the Inquisition was enough. But, being a good Christian, Torquemada said that no blood must be shed. However, he conceded that people did often die under torture. If this happened, the inquisitor must immediately seek absolution from a fellow priest. Torquemada gave all his priests the power to absolve one another of murder.

The inquisitors did not use the word torture, naturally. Prisoners were simply put to 'The Question'. There were five carefully thought-out stages to The Question. The first was the threat. The prisoner would already have heard about the cruel methods that the Inquisition employed, but the inquisitors felt it was their duty to remind the prisoner of the danger they faced in the hope that they would become weak with fear.

The second was the journey to the torture chamber. The victim would be take ceremonially in a procession by candlelight. Also lighting the way would be braziers which would take on their own terrifying significance. The torture chamber would be dark and dismal. The victims would be given a little time to glance around it and see the hideous devices that were employed. They would see them being used on other victims who had refused to confess, and they would see the torturers, who wore black hoods with eyeholes cut in them.

In the third stage, the prisoner would be seized and stripped. This would leave them naked and vulnerable. The fourth stage was to introduce the victim to the particular instrument that was to be used on them and strap them on to it. Only then, in the fifth and final stage, would the pain begin.

It was against the law to repeat The Question. Once a victim had been tortured and survived, they could not be tortured again. However, there was no law against continuing the torture. It could go on day after day, week after week, with any interval merely being a 'suspension'.

Although the rack was used by the Inquisition, most prisoners were subjected to the strappado and squassation. If that did not work the water torture was used. The accused would be tied to a sloping trestle so their feet would be higher than their head. The head would be held in place with a band of metal. The nostrils would be sealed with wooden pegs and the jaw opened with piece of iron. A piece of linen would be put over their mouth and water would be pored down their throat, carrying the linen with it. The victim would swallow automatically pulling the linen into the gullet. They would cough and retch and reach a state of semi-suffocation. When they struggled the ropes would cut into them. More and more water would be brought. Up to eight jars were sometimes used.

Sometimes the Spanish Chair was also used. This was an iron chair with metal bands that held the victim so they could not move. Their bare feet would be put in stocks next to a brazier. Their feet were covered in fat and slowly allowed to roast. Fat was applied so that the flesh did not burn too quickly. Sometimes the victim had to be taken to the *auto-da-fé* in the chair because their feet had been completely burnt away. Flogging was also used and fingers and toes were cut off, usually one a day.

One Jew who converted to Christianity was delivered to the

Inquisition by a servant who he had had whipped for stealing. He refused to confess to heresy. He had a linen bag tied over his head so tightly he almost suffocated. When it was taken off, he was asked to confess. He refused. His thumbs were bound so tightly that blood spurted up from under the nails. Next his limbs were attached to pulleys and the ropes jerked violently that his joints were dislocated. Then he was struck on the shins so viciously that he fainted with pain.

Finally he was tied up so tightly that the ropes cut into his flesh. He was only released when he had lost so much blood that his torturers feared he might die. Not that they cared, but it was much better for all concerned that, if people were going to die, they did so at the *auto-da-fé*. Public burning was a far more effective way of instilling the fear of God in other people. This particular man did not suffer that terrible fate. He was forced to wear the *sanbenito* – the garment of shame – for two years, then he was banished from Seville.

A Scotsman named William Lithow was arrested in Malaga, accused of being a spy. As a Protestant he was taken before the Inquisition as a heretic. When he refused to convert to Catholicism, weights were put on his legs. The torture left him unable to walk. He held in a prison that was overrun with vermin. His beard, his eyebrows and his eyelids were so infested he could barely open his eyes. Every eight days, they were swept off him. He was given a pint of water every other day. His cell had no bed, blanket, pillow or window.

After forty-seven days, he was taken by carriage to the torture chamber where he was racked for five hours. His torturers were so clumsy that they took an inch of flesh off his heel. From then on, the carriage drew up outside his cell every morning at the same time, so that he would think he was being taken back to the rack. When he still refused to convert, he was kicked in the face by the inquisitor and sentenced to eleven different tortures. Finally, he was taken to Granada to be burnt.

Two slaves – a Turk and a black woman – were to look after him until he was well enough to be burnt. They were very kind to him and another servant, a Flemish boy, was so impressed by his courage that he got word to the English ambassador who rescued him.

The inquisitors were particularly fond of torturing attractive young women. In Cordova, one 15-year-old girl was stripped naked and scourged until she bore testimony against her mother.

In Toledo, a woman named Elvira del Campo was charged with not eating pork and putting out clean linen on a Saturday. Terrified of torture, she admitted that these were criminal acts, but denied any heretical intentions. The inquisitors were not satisfied. When they sent her to be tortured, she fell on her knees and begged them to tell her what they wanted her to say.

She was taken to the torture chamber where she was told to tell the truth, but she had nothing to say. She was stripped naked and asked again. Her suffering was detailed in the records of the Inquisition at Toledo.

'Señors,' she said. 'I have done all that is said of me and I bear false-witness against myself, for I do not want to see myself in such trouble. Please God, for I have done nothing.'

She was told not to bear false-witness against herself but to tell the truth. They began tying her arms.

'I have told the truth, what more do I have to tell?' she asked.

A cord was tied around her arms were twist until she screamed.

'Tell me what you want as I don't know what to say,' she said.

The torture continued in this way for some time, while all the unfortunate woman could do was beg to be told what she should confess to, as she did not know.

On being asked once again she wished to tell the truth, she was threatened with the water torture. She replied that she could not speak and that she was a sinner. The linen was then placed in her mouth. 'Take it away,' she screamed. 'I am strangling. I am sick.'

A jar of water was them poured down her throat. Afterwards she was told to tell the truth. She begged to be allowed to confess, she was dying. The inquisitor told her that the torture would continue until she told the truth. She had to tell it. Then she was repeatedly cross-questioned, but she said nothing. Seeing she was exhausted by the torture, the inquisitor ordered it to be suspended.

All this had been noted down by a secretary who attended the torture sessions. On this occasion, Elvira del Campo seems to have got off lightly. Only one jar of water was poured down her throat and, according the secretary's meticulous notes, she did not scream or cry very much. But her sufferings were by no means over.

She was left for four days. By this time her limbs had stiffened, making any renewed torture doubly painful. Then she was brought back to the torture chamber again. This time when she was stripped, she broke down completely and begged to be allowed to cover her nakedness. It made no difference. Her interrogation and torture continued. This time her replies were even less coherent than before. Eventually, she confessed to Judaism, repented and begged for mercy. The torture was then suspended once more.

Legally, confessions extracted under torture were not valid. So twenty-four hours later, she was taken back to the Holy Office, where her confession was read out. Under oath she had to swear that it was correct in every detail. If she did not, the suspended torture would be resumed. That done, she was reconciled to the Church at a public *auto-da-fé*.

There were other, worse, tortures. In the prison of the Inquisition at Toledo, a statue of the Virgin Mary covered with nails and blades was found. When a lever was pulled, the Virgin Mary's arms embraced the victim, whose naked flesh was pulled on to the spikes in a vicious mockery of the faith. But probably the most nauseating torture involved a number of mice that were placed on the victim's stomach. A large dish was put over them upside down. A fire was lit on top of the bowl. As it grew hotter the mice would panic and try and get away from it. The only way out was for them to burrow through the victim's flesh. When the Holy Office had extracted a confession, it 'abandoned' its victims to secular authorities with the usual plea for mercy. Again, the secular authorities did not dare to show mercy. If they did, they risked being hauled in front of the Inquisition themselves.

Even the inquisitors admitted that mistakes were made. Thousands of good Catholics were falsely accused, tortured into making a confession and unjustly condemned to death at the *auto-da-fé*. But they were privileged. They were being allowed to die for the faith, For their glorious death, they would be admitted straight to paradise, so they had nothing to complain about.

Sometimes the Church was merciful. Those reconciled with the church and spared had to be whipped half-naked though the streets in a procession to the local cathedral six Fridays in succession as an act of penitence. After that, they would never be able to hold any rank or office, or wear fine clothes or jewellery. One fifth of their money would also be forfeit to the Inquisition. But those unreconciled suffered public burning at the auto-da-fé.

Auto-da-fé is the Portuguese for 'Act of Faith'. In Spanish it is *auto-de-fé* but, for historic reasons, the Portuguese variant has been co-opted into the English language. These ghastly rituals took place on Sundays or other holy days, because more people would be able to watch.

The evening before the *auto-da-fé* the accused were brought before the Inquisition and told whether they would live or die. Every person condemned would then be allotted two priests to wrestle for their souls. Although the condemned were bound to die, it was still possible to save their souls. In that case, if they were reconciled with the church, they would be strangled before the flames reached them.

Everyone found guilty had to wear a tall cap like a mitre called a *coraza* and a *sanbenito*. This was a loose-fitting tunic made of yellow sackcloth that came down to the knees. It was a garment regularly worn by penitents. Those found guilty of lesser crimes would be sentenced to wear the *sanbenito* on Sundays, say, or for a specific period. Normally, they would have blood-red crosses sewn on them. But the sanbenitos worn by those facing the *auto-da-fé* were decorated with flames and devils prodding the fires with pitchforks. If the flames pointed downwards, the Inquisition had been merciful and the wearer would be strangled. But if they pointed upwards, the victim would be burnt alive.

The next morning at around six o'clock the victims were lined up outside the prison in their *sanbenitos* with a rope around their necks and their hands tied together. Then they marched off in a procession led by priests bearing green crosses – the symbol of the Inquisition – draped in black material. Next came the alguazils. As well as arresting suspects and visiting victims in jail, urging them to repent, they were also charged with protecting the inquisitors – who were not always popular figures in the community.

Next came a priest carrying the host. Over his head was a canopy of scarlet and gold carried by four men. When he approached, the men, women and children in the crowd had to fall to their knees. If they did not, they risked being called in front of the Inquisition.

Then came more *alguazils*, followed by lesser criminals, some of whom bore the marks of torture. Those who were to be burnt came next, each flanked by two Dominican friars in their white vestments and black hoods. Often they were still trying to save the soul of victim. Then came the bodies of those who had been found guilty after their death and had been dug up for punishment. After them were the effigies of those who had fled Spain rather than face the Inquisition, carried on green poles. The effigies wore the *sanbenitos* and *corazas* of the condemned.

After them came the inquisitors. They were flanked on one side by banners emblazoned with the arms of the pope, entwined with those of Ferdinand and Isabella. On the other side were the arms of the Inquisition. Behind came more *alguazils* and other minor officials. The entire procession was flanked by soldiers carrying halberds, and bringing up the rear was the crowd who followed the procession to the cathedral square.

Once there, each victim was read a list of their crimes, then a sermon was preached. Often there were several hundred victims and this process could take all day. The victims were made to sit on benches swathed in black crepe. The benches were set on a platform so the crowd could see those who had been condemned. Being good Catholics the crowds shouted insults at the victims and humiliated them. It was not unusual to set fire to Jews' beards. This was called 'shaving the New Christians'. All the while, priests and monks harried the victims, still working hard to get a last-minute repentance.

The inquisitors sat on another platform surrounded by their black draped green crosses. Incense was burnt – a wise precaution as there were usually a large number of freshly disinterred bodies around.

Mass was then celebrated, followed by another sermon. Following that the Grand Inquisitor stood up and led the crowd in the oath. The onlookers were required to fall to their knees and swear that they could defend the Holy Office against all its enemies. They would be faithful to it in life and in death. They would do whatever it asked of them. And they swore that they would pluck out their right eye or cut off their right hand if that was what it asked of them. (Ferdinand and Isabella refrained from saying this oath. So did the Spanish monarchs that succeeded them – with the exception of Philip II who was a zealot.) It was at this point the Church washed its hands of the victims. It had done all it could for the sinners. Now they abandoned them to the secular authorities for the punishment to be carried out. The charges were read out again, this time by the secular authorities. The Grand Inquisitor then made a public plea for mercy, asking disingenuously that their blood not be spilt. And it was not going to be: that was the reason they were burnt.

The victims were then take up to the *quemadero* – the place of burning. This was a field where the stakes had already been set up and the faggots piled high. The victims were tied to the stakes. They were asked if they wanted absolution, the lucky ones were garrotted, then the faggots were lit. Monks chanted. People cheered. The inquisitors feigned shock at the wickedness of the world. And the smell of roasting flesh permeated the air.

After condemning two thousand people to death in this fashion, Torquemada himself died peacefully in his bed in 1498. He was a happy man. He had lived to see the Muslims expelled from Granada and his own persecution had resulted in the expulsion of the Jews from Spain in 1492. At the time many people called him the 'Saviour of Spain'. Indeed, many of the Grand Inquisitors that followed him were worse than he was. At its height, the Spanish Inquisition had fourteen tribunals set up in Spain, Mexico and Peru. The Spanish Inquisition established itself in Sicily in 1517, although efforts to set up in Naples and Milan failed, and in 1522, the emperor Charles V introduced it to the Netherlands in an effort to stamp out Protestantism, and keep the Dutch people in political subjugation.

Although Torquemada was primarily interested in burning heretics, in 1494, the Inquisition began to argue that, if witches truly did visit sabbats, then they were apostates, or if sabbats were a delusion, they were heretics. Either way, they were condemned. The Spanish Inquisition burnt its first witch in 1498. Her name was Gracia la Valle and she was burnt at Zaragoza. Another execution took place the following year, and three witches were burnt in 1500. Thirty were burnt in Biscay in 1507. Two more were killed in 1512 and another in 1522.

In 1526, the secular courts joined the witch craze and mass trials were held in Navarre. Another mass outbreak at Navarre the following year and one in Biscay in 1528 were initiated by individual inquisitors. Meanwhile, the Supreme Council of the Inquisition – the Suprema – was having second thoughts about witchcraft and held a meeting to decide the matter. The first question to be decided was whether witches really committed the crimes they confessed. A majority of six to four decided that they did. If so, should they be 'reconciled' to the Church, or handed over to the civil authorities for execution? The majority favoured reconciliation, unless murder was alleged when they should be handed over for trial. If their crimes were an illusion, the Suprema could not decide on a suitable punishment. However, they did decide that the crimes fell under the jurisdiction of the Inquisition. The vote was split on whether they could convict on the strength of a confession without any supporting evidence. The future Inquisition General Cardinal Fernando de Valdes decided that a confession alone was sufficient only in cases that attracted minor punishments.

This restrained attitude of the Suprema quietened a further witch hunt in Navarre in 1530 and in Galicia in 1551. It was still hard to restrain individual inquisitors and, in 1600, the Inquisition assumed jurisdiction over all kinds of sorcery.

In 1609, the French witch hunter Pierre de Lancre began work in the Basque country. A wealthy lawyer, Lancre had been convinced of the truth of witchcraft when, in 1599, returning from a pilgrimage to the Holy Land curtailed at Naples, he saw a girl changed into a boy by the devil in Rome. He rode into the Basque country armed with a commission from King Henry IV. However to restrain his excesses, the Parlement of Bordeaux added its president, D'Espagnet, to his investigating committee. But D'Espagnet resigned on 5 June, leaving Lancre a free hand.

Lancre maintained that the Labourd region had become a haven for the devils expelled from Japan and the East Indies by Christian missionaries. Indeed, English wine buyers visiting the area had seen hordes of these demons flying in the skies. As early as 1576, forty witches had been burnt there. But by 1609, Lancre said, the devils had converted the majority of the people there. The area was 'a hive of witches'. Well-organised sabbats were held in Hendaye in the Pyrenees, the public square in Bordeaux – or even as far away as Newfoundland. An average attendance was 12,000 – but some had seen as many as 100,000 witches, including 2,000 children, at a sabbat. This was because local witches were fined ten sous or one eighth of a crown for non-attendance. Even Lancre himself was not free from their influence. He complained that, while he was asleep on the night of 24 September 1609, a Black Mass was said in his bedroom.

Under torture, 17-year-old Marie Dindarte described how, on the night of 27 September 1609, she had anointed her naked body with ointment and flew through the air. Unfortunately, she could not produce the ointment in evidence in court because the devil was angry with her for revealing their secret and had hidden it. Sixteen-year-old Marie de Naguille and her mother Saubadine de Subiette revealed how the devil came to wake them when it was time for the sabbat and opened the windows for them to fly out. Fifteen-year-old Marie de Marigene and three friends rode to Biarritz on the devil in the shape of an ass, and Father Pierre Bocal of Siboro admitted saying a Black Mass at the sabbat for twice his regular stipend.

Lancre was particular adept at wringing detailed descriptions of their sexual encounters with the devil out of these young girls, arguing that to doubt the validity of these confessions was to doubt the Church. As wholesale burnings got underway, panic spread through the population: the work of the devil, Lancre said. Even the clergy began to oppose him. Lancre then burnt three priests and the Bishop of Bayonne, Bertrand d'Echaux, had to rescue five others from Lancre's jails.

However, when 5,000 Basque fishermen returned from the summer fishing off Newfoundland to find their wives and children had been burnt, they turned into a howling mob. Lancre withdrew leaving, he reckoned, some 30,000 witches unburnt – though in his entire career he burnt some 600. He also contributed greatly to the literature. In 1612, he published *Tableau de l'constance de mauvais anges [Description of the Inconstancy of Evil Angels]*, in 1622 *L'Incredulité et mescréance du sortilège [Incredulity and Misbelief of Enchantment]* and in 1627 *De Sortilège [Witchcraft]*. He died in France in 1631 and was buried in a tomb inscribed in Euskera, the Basque language. His estate went to his grand-nephews, but he bequeathed his extensive library to his illegitimate son, a Jesuit.

Another witch panic broke out in Navarre in 1610. Lancre maintained that it had spread from Labourd, which he considered was the centre of the pestilence. The secular authorities at Logrono began arresting suspects, extracting confessions and burning witches before Inquisition could intervene. Jealous of its powers, the Suprema sent three inquisitors who found over 280 adults worshipping the devil, along with numerous children who were considered too young to burn. Forty witches were taken before the local inquisition. Many more were thought to be in the surrounding areas and they gathered information on twenty large sabbats.

The Inquisition then joined with the Crown and the bishops on a joint crusade to rid Spain of witches. They organised a two-day auto-da-fé beginning on 7 November 1610 where the witches would be burnt. But this did not turn out to be the spectacle they had planned. King Philip III did not show up and many of the witches recanted and were reconciled to the Church. Of the fifty-three people condemned, twenty-nine were witches. In the end, only six were burnt alive and their confessions were not very convincing. They said they had eaten the decaying body of a dead relative. Another six accused witches had died in prison.

On 26 March 1611, the Suprema reversed its hard line and ordered an Edict of Grace, allowing witches a period to repent without penalty. They sent Alonzo Salazar de Frias to the area to administer the edict. Over the next eight months he interviewed 1,802 self-confessed witches – 1,384 of them were children aged between twelve and fourteen. Eighty-one of them recanted their confession. It was

The Spanish Inquisition

thought that more would have done so if they had not feared execution for perjury.

Salazar wrote a report that ran to 5,000 large sheets. He found witnesses who said that they had seen self-confessed witches in other places when they were supposed to be at the sabbat. Witches often disagreed where the sabbats were held. Girls who confessed having sex with the devil were found to be virgins. Boys said that sabbats had been held in places where Salazar's own secretaries at been at the time and seen nothing. Salazar could find no external evidence for witchcraft. Confessions were extracted by torture and allegations by bribery. One young beggar denounced 147 people. In all, Salazar revealed that 1,672 of the accused had been charged on perjured testimony. He concluded, 'My experience leads to the conviction that, of those availing themselves of the Edict of Grace, more than three-quarters have accused themselves and their accomplices falsely. I also believe that they would come freely to the Inquisition to revoke their confessions, if they thought they would be received kindly without punishment.'

Although other inquisitors investigating the Navarre witch panic objected, Salazar was allowed to formulate a code of conduct which was issued on 13 August 1614. It insisted that external evidence was presented in witch trials. Witness were to be allowed to retract their accusations without fear of torture. Confessions were to be thoroughly investigated. Tribunals could not convict except by unanimous verdict, and details of witchcraft cases had to be forwarded to the Suprema. All pending cases were dropped. Property was no longer to be expropriated and the property of the victims at Lograno was to be returned to their relatives.

A few isolated witch trial occurred in 1622, 1637, 1640 and 1641, but there were no convictions with the Suprema consistently acting as a restraining influence. There were maybe half-a-dozen witch trials after that, but no one was executed for witchcraft in Spain after 1611. The Spanish did, however, continue to believe that witches made pacts with the devil long after the rest of Europe was ridiculing it. On 15 October 1818, a tribunal in Seville sentenced Ana Barbero to two hundred lashes and six years exile – later remitted to eight years in a

185

prison for prostitutes – for blasphemy, superstition and making a pact with the devil.

Napoleon attempted to suppress the inquisition when he occupied Spain in 1808 and it was finally halted in 1834: the last *auto-da-fé* took place in Mexico in 1850. Estimates of how many people perished in the *autos* vary wildly. But they probably run into the hundreds of thousands. From their inception, the proportion of the cases involving witchcraft grew steadily. Between 1575 and 1610, only one and a half per cent of the cases at the inquisition at Toledo related to witchcraft. Between 1648 and 1749, the proportion rose to over 8 per cent. However, in 1780-1820, the forty years preceding the suspension of the Inquisition, nearly 70 per cent of the trials were for superstition – that is, they did not involve *maleficia*.

The majority of the victims were women, some of them in their nineties. Children as young as twelve or thirteen frequently burnt after their parents had been condemned. In 1659, two 10-year-old girls were burnt in Toledo.

Two elderly nuns were burnt alive in Evora in 1673 with the name of Jesus on their lips. They had lived blameless lives in a convent for over forty years. Garcia d'Alarcon was said to be the most beautiful woman in the country when she was burnt by the Inquisition in Granada 1593. Isabelle, the wife of Francisco Dalos of Ciudad Real, first appeared before the inquisition at the age of 22. She was arraigned five more times and spent eighteen years of her life in the prisons of the Inquisition. Her final trial began in 1665, when she was 80. It lasted until 1670. She was tortured three times and eventually died. The Inquisition then sentenced her to a double punishment burning her body along with an effigy. Foolishly she had neglected to confess before she expired in the torture chamber, so she had also died in a state of sin.

One of the most famous victims of the *auto-da-fé* in the New World was Doña Ana de Castro, a socialite in Lima. Her love affairs were legendary and it was said that she even shared her favours with the viceroy. It was possibly a rejected lover or a jealous rival who told the Inquisition she was secretly practising Judaism. She was burnt in 1836.

In Sicily, a renegade Augustin Friar named Diego Lamattina got his own back. In 1657 he was charged with being a heretical blasphemer, despiser of the sacraments and an insulter of sacred images. When he was in prison, he was visited by the Inquisitor General, whose brains he dashed out with his manacles.

Balthazar Lopez was an incorrigible joker. As court saddler in Castile, he had amassed a small fortune. After taking a trip abroad in 1645, he was arrested. Along with fifty-six others he faced the flame at the great *auto-da-fé* held at Cuena in 1654. As they approached the *quemadero*, his confessor exhorted him to rejoice as the gates of Paradise were soon to be opening freely for him.

'Freely,' scoffed Lopez. 'The confiscation of my property has cost me two hundred thousand ducats. Do you infer that I have been swindled?'

At the *brasero* – the brazier – he noticed that the executioner, Pedro de Alcalá, was making a clumsy job of strangling two of his fellow victims.

'Pedro,' Lopez said. 'If you can't strangle me better than you are doing to those two poor souls, I'd rather be burned alive.'

The executioner then tried to bind his feet.

'For God's sake,' said Lopez, finding this the final indignity. 'If you bind me, I won't believe in your Jesus.'

Then he threw down the crucifix he was holding. The priest finally managed to persuade him to take it back and ask for forgiveness. As the executioner started to strangle him, the priest asked if he was truly repentant.

'Father,' said the dying man. 'Is this any time to joke?'

A sixteenth-century tribunal. An accused man is tortured in front of the members of the court by stretching with weights and pullies. Confessions extracted by such means were usually false as the victim would rather lie than endure further agonies. Engraving copied from the original woodcut by J. Millaeus.

The Witch of Umbria

L
IKE SPAIN, Italy was more interested in burning heretics than witches. However, on 20 March 1428 a woman named Matteuccia di Francesco from the castle of Ripabianca di Deruta was tried for witchcraft in the main square of Todi, near Perugia in Umbria, central Italy. Thirty charges were brought against her in the Court of Malefactors under Captain Lorenzo de Surdis. They included smearing her entire body with an 'ointment' that was considered to be an instrument of magic and riding on the devil, who she had evoked in the shape of a goat. In this way she could travel over water and 'through the wind'.

On her flying goat she went to a meeting at the 'walnut tree of Benevento' with 'very many witches, enchanted spirits, infernal demons and the greater Lucifer, who, presiding at the meeting, ordered her and the others to go around destroying children and other wicked things'. They also smeared each other with an oil made from the fat of vultures, the blood of bats, babies' blood and other unsavoury ingredients.

'After hearing this order, Matteuccia attended the meetings many times and instigated and informed by the devils she went to children about one year to suck their blood from their throats or noses so as to be able to make the ointment,' the indictment said. She visited the walnut tree on Mondays, Saturdays and Sundays between March and

December. In September 1427, she transformed herself into a witch by smearing herself with the ointment, then went to the house of a woman called Andreuccia in the castle of Montefalco, where she beat and sucked the blood of a child who was not yet a year old. 'After this time child grew ill and pined away.' Other babies had been similarly abused. These included the eight-month-old son of the Angelino family in the castle of Andria in the district of Perugia, the seven-month-old daughter of Andreuccio and Caterina of the castle of Rotacastelli in the district of Orvieto and the baby daughter of Mecarello who was sleeping in a cot in a villa Rotello in the district of Orvieto where she had gone to make enchantments.

Matteuccia also dispensed marital aids. A wife living in the castle of Collemezzo came to her complaining that her husband humiliated her and treated her badly and asked her for a remedy. Matteuccia gave her 'an egg and a herb called *Costa cavallina*', telling her to give them to her husband. After he had eaten them he would 'become infatuated for a few days'. The woman followed Matteuccia's instructions but the plan backfired as 'the man being infatuated was furious for three days'.

Other women who had trouble with violent or uncaring husbands or lovers were told to make images of them in wax, which she wrapped in a thread spun by a virgin. The figure was then to be put under the man's bed – or in one case melted on a hot brick – while a spell was chanted. One woman from the castle of Pacciano near Perugia who wanted to seduce the man she loved was told to capture a few swallows. They were to be burnt and the powder fed to the man in a drink. Yet another woman from the castle of San Martino in the district of Perugia who wanted 'amorous favours' from her husband who was living with another woman was told to feed a small swallow on sugar, then give it to her husband along with some wine diluted with water she had used to wash her feet. And a woman from Mercatello whose husband preferred the company of other women was told to burn some of her hair and give the ashes to him to eat. Whether this worked is not recorded.

She also gave out a herb that was supposed to be administered to a potential love diluted in water that the seducer had washed their hands and face in, and she also made charms made from hair wrapped in a piece of cloth that, when put under the bed or under the door, would make husbands love their wives or wives love their husbands. One poor woman was having trouble with a priest at the castle of Prodo in the Orvieto district, who 'did not look after and make love to her every day, but instead beat her'. He got the melted wax treatment and the woman later reported that it had worked.

In May 1427, a woman named Caterina from Castello della Pieva asked Matteuccia for a potion to stop her getting pregnant. She was not married, but she wanted to go on seeing the local priest every day and she did not want her parents to discover the affair.

Another women wanted a man to abandon his wife and love her instead. Matteuccia told her to 'wash her hands and feet facing backwards and with her knees bent and when she had done so to take the water and throw it where the man and woman were going to pass'. This apparently made the man and his wife hate each other.

As well as promoting 'amorous favours', she could also deny them. She would take a holy candle, set light to it and bend it at the junction of three roads where a lover would pass. As long as the bent candle was kept in a safe place the man or woman the magic was directed against could not have sexual intercourse. Matteuccia did this for a young man whose lover had been given to another by her parents and, apparently, ruined the poor girl's wedding night.

The magic ointment she was accused of smearing on herself was made from the meat or fat from dead bodies mixed with powder from pagan bones – that is, bones from people who had not been baptised – herbs, locks of hair, birds feathers, mice and the hooves of she-mules all burnt and ground to a powder. The preparation was put to diverse uses, including '...to cure invalides, to spread hatred and to evoke more enthusiasm in tired or deluded lovers'.

When patients came to her who were suffering from pain in the limbs, she spat on the floor, held a lighted candle in her hand and asked them to recite a spell three times. These spells were in fact popular religious invocations, but were apparently 'profaned by a diabolic spirit'. Then three grains of salt were thrown in the fire. She told 'people possessed by a spirit' to get hold of pagan bones and take them to a cross-roads, where they should leave them after reciting nine Pater Nosters and nine Ave Marias, along with a spell of her own making. After nine days they should return to the place and the spirit would return to the bones. Apparently this worked on a man who was so mad that he had been sleeping on top of a tomb in 1426. Even so, it was considered that she was 'adding evil to evil'. She cured a young man at the castle of Panicale in the district of Perugia of his derangement when she burnt a feather tied to a piece of cloth which she found under his pillow. It had been a charm of another witch. And she cured a young woman who had fallen ill after being bewitched by her lover's wife. Again she burnt the other witches' charms – in this case three blackened mice, wrapped in linen.

When a paralysed man was brought to her, she prepared a potion of herbs to cure him. She did this 'consciously, purposely, criminally and with intent to harm and make a profit,' the indictment said – the paralysis being the will of God, presumably. Worse, she had been getting away with this sort of thing for four years.

Curiously, Matteuccia had only been discovered to be a witch when St Bernardino, who was on a preaching tour from Siena, turned up at Todi and put a stop to her activities. Apparently, she had been helping a mercenary captain called Braccione Fortebracci da Montone who had recently captured Todi. One of his men had helped her fish a dead body out of the Tiber which she used to cook up her spells. She was also involved in a plot to embezzle 42 florins from the company that was rebuilding the fort. The chief embezzler was fined 225 florins. Matteuccia's sentence was rather more severe – being 'universally recognised as a woman of bad ways and habits, a public enchantress, sorceress and witch... ignoring God but rather following the enemy of mankind'.

Fortunately Matteuccia 'confessed spontaneously and saying that she had no defence'. According to Captain Lorenzo, she had been given time to prepare a defence, but neither she or anyone else had taken advantage of this. What is more, under interrogation, she confirmed all the names, dates, times and places in the indictment. The verdict was not in doubt and Lorenzo decided that she must be made an example of 'to all those who would like to carry on similar activities'. He sentenced her to 'be put on a donkey with her hands tied behind her back and, with a paper hat on her head, to be taken to a public place where one usually administers punishment or to any place inside or outside the city by choice of the nobleman Ser Giovanni di Ser Antonio di S. Nazzaro da Pavia and there she should be burned so that the guilty one dies and her spirit be separated from her body'.

The sentence was proclaimed to accompaniment of church bells and the fanfares of heralds. It was carried out by the soldiers on hand straight away and witnessed by Alvisio di Rinaldo of the quarter Nidola and the parish of St Felice, Gaiello di Marcuccio of the quarter della Valle and the parish of St Salvatore, Pietro di Simone of the quarter of della Valle and the parish of St Quirico and Pietro di Giovanni of the quarter Camucia and the parish of St Maria. The public notary Novello Scuderij da Vassano wrote down all the details, adding a sketch of woman with dishevelled hair to represent the witch. He then affixed the imperial seal, adding that this had been done in the time of the Holy Father Pope Martin V, who had, incidentally, defeated Braccione Fortebracci da Montone at the battle of L'Aquila and was to take over the rest of northern Italy in 1429.

A group of supposed witches being beaten in front of King James I (King James VI of Scotland). James was a convinced witch hunter, who personally took part in the interrogation of many suspected witches.

9

Hammer of the Scots

SCOTLAND WAS SECOND ONLY to Germany in the barbarity of its persecution of witches. In Scotland, however, it was not the Jesuits and the Catholic Inquisition who held sway but the Presbyterian clergy. Calvinists had brought the belief in witchcraft back from the Continent. If anything, the laws in Scotland were even more heavily biased against the accused than they were on the Continent. The suppression of any opposition was complete and the Scots were only limited in the cruelty of their tortures by their lack of technical sophistication at that time.

Although the folklore of sorcery was just as widespread in Scotland as in other European counties, there were no witch-burnings until the Reformation and few trials before the end of the sixteenth century. To start with, as in England, witch trials were instigated initially for political ends. In 1479, the Earl of Mar was accused of trying to kill his brother, King James III, by witchcraft. Then in 1537, Lady Glamis was burnt for using charms against King James V. In 1590, Lady Foullis was charged with employing charms, poisons and wax dolls against Lady Balnagowan, so she could steal her husband, but she was acquitted by a jury of her tenants.

A specific statute banning witchcraft was introduced by Mary, Queen of Scots, in 1563. This also prohibited fortune-telling and beneficial sorcery, and deemed those seeking the help of a witch to be as culpable as the witches themselves. The new law started a steady stream of witch trials. In 1576, Bessie Dunlop of Lyne, Ayrshire, was burnt for being a member of a coven comprising four men and eight women, and for receiving herbal cures from the Queen of the Fairies. Allison Peirson of Byre Hills, Fifeshire, was burnt in 1588 for trade with the Queen of Elfame and prescribing magical potions. Apparently, she had recommended that the Bishop of St. Andrews cure his hypochondria with boiled capon and spiced claret. But the Scottish witch trials did not really take off until the accession of James VI – later to become James I of England – in 1567. A deeply superstitious man, though initially sceptical about witches, James soon became convinced and, in 1591, he personally supervised the trial and torture of the notorious North Berwick Witches.

The witch hunt began in Tranent, a small town in the famine-ravaged East Lothian nine miles east of Edinburgh, where the deputy bailiff David Seaton grew suspicious of the night-time activities of his young servant girl, Gilly Duncan. She had acquired a reputation for curing 'all such as were troubled or grieved with any king of sickness or infirmity' which, to Seaton, seemed devilish and unnatural. So he tortured her, crushing her fingers in a vice and tying a rope around her head and jerking it. Naturally, he also had to search the young woman's body for the devil's mark, which he found on her throat. She then confessed that she had succumbed to the 'wicked allurements and enticements of the devil'. Her dutiful employer then handed her over to the authorities.

She was then forced to reveal her accomplices, who were rounded up. Among the numerous people in the vicinity of Leith and Edinburgh she named were the elderly and well-educated Agnes Sampson, Dr John Fian, the schoolteacher at Saltpan, and Barbara Napier and Euphemia Maclean who were 'reputed for as civil honest women as any that dwelled with the City of Edinburgh'.

Agnes Sampson was said to be 'of a rank and comprehension above the vulgar'. So she was taken to Holyrood Castle where she was examined by James VI himself. 'She stood stiffly in the denial of all that was laid to her charge' and was 'grave and settled in her answers'. As a result, 'all her hair was shaven off, in each part of her body'. The devil's mark was then found on her pudenda. She was then fastened to the wall of her cell with a witch's bridle. This was a metal device that was forced into the mouth, so that two sharp iron prongs stick into the tongue, while another two stick into the cheeks. She was forced to go without sleep, then ropes were twisted around her head, then jerked about in all directions causing 'a pain most grievous'. After this she admitted the fifty-three charges in the indictment against her, which largely concerned using charms to cure ailments. She confessed to using simple charms and the white paternoster 'open, heaven's gates'. Then she admitted using this 'black' paternoster:

> Four nooks in this house, for holy angels
> A post in the midst, that's Christ Jesus,
> Lucas, Marcus, Matthew, Joannes,
> God be into this house and all that belongs to us.

Although his hardly constitutes invoking the name of the devil, even her innocent bedtime prayer 'Matthew, Mark, Luke and John/The bed be blessed that I lie on' was held to be a devilish incantation at her trial.

She had a familiar in the form of a dog named Elva, who lived in a well, and made use of magic powders. Worn down by torture and interrogation, she finally admitted to attending a sabbat on Allhallows Eve with six men and ninety women – though this was inflated to two hundred by the contemporary tract *News from Scotland* published in 1591. After drinking they sailed in 'riddles or sieves' to North Berwick. There Gilly Duncan played the Jews' harp and they danced a reel with the men turning 'nine times widdershins [anti-clockwise] about and the women six times'. Black candles were lit in the church and the devil in the form of a man commanded them to 'kiss his buttocks, in a sign of duty to him, which being put over the pulpit bare, everyone did as he enjoined them'. They also discussed ways of harming the King, and raised a storm when he went to Denmark to collect his bride Anne. King James was so taken with this story he got Gilly Duncan to play

'Gyllstripes' on the Jew's harp 'to his great amusement and pleasure'.

Although James declared that all witches were 'extreme liars', he believed Agnes Sampson when she told him that she knew what had occurred between James and his 15-year-old queen on their wedding night. According to *News from Scotland*, Agnes:

> *declared unto him the very words which had passed between the King's majesty and his Queen at Oslo in Norway the first night of their marriage, with their answer to each other. Whereat the King's majesty wondered greatly, and swore by the living God that he believed that all the devils in hell could not have discovered the same, acknowledging her words to be most true and therefore gave the more credit to the rest which is before declared.*

James continued his interrogation and Agnes was forced to come up with more and more fanciful confessions. She admitted raising storms by baptising a cat and throwing it in the sea with the severed limbs of a dead man tied to each of its paws. She had made magic powder from a winding sheet and the joints of a corpse. With others of her ilk, she had made a wax dummy of the King and melted it. She collected the venom from a toad after hanging it up for three days. Then she tried to get hold of some of James's underwear so that she could smear the venom on it to make him feel 'as if he had been lying upon sharp thorns and ends of needles'. Her torment only ended when she was strangled and burnt as a witch.

As the sister-in-law of the Laird of Carschoggill, Barbara Napier was well connected. Nevertheless she was accused of associating with Agnes Sampson and Richard Graham, another notorious sorcerer. She was indicted for 'many treasonable conspiracies undertaken by witchcraft to have destroyed the King's person by a picture of wax...and for drowning a boat between Leigh and Kinghorne, wherein sixty persons were lost'. But when the accusations were heard, the jury at the Edinburgh assizes dismissed the case. James was furious. He charged the jury with 'wilful error on assize, acquitting a witch'. He intervened, he said, 'for an example in time coming, to make men to be more wary how they give false verdicts' and he demanded that Barbara be strangled and burnt at the stake and her property be forfeited to him.

He explained his position on 7 June 1591 in his famous Tolbooth Speech:

> For witchcraft, which is a thing grown very common amongst us, I know to be a most abominable sin, and I have been occupied these three quarters of this year for the sifting out of them that are guilty therein. We are taught by the laws of both God and men that this sin is most odious. And by God's law punishable by death. By man's laws it is called maleficium or veneficium, an ill deed or poisonable deed, and punishable likewise by death.
>
> The thing that moved [the jury] to find as they did, was because they had no testimony but of witches; which they thought not sufficient. By the civil law I know that such infamous persons are not received for witnesses, but in matters of heresy and lesae majestatis. For in other matters it is not thought meet, yet in these matters of witchcraft good reason that such be admitted. First, none honest can know these matters. Second, because they will not accuse themselves. Thirdly, because no act which is done by them can be seen.
>
> Further, I call them witches which do renounce God and yield themselves wholly to the Devil; but when they have recanted and repented, as these have done, then I account them not as witches, and so their testimony sufficient.

The speech was published in full the following day, 8 June 1591.

The jury agreed to 'yield themselves to the King's will'. Barbara Napier was duly sentenced, but pleaded pregnancy. Later, 'nobody insisting in the pursuit of her, she was set at liberty'.

Dame Euphemia Maclean also discovered that lofty connections were not necessarily a protection. She was the daughter of Lord Clifton and the wife of Patrick Moscrop, a man of wealth and influence – wealth enough for six lawyers to take the risk of defending her. However, she was Catholic and a friend of the Earl of Bothwell, cousin, heir and a former lover of the bisexual James who had fallen out of royal favour. She refused to confess any of the bewitching and cures alleged against her. The jury took all night to consider their verdict. Even then the foreman had to be dismissed before they found her guilty as charged. James saw to it that she was to be 'burned in ashes alive to the death' without the mercy of being strangled beforehand.

Bothwell himself was charged with witchcraft and imprisoned in Edinburgh Castle. He escaped in 1591, but was deprived by parliament of his lands and titles. In 1591 he attempted to seize Holyroodhouse, and in 1593 he succeeding capturing the King, forcing from him the promise of a pardon which was not forthcoming. Forced to take refuge in France in 1595, he died at Naples in extreme poverty.

Richard Graham was accused of helping Bothwell bewitch the king. James again had a hand in the interrogation and Graham was burned 'for witchcraft and sorcery' in February 1592, in a mass execution. But the conspirator who suffered most horribly was Dr Fian, the schoolmaster from Saltpan, who was accused of being the ringleader. On 26 December 1590, he was charged with twenty counts of witchcraft and high treason. These included:

- Making a pact with Satan, who appeared to him when he lay musing on how he could revenge himself on a workman for not having finished whitewashing his room on time
- Receiving the devil's mark from Satan
- Conspiring with Satan to wreck the ship carrying the King to Norway by throwing a dead cat into the sea
- Giving homage in a North Berwick church to Satan – a 'mickle black man with a black beard sticking out like a goat's beard, and a high ribbed nose, falling down sharp like the bill of a hawk, with a long rumpled tail'
- Looting graves for corpses to be used in making charms – as witnessed by others who had confessed under torture.
- Having 'ecstasies and trances, lying by the space of two or three

hours dead, his spirit taken, and suffered himself to be carried and transported to many mountains'.

He also flew through the air, opened locks by blowing on them, raised storms, carried powerful magic candles on his horse, seduced a widow and used love charms – though he seems, sadly, to have made a cow lovesick, rather than the young lady that he intended.

King James personally watched his torture which was detailed in *News from Scotland*. It began with the 'thrawing of his head with a rope'. A rope was bound around his head and jerked in all directions. After an hour, Dr Fian was urged to confess 'by fair means'. He refused.

The Spanish boots were then used on him. After the third application, he passed out. This was considered to be a trick of the Devil, so his torturers searched his mouth for charms and found two pins 'thrust up into his head'. There can be little doubt that the torturers put them there because, afterwards, he renounced all 'conjuring, witchcraft, enchantment, sorcery and such like' and confessed everything that was put to him as 'most true, without producing any witness to justify the same'.

Despite the terrible injuries that would have been done to his feet and legs by the Spanish boots, *News from Scotland* says that he escaped from prison the next night and made his way back to his home in Saltpans. This King immediately 'commanded a diligent enquiry to be made for his apprehension... By means of whose hot and hard pursuit, he was again taken and brought to prison.' However, when he was brought back before the King, he recanted his confession. He was searched again in case he had 'entered a new conference and league with the Devil'. Nothing was found so he was 'commanded to have a most strange torment'. This time:

> *His nails upon all his fingers were riven and pulled off with an instrument called in Scottish a turkas, which in England we call a pair of pincers, and under every nail was thrust in two needles over even up to their heads. At all which torments notwithstanding, the doctor never shrunk any whit, neither would he then confess it the sooner for all the tortures inflicted on him.*

The Spanish boots were applied again and Dr Fian 'did abide so many blows in them that his legs were crushed and beaten together as small as might be, and the bones and flesh so bruised that the blood and marrow spouted forth in great abundance, where they were made unserviceable forever'.

Despite this he denied all the accusations made against him and maintained that his original confession 'was only done and said for fear of pains which he had endured'. But James had already decided that he was going to die 'for example's sake, to remain a terror to all others hereafter, that shall attempt to deal in the like wicked and ungodly actions as witchcraft'. Having been convicted and sentenced, Dr Fian was strangled then 'immediately put into a great fire, being provided for that purpose, and there burned in the Castle Hill of Edinburgh, on a Saturday in the end of January'.

By the time James VI got in on the act, the intellectual tide on the Continent was turning against witchcraft. In 1563, Johan Weyer, the physician to the Duke of Cleves, published *De Praestigiis (On Magic)*. Though he believed in the devil, Weyer thought that women who believed that they had made a pact with the devil were suffering a hallucination induced by the devil himself. He also believed any harm done was caused by the devil. As a protestant and a doctor, he was scathing about clergymen who, at the first sign of illness, claimed that the patient was bewitched and took money for exorcism. The witch hunts themselves were the work of the devil, he maintained, saying that, 'daily experience shows what execrable alienation from God, what fellowship with the Devil, what hatred between relatives, what strife between neighbours, what enmities among the presents, what feuds between cities, what frequent slaughter of the innocent, are caused by the most fruitful mother of calamities, the belief in the sorcery of witches.'

In *De Praestigiis*, Weyer condemned the witch-hunters whose innocent victims were 'constantly dragged out to suffer awful torture until they would gladly exchange this most bitter existence for death' and would willingly confess 'whatever crimes were suggested to them rather than be thrust back into their hideous dungeon amid ever recurring torture'.

People were condemned by 'malicious accusation or the mistaken suspicion of illiterate and ignorant peasant'. Old women 'deceived or possessed by the Devil' were then 'turned over to be slaughtered by the most refined tortures that tyrants could invent, beyond human endurance. And this cruelty is continued until the most innocent are forced to confess themselves guilty. So it happens that the time comes when these bloodthirsty men forced them to give their guiltless souls to God in the flames of the pyre rather than to suffer any longer the tortures inflicted on them by these tyrants.' Otherwise, if they died at the hands of the torturers, Weyer said, 'when brought out, lo, the joyful cry goes up that they have committed suicide (as indeed they might, what with the severity of their agonies and the squalor of the jail), or that the Devil had killed them.'

Then in 1584, the Englishman Reginald Scot published *Discovery of Witches* which set out to ridicule the very idea of witchcraft. On the topic of ligature, for example, he relates the tale of a young man who, after fornicating, finds himself emasculated. So he 'went to a witch for the restitution thereof. She brought him to a tree, when she showed him a nest, and bade him climb up and take it. And being in the top of the tree, he took out a mighty great one, and showed the same to her, asking her if he might not have the same. Nay, quoth she, that is our parish priest's tool, but take any other which thou wilt. And it is there affirmed, that some have found twenty, and some thirty of them in one nest, being there preserved with provender, as it were a manger... These are no jests, for they be written by them that were and are judges upon the lives and deaths of those persons.'

King James called Scot's book 'damnable'. Indeed in Scotland in 1590, Janet Clark and Janet Grant were convicted of taking the penises of some men and giving them to others. When James acceded to the throne of England in 1603, he ordered all the copies of Scot's book burned. Fortunately for Scot, he had died four years earlier in 1599, otherwise he may well have suffered the same fate as his book.

To counter this trend of disbelief in witches, James himself set out to prove that 'such assaults of Satan are most certainly practised and that the instruments therefore merit most severely to be punished'. So in 1597 in Edinburgh James published his own book, *Demonology*. In it, he paraded the fact that he did not believe in lycanthropy; he did however believe in the devil's mark and 'swimming'.

On his accession to the throne of England in 1603, he published a new edition of *Demonology* in London. And within a year, James had forced the English parliament to pass a Witchcraft Act. This started the English witch hunt, but James could not persuade the English to burn their witches or to torture them.

One peculiarly Scottish torture was forcing the accused to wear a hair shirt steeped in vinegar which took their skin off. The Scots would also keep witches in solitary confinement, keep them awake for long periods and force them to lie naked on a cold stone floor.

In June 1596, 'a known notorious witch' named Alison Balfour was kept in the 'caspie claws' – an iron vice that crushes the arms – for forty-eight hours in Edinburgh Castle. While she endured this, she had to watch her 7-year-old daughter tortured with 'pilliwinks' or thumbscrews, her 81-year-old husband pressed under seven hundred pounds of iron bars and her son put in the 'Spanish boots', whose wedge was given fifty-seven blows, turning his bones into pulp. Her servant Thomas Palpa, who was also implicated was kept in the caspie claws for 264 hours, scourged with 'ropes of such sort that they left neither flesh nor hide upon him'. The English were appalled by such barbarity. In 1652, the English Commission for the Administration of Justice took testimony from two fugitive witches from the Highlands, who related how six of them had been hung up by their thumbs, whipped and burnt in the mouth, on the head and between the toes. The other four had died under this torture.

In Scotland, the Privy Council appointed commissions of eight local dignitaries to investigate any alleged witchcraft. Often these commissions also had the power to sentence the accused to death. With three or five of the commissioners acting together, if evidence of witchcraft was found, they would authorise the sheriff to summon an assize of no more than forty-five men, fifteen of whom would sit as a jury. There were numerous witch-hunting commissions. On 7 November 1661, for example, fourteen such commissions were authorised. Another fourteen were authorised on 23 January 1662, and there was no shortage of work for them. The General Assembly of the Kirk of Scotland in 1640 and 1642 ordered ministers to search out suspected witches. The minister and the elders of the church would meet as a 'presbytery' to come up with charges. It is no accident that the worst persecutions – 1590–97, 1640–44 and 1660–63 – coincide with the height of Presbyterianism.

Unusually, in Scotland, the accused was allowed a lawyer, though most witches were too poor to afford one. If someone had the 'general reputation' of being a witch, that was usually enough to secure a conviction. A confession was not necessary. But once the indictment had been drawn, the accused was not allowed to contradict it, even when it was clearly wrong. In 1629, Isobel Young of Eastbarns was accused of cursing a man who then lost the use of his leg and stopping a water mill twenty-nine years earlier. She argued that the man had been lame before she cursed him and that the water mill had broken down due to natural causes. The prosecutor, Sir Thomas Hope, pointed out that in her defence she had merely contradicted the indictment, which was not allowed. She was convicted, strangled and burnt.

In 1597, following the publication of James VI's *Demonology*, the witch craze in Aberdeen hit a new peak. Twenty-four men and women were burnt for bewitching animals, turning milk sour, dancing with the devil around the town cross, using ligature to make men unfaithful to their wives and making love charms out of bent pennies and red wax wrapped on cloth. One of the first to die was Janet Wishart, who had used a spell to make Alexander Thomson alternately sweat and shiver. Andrew Webster and others died when she put the evil eye on them. She dismembered a corpse hung on the gallows, threw out live coal to raise storms and sent phantom cats to give people nightmares.

One of the convicted witches tried to delay her own burning by naming others. She said that she had seen over 2,000 witches at a great gathering at Atholl. 'She knew them all well enough, and what mark the devil had given them severally to every one of them. There was many of them tried by swimming in the water, by binding of their two thumbs and their great toes together; for being thus cast in the water, they floated always above.'

Janet Wishart was burnt with another witch named Isabel Crocker in February 1596. Being Scots, they were presented with itemised bills:

	Shillings	pence
For twenty loads of peat to burn them	40	0
For a boll [six bushels] of coat	24	0
For four tar barrels	26	3
For fir and iron barrels	16	8
For a stake and the dressing of it	16	0
For four fathoms [24 feet] to tows [hangman's rope]	4	0
For carrying the peat, coals and barrels to the hill	8	4
To one justice for their execution	13	4

In all they were charged £11 10s. Others got off with a branding on the cheek, costing just six shillings and eight pence. But all tortures had to be paid for, item by item.

On 19 November 1636, William Coke and his wife Alison Dick were burned for witchcraft at Kirkcaldy. To help them burn they were dressed in special hemp garments made for the occasion and placed in barrels of tar. But they were too poor to pay up, so the kirk and the town council received a bill for:

	£	s	d
For ten loads of coal to burn them	3	6	8
For tows		14	0
For hurden [hemp fabric] for jumps [short coats] for them	3	10	0
For making them		8	0
For one to go to Finmouth for the laird to sit upon their assize as judge		6	0
For the executioner for his pains	8	14	0
For his expenses here		16	0

On 10 March 1607, Isobel Grierson, the wife of John Bull, a workman in Prestonpans, not far from Edinburgh, was indicted on six counts of witchcraft. They were:

1. *Conceiving cruel hatred and malice against Adam Clark : or over a year and a half, Isobel Grierson used all devilish means to be avenged on him. Especially during November, 1606, between eleven and twelve o'clock, 'in the likeness of her own cat, accompanied with a great number of other cats, in a devilish manner, entered within their house, where they made a great and tearful noise; whereby the said Adam, then lying in bed with his wife, and servants that were then in the house, apprehended such a great fear that they were likely to go mad'. A servant was dragged by the hair around the house by the devil who appeared in the form of a black man. She was ill for six weeks afterwards.*

2. *For rancor against William Burnet, husband of Margaret Miller – now a widow – who Isobel Grierson sought to kill 'by devilish and ungodly means – as a manifest sorcerer and witch'. In January 1650, she threw a piece of raw meat at his door. Then the devil appeared each night for six months in his house in the likeness of a naked infant. The devil also appeared in the form of Isobel Grierson who 'in an unhonest and filthy manner, pissed upon the said Margaret Miller and in diverse parts of the said house'. William Burnet then pined away and died in 1605 'in great dolor and pain'. Isobel was accused as 'art and part of the said former William's death and sickness'.*

3. *Isobel was also indicted for casting sickness on Robert Peddan nine years earlier in October 1598. After pining away for some time, he remembered he owed Isobel nine shillings and fourpence. Peddan had refused to pay the debt and Isobel said 'he should repent it'. When he paid up and asked Isobel to restore his health, he recovered.*

4. *Also Robert Peddan charged that, while passing an open window in his house in June, 1606, Isobel had stretched out her hand and stroked the cat. At the time Peddan was brewing ale. Immediately the brew turned 'altogether rotten and black, thick like gutter dirt, with a filthy and pestilent odour, that no man might drink nor feel the smell thereof'.*

5. *Isobel was also charged with conceiving a deadly intent against Robert Peddan's wife, Margaret Donaldson. Margaret had fallen ill in 1600 and believed that Isobel Grierson had bewitched her. She asked the neighbours to arrange a reconciliation, after which she got better. But when Isobel thought that Margaret was defaming her as a witch, she threatened her with the words, 'The faggot of hell light on thee, and Hell's cauldron may thou seethe in.' Margaret fell ill again and it took her nine weeks to recover. Then in December 1606, she bumped into Isobel again, who said, 'Away, thief, I shall have thy heart for spreading rumours about me so falsely.' And Margaret promptly fell ill again.*

6. *The final indictment is the most damning. It accused Isobel Grierson of being 'a common sorcerer and a witch, and abuser of the people, by laying in and taking off sickness and diseases, and using all devilish and ungodly means to win her living; and a user of charms and other devilish practices'.*

This final charge needed no witnesses, but those involved were called to testify on the other counts. The jury found her 'culpable and convicted of all and sundry the heads and points of the dittay [indictment] above written'. Isobel was strangled and burnt on Castlehill Edinburgh, and her property was forfeit to the king.

Margaret Barclay, the wife of Archibald Dean, a burgess of Irvine, Ayrshire, fell out with her brother-in-law and his wife. Things got so bad that Margaret took them before a church court. The kirk tried to mediate, but Margaret was not a very forgiving soul. When her brother-in-law set sail for France with the town provost Andrew Tain, it was said she wished that the ship would sink so 'partans [crabs] might eat the crew'.

Later a tramp named John Stewart was passing through Irvine and told of a ship sinking near Padstow in England. Its loss was confirmed by two surviving sailors. Margaret Barclay was arrested for witchcraft, and Stewart for precognition. Under torture, he said that Margaret had sought his aid against 'such persons as had done her wrong'. He also said that he had seen her making wax images of Andrew Tain and the ship in a deserted house along with Isobel Insh. Isobel's 8-year-old daughter was seized and 'confessed' that she too had been present in the deserted house. When it got dark, she said, a demonic dog shone light from its mouth and nose, so that they could continue work on the figurines. Afterwards Margaret had sworn the child to secrecy with the promise of a new pair of shoes. Previously Stewart had made no previous reference to the child, but he now agreed that the 'little snatchet' was present. However, although Stewart was kept under heavy guard with his arms in fetters, on the morning of his trial in 1618, he managed to strangle himself with the ribbons of his bonnet.

Isobel Insh had also been tortured into confession, then locked in the church belfry. She managed to escape onto the roof, but slipped and fell, dying five days later. This left Margaret Barclay alone to face the charges and it was now her turn to face what local landowner, the Earl of Eglinton, called a 'most safe and gentle torture'. This was done by putting her 'two bare legs in a pair of stocks, and thereafter by on-laying of certain iron gauds [bars]'. When she could stand no more she cried: 'Take off! Take off! And before God I shall show you the whole form.' The bars were removed, but left in front of her. Even so, the confession was entered in evidence as having been made 'without any kind of demand, freely'. She also implicated Isobel Crawford.

Margaret's husband acted as her lawyer at her trial and she recanted.

'All I have confessed was in the agony of torture, and before God, all I have spoken is false and untrue,' she said. Nevertheless she was found guilty, strangled and burnt.

Isobel Crawford showed considerable courage under torture – 'admirably, without any kind of din or exclamation, suffered above thirty stone [420 lbs] of iron to be laid on her legs, never shrinking there-at in any sort, but remaining, as it were, steady'. But as the iron bars continued to be piled on she began to confess anything that was put to her, including sexual relations with the devil. Once the torture ended, she retracted her confession. She died impenitent and refused to absolve her executioner.

In 1623, Isobel Haldane was charged with witchcraft in Perth, Tayside. The following comes from the court records of her trial:

15 May 1623

Isobel Haldane, suspect of witchcraft, being convened before the Sessions of Perth, after prayers made to God to open her heart and loose her tongue to confess the truth:

Q. If she had any skill of curing men, women or bairns that were diseased?

A. None.

Q. If she cured Andrew Duncan's bairn?

A. According to the direction of Janet Kaw, she went with Alexander Lokart down to the Turret-port, took water from thence brought it to Andrew Duncan's house, and there, upon her knees, in the name of the Father, Son and Holy Ghost, washed the bairn. After that, took the water, with the bairn's sark [shift], accompanied by Alexander Lokart, and threw both in the burn; but in the going, she spilled some, which she regrets bitterly, because had any one stepped over the place, the disease would have been transferred from the sick child to him.

Q. If she had any conversation with fairy folk?

A. Ten years since, lying in her bed, she was taken forth, whether by God or the Devil she knows not, and was carried to a hillside. The hill opened and she entered there. She stayed three days, viz., from Thursday to Sunday at twelve o'clock. She met a man with a grey beard who brought her forth again.

Witness John Roch swears: About the same time, he being in James Christie the wright's shop, having the wright make a cradle for him, because his wife was near down lying [in child-birth], the said Isobel Haldane came by, desired him not to be so hasty, for he needed it not; his wife should not be delivered of her child till that time five weeks. And the bairn should never lie in the cradle, but be born, baptised and never suck, but die and be taken away. And as the said Isobel spoke, so it came to pass in every point.

Q. How she knew it?

A. The man with the grey beard told her.

Witness John Roch swears: The said Isobel Haldane came to Margaret Buchanan, spouse to David Rind, being in health, at her ordinary work, and desired her to prepare for death, for before Easter Eve, which was within a few days, she would be taken away. And as she said, so it was: before that term, the woman died.

Q. How she knew the term of life?

A. She had enquired at that same man with the grey beard, and he had told her.

16 May 1623

Witness Patrick Ruthven, skinner in Perth, swears: He being bewitched by Margaret Hornscleugh, Isobel Haldane came to see him. She came in to the bed and stretched herself above him, her head to his head, her hands over him and so forth, mumbling some words, he knew not what they were.

Confessed. Before the said Patrick was bewitched, she met him and forbade him to go until she had gone with him.

19 May 1623

Witness Stephen Ray of Muirton swears: Three years since, that Isobel Haldane having stolen some beer forth of the Hall of Balhoussie, he followed her and brought her back again. She clapped him on the shoulder, saying, 'Go thy way! Thou shalt not win thyself a bannock [piece] of bread for a year and a day.' And as she threatened, so it came to pass. He pined away, heavily diseased.

Confesses taking away the beer and the disease of the man. She only said, 'He that delivered me from the fairy folk shall take amends on thee.'

Confesses she went silent to the Holy Well of Ruthven, and returned silent, bringing water from thence, to wash John Gow's bairn. When she took the water from the well, she left a part of the child's dress at it, which she took with her for that effect; and when she came home, she washed the bairn therewith, in like manner she had done the like to John Powryis' bairn.

21 May 1623

Confesses she had given drinks to cure children, among the rest, that David Morris' wife came to her, and she sent forth her son to gather fochsterrie [star grass] leaves, whereof she directed the child's mother to make a drink.

Witness Mrs David Morris swears: The said Isobel Haldane, unrequested, came to her house and saw the child. Said 'it was changeling taken away'. Took in hand to cure it; and to that effect gave the child a drink, after the receipt whereof the bairn died.

These records are witnessed by:

William Young, scribe to the Presbytery of Perth, at command of the same, with my hand and 'Jonathan Davidson, notary public and clerk to the Session of Perth, at their command and direction, with my hand.

Isobel Haldane's trial continued on 22 and 26 May, during which she made more confessions:

Q. Where had she learned her skill?
A. When I was lying in childbed lair, I was drawn forth from my bed to a dub [stagnant pond] near my house door in

Dunning, and was there puddled [confused] and troubled.
Q. By whom was this done?
A. By the fairy folk, who appeared some of them red, some of
them grey, and riding upon horses. The principal of them that
spake to me was a bonny white man, riding upon a grey horse.
He desired me to speak of God, and do good to poor folks; and
he showed me the means how I might do this, which was by
washing, bathing, speaking words, putting persons through
hasps of yarn and the like.

Although the worst that can be alleged against this poor woman is that she introduced personal hygiene to Scotland, it seems certain that she was convicted and burnt.

Between 13 April and 27 May 1662, apparently without the aid of torture, a young attractive red-haired girl named Isobel Gowdie made a series of astonishing confessions to the elders of her local kirk in Lochloy, near Auldearne in Morayshire. Bored by marriage to a dull farmer, she said that she had become a witch and had attended Sabbats for fifteen years. She claimed that in 1647, she had made a pact with the devil at the church at Auldearne. She had renounced Christ and had been rebaptised in her own blood which the devil sucked from her. He gave her the new name Janet and, when she had swore allegiance to him with one hand on the top of her hand and the other on the sole of her foot, he gave her the devil's mark, concluding the service with a reading from a black book from the pulpit. A few nights later she went to a meeting where the devil had sex with her and twelve other women worshippers. At later meetings, two children were sacrificed in the Devil's name and their bodies and blood were used in satanic rites.

In return she got the power to turn herself into various animals. She could also fly thought the air with the cry, 'Horse and hattock [little hat], in the Devil's name.' She rode a piece of straw because, if she left her broomstick or stool beside the bed, it would delude her husband that she was still there.

On her way to the sabbat, she could shoot down Christians who saw her and did not bless themselves.

Grace was said before the sabbat banquet:

> *We eat this meat in the Devil's name,*
> *With sorrow and sighs and mickle shame;*
> *We shall destroy both house and hold;*
> *Both sheep and cattle in the fold,*
> *Little good shall come to the fore,*
> *Of all the rest of the little store.*

The thirteen witches in her coven each had their own devil and familiar whose names included Red Reiver, Roaring Lion, Robert the Rule, Roie and Swein. Isobel told the judges that they spent their time raising storms by hitting a wet rag against a stone and reciting this spell:

> *I knock this rag upon this stone*
> *To raise the wind in the Devil's name;*
> *It shall not lie, until I please again.*

To turn themselves into a hare, the witches would recite three times:

> *I shall go into a hare,*
> *With sorrow and sigh and mickle care;*
> *And I shall go in the Devil's name*
> *Ay while I come home again.*

When they wanted to turn themselves back again they said:

> *Hare, hare, God send thee care;*
> *I am in a hare's likeness just now,*
> *But I shall be in woman's likeness even now.*

There were minor variations to turn into another animal. For example:

> *I shall go into a cat,*
> *With sorrow and sigh and a black shot.*
> *And I shall go in the Devil's name*
> *Ay while I come home again.*

She also admitted turning into a jackdaw and shooting arrows, sharpened by elf boys, to kill people. The Devil would be very angry if they missed their target. If one of the witches failed to turn up to a sabbat or disobeyed his orders, he would beat them. Although Alexander Elder was too weak to resist and was beaten often, Margaret Wilson would fight back, while Bessie Wilson 'would speak crusty with her tongue and would be belling against him soundly'. But usually they fled crying 'Mercy! Mercy! Our lord!'

The court records have been lost, but it can safely be assumed that she was executed.

Margaret Dunhome – also known as Dinham or Dollmune – was executed at Burncastle in 1649. John Kincaid was paid £6 for 'brodding' – or pricking – her. The executioner charged £4 14s, including three dollars expenses. Another three pounds was paid for 'meat and drink and wine for his entertainment', plus forty shillings for a man with two horses to fetch him and take him home again. Two guards got thirty shillings a day for thirty days – £45 – and the entire bill came to £88 14s in Scottish pounds, which were valued at one sixth of an English pound. However, whoever added it up added an extra £4, presenting a bill for £92 14s in all. Margaret Dunhome's goods were disposed of for £27, so a bill of £65 14s was presented to the owner of the estate where she had her cottage.

Another unprompted confession came from Major Thomas Weir in 1670. Born in Lanark in 1600, he served as a lieutenant in the Scottish Puritan – Covenanter – army in the English Civil War. After the war he became a civil servant and an admired religious fanatic. Suddenly at the age of 70 he began confessing a lifetime of terrible sins. At first no one believed him and when he persisted the Provost sent for a doctor. But Weir was found to be sane and 'his distemper only an exulcerated conscience', so the Provost was forced to arrest him.

Major Weir came to trial on 9 April 1670, indicted on four counts:

1. *The attempted rape of his sister, Jane Weir, when she was ten. Continued incest with her from when she was sixteen to fifty when he 'loathed her for her age'.*
2. *Incest with his stepdaughter, Margaret Bourdon, the daughter of his deceased wife.*

3. Adultery with 'several and diverse persons'. This included fornication with Bessie Weems, 'his servant maid, whom he kept in the house...for the space of twenty years, during which time he lay with her as familiarly as if she had been his wife.

4. Bestiality with mares and cows, 'particularly in polluting himself with a mare upon which he rode to the West Country, near New Mills'.

Although he was not formally charged with witchcraft, his sister Jane was. She was also charged with incest and 'most especially consulting witches, necromancers and devils'. And she confessed.

The Weirs' sister-in-law Margaret testified that, at the age of 27, 'she found the Major, her brother [-in-law], and her sister [-in-law], lying together in the barn at Wicket-Shaw, and that they were both naked in the bed together, and that she was above him, and that the bed did shake, and that she heard some scandalous language between them'. There was also a witness to the Major's bestiality with a mare in 1651 or 1652. A woman had seen him in the act and complained. But no one had believed her and she was 'whipped through the town by the hands of the common hangman, as a slander of such an eminent holy man'.

Jane Weir admitted that, many years before when she had been a schoolteacher in Dalkeith, she had sold her soul to the devil, saying in the presence of a little woman 'All my cross and troubles go to the door with me.' She had a familiar who span 'extraordinary quantities of yarn for her, in a shorter time than three or four women could have done the same'. In 1648, she and her brother had been 'transported from Edinburgh to Musselburgh, and back again, in a coach and six horses, which seemed all of fire'. Jane also provided the clinching evidence of her brother's witchcraft. His thornwood walking stick which was decorated with carved heads, she said, was a wand. Then people remembered that the Major always leaned on his walking stick when praying, as if drawing inspiration from the devil.

The jury found against Jane Weir on a unanimous vote. Major Thomas Weir was convicted by a majority verdict. He was strangled and burnt on the execution ground between Leith and Edinburgh on 11 April 1670. Sixty-year-old Jane was burnt the following day at the Grass Market in Edinburgh. On the ladder, she was unapologetic. Addressing the spectators, she said, 'I see a great crowd of people come hither today to behold a poor old miserable creature's death, but I trow [think] there be few among you who are weeping and mourning for the broken Covenant.'

Weir's house in Edinburgh lay empty for a century and was thought to be haunted. When an impoverished couple finally moved in, they fled after a single night. The house lay empty for another fifty years before it was demolished.

As the seventeenth century drew to a close, witch trials in England were petering out. But the Scots were still firm believers. In 1678, the King's Advocate Sir George Mackenzie wrote 'That there are witches, divines cannot doubt, since the word of God had ordained that no witch shall live; nor lawyers in Scotland, seeing our laws ordains it to be punished with death.' That same year, Sir John Clerk refused even to sit on a commission to investigate witchcraft. In 1691, the book *Secret Commonwealth* was published by the Reverend Robert Kirk, minister at Aberfoyle, which spoke of finding the devil's mark. Then in 1696, a new witch scare was started near Paisley in Renfrewshire by Christine Shaw, the 11-year-old daughter of the Laird of Bargarran.

On Monday, 17 August 1696, Christine saw a 'well formed lass' stealing a drink of milk and threatened to tell on her. The lass in question, Katherine Campbell – said to have 'a proud and revengeful humour' – then made a terrible mistake. She said that she wished the devil would hurl Christine's soul into the pits of hell. Four days later a woman of poor reputation named Agnes Naismith asked Christine how she was and got a cheeky reply. The following day, 22 August, Christine had a fit. Her body convulsed. She swallowed her tongue and she cried out that Katherine and Agnes were tormenting her. During the fits, it is said that Christine vomited up egg shells, feathers, balls of hair, gravel, hay, candle grease, small bones and crooked pins – all things she claimed that her tormentors had made her swallow. To keep them at bay she quoted the Bible, and soon her convulsions ceased. Two physicians, Dr. Matthew Brisbane and Dr. Marshall, examined her but could find nothing wrong.

On 19 January 1697, the Privy Council of Scotland appointed an investigating commission to investigate witchcraft in Bargarran. By then Christine had a whole catalogue of accusations: her grandmother, Jean Fulton; her three cousins – 'squint-eyed' 14-year-old James Lindsay, 11-year-old Thomas Lindsay and 17-year-old Elizabeth Anderson; the upper-class Margaret Lang – 'a person of extraordinary gravity and wisdom' – and her 17-year-old daughter Martha Semple. These last two had the money to flee, but Margaret said, 'Let them quake that dread and feat that need; but I will not gang (go).'

Others were not so brave. Elizabeth Anderson named others until, eventually, twenty-one were indicted. Christine claimed that these witches – as spectres – molested her and when they were forced to touch her she had a fit. On 11 February the local kirk held a service asking for Christine's release but the constant attention of ministers seemed to encourage her.

Within two months the investigating commission submitted its report which included the confessions of Jean Fulton's three grandchildren – James and Thomas Lindsay, and Elizabeth Anderson. They said that their grandmother had taken them to a sabbat where they had been given a piece of the liver of an unbaptised child. They had refused to eat it, that was why they could speak out. The other accused witches, who had eaten it, could not confess.

They also admitted strangling two children who had been found dead, and killing a minister who had died some time before by sticking pins into a wax effigy. They had also overturned a ferry, drowning two. Elizabeth Anderson said that she had seen the devil talking to her father, Agnes Naismith and others in Bargarran's yard. They had been plotting to murder Christine Shaw 'by the stopping of her breath'. She also recalled at the age of ten flying to a sabbat with her father.

A new commission was appointed on 5 April 1697, this time with capital powers. The judges extracted two more confessions, then put their indictments before a jury on 13 April 1697. The prisoners were already proven witches. Devil's marks had been found. And the Lord Advocate warned the jury that if they acquitted them, 'they would be accessory to all the blasphemies, apostasies, murder, tortures and seductions, whereof these enemies of heaven and each should be guilty'. Even so, it took the jury seven hours to deliberate. They returned seven guilty verdicts. Katherine Campbell, Agnes Naismith, Margaret Lang and Martha Semple were burnt in George Street, Paisley on 10 June 1697, along with three men including 14-year-old James Lindsay.

They were supposed to have been strangled before they were burnt but, according to one account, they were taken down from the gallows and flung into the fire too quickly, so some were burnt alive.

After the burnings, Christine's fit stopped and in 1718 she married a minister. After his death she became a prominent businesswoman. Long after her death, a small hole was found in the wall next to the bed in her room, which had been kept as it was. It is thought that the egg shells, feathers, balls of hair, gravel, hay, candle grease, small bones and crooked pins she vomited up had been pushed through that hole by an accomplice.

Pamphlets about the case of Christine Shaw were circulated widely and may had been responsible for another outbreak in the seaport of Pittenweem, after a minister read them at least twice to the adolescent Patrick Morton. At the age of sixteen, in 1704, he was working at his father's smithy when he was asked to forge some nails for Beatrix Laing, the wife of a former treasurer of Pittenweem. Busy with another job, Patrick said that he could not oblige her. She left 'threatening to be revenged, which did somewhat frighten him'. Next day he saw Mrs Laing throwing hot coal into water, which he took to be a sign of witchcraft. Soon he lost all strength in his limbs, lost his appetite and became gaunt. In May 1704, he began suffering epileptic fits. His stomach swelled up. He had trouble breathing and suffered spasms where he went rigid swallowed his tongue. He also had marks on his arms where witches had pinched him, like those exhibited by the children at Salem. Morton claimed that Beatrix Laing, Mrs Nicholas Lawson and others were haunting him. The minutes of the kirk sessions record that, 'His condition is much about the same with that of Bargarran's daughter in the west.' And on 19 May 1704, he told the minister than he would have no peace until Mrs Laing was punished.

Although there was no vomiting this time, Morton suffered hallucinations and wrote an account of one of them. He saw Satan standing in the bed and who said to him, 'My child, I will give you a silver suit and silver tressing about your hat, if you will confess that there is no Saviour; though two of my dear children [Mrs Laing and Mrs Lawson] suffer punishment, yet it shall be well with you hereafter.'

The accused were arrested on 13 June 1704, after a petition to the Privy Council. Despite her social standing, Mrs Laing was searched for the devil's mark, kept without sleep for five days and nights, and tortured brutally. She confessed and named Mrs Nicholas Lawson, Isobel Adams, Janet Cornfoot and others. Immediately the torture stopped she recanted. So she was put in the stocks, then transferred to 'Thieves' Hole' and kept in 'a dark dungeon where she was allowed no manner of light or human converse' for five months. Even the Privy Council found the zeal of the local magistrates a little excessive and released her, with the other accused, on payment of a fine of eight Scottish pounds – about the price of three pairs of blankets. However, the hysteria in Pittenweem had not died down and she could not go home. She died 'undesired' in St. Andrews.

Isobel Adams confessed that 'about a fortnight after Martinmas [11 November], she came to Beatrix Laing's, and that she saw a little black man with a hat and black clothes, sitting at the board end, and Beatrix said, 'Here is a gentleman that will fee [hire] you.' Upon which she engaged, and the devil kissed her, and told her that he knew she was discontented with her lot, and that in his service, 'she should get riches as much as she could wish. And that on New Year's Day thereafter, the devil appeared to her in Thomas Adams' house, and there she renounced her baptism vows; and likewise acknowledges that she was in Macgregor's house with Beatrix Laing, Mrs Lawson, Janet Cornfoot and Thomas Brown, upon a design to strangle said Macgregor.'

Isobel Adams was also freed on payment of an illegal fine, but Thomas Brown starved to death in prison. Janet Cornfoot was tortured on charges of bewitching Alexander Macgregor. After being flogged by the parish minister Patrick Cowper, she confessed, but then retracted. In case her recantation gave heart to any of the other accused, she was taken from the dungeon and held alone in the steeple, but escaped.

On the night of 30 January 1705, the mob caught up with her. They tied her up and beat her, then dragged her to the shore. There they strung her from the line running from a ship to the shore and pelted her with stones. Taking her down, they beat her again, then put a door on her, piled stones on it and crushed her to death. 'And to be sure it was so, they called a man with a horse and sledge, and made him drive over her corpse backward and forward several times.'

Neither the minister nor the magistrate tried to break up the mob, though the bailiff had succeeded in dispersing them earlier. She was refused a Christian burial and the leaders of the mob were not prosecuted. Soon after Patrick Morton was exposed as a liar.

New intellectual backing was given to the witch-craze by the *Trial of Witchcraft* published by the Reverend John Bell, the minister at Gladsmuir, in Glasgow in 1705, which still accepted the devil's mark as fact. But on 3 May 1709, Elspeth Ross became the last person to be tried before the Court of Justice on the general charge of being a notorious witch. She was branded and banished. In 1718, the King's Advocate Robert Dundas reprimanded the deputy sheriff of Caithness for taking proceedings against witches without notifying him first. The case involved William Montgomery who was trying to rid himself of a plague of cats. When he slashed at two of them, it was said two witches died. Dundas also refused to take action against the Calder witches, accused by the son of Lord Torphichen, a possessed child. The charges were dropped, but two of them died in prison. However in June 1727, Janet Horne was burnt at Dornoch for having used her daughter as a flying horse – the devil having shoed her so that she was permanently lame. But the judge, Captain David Ross, dismissed the charges against the daughter.

The Scottish Witchcraft Act was formally repealed in June 1736, but the divines of the Associated Presbytery passed a resolution reaffirming their belief in witchcraft in 1773. It is estimated that, in all, 4,400 witches were burnt in Scotland.

A coven of witches take to their broomsticks in this mid nineteenth-century illustration. The nearest appears to be experiencing difficulties.

The Irish Experience

I N IRELAND, no more than half a dozen witch trials were recorded. In 1317 Bishop Richard de Ledrede of Ossory, a Franciscan trained in France who was described as a 'vile, rustic, interloping monk' by the Seneschal of Kilkenny, discovered in his diocese the presence of 'a certain new and pestilential sect...who attempt to hinder the salvation of souls'. And in 1324, he accused Dame Alice Kyteler, four times married and the wealthiest lady in Kilkenny, of heretical witchcraft. There were seven indictments against her, her son by her first marriage and their servants:

1. *To make their sorcery effectual, they denied God and the Catholic Church and abstained from all Christian duties.*
2. *They sacrificed living creatures, especially cocks, to Robert Artisson, a demon and 'one of the poorer classes of hell'.*
3. *They sought knowledge of the future from the devils.*
4. *They parodied religious ceremonies in nocturnal meetings, which they concluded by extinguishing candles and saying 'Fi! Fi! Fi! Amen.'*
5. *To incite love and hatred or to kill or injure men and beasts, they made powders and ointments from intestines of sacrificial cocks, 'certain horrible worms', herbs, the*

      nails of dead men, hairs, brains of unbaptised children, all
      boiled in the skull of a beheaded robber over a fire of oak
      wood.

6.   Lady Alice possessed magic powders. These were found
      by her fourth husband, John le Poer, and forwarded to the
      Bishop. All her other children joined in a complaint that
      she had killed her husbands and by magic robbed them of
      their inheritance.

7.   Lady Alice had sexual relations with Robert Artisson, who
      sometimes appeared as a cat, a shaggy black dog or a
      black man carrying a rod of iron.

However, Dame Alice had powerful friends. When she was arrested, the Lord Justice got her released. When Bishop de Ledrede arrived at the secular court to demand her arrest by the civil authorities, he was physically ejected, twice. But when de Ledrede persisted, Dame Alice fled to England. With the connivance of John Le Poer, her son was imprisoned for nine weeks. Her maid Petronilla de Mear was flogged until she confessed that she had been to nocturnal orgies, that she had made sacrifices to Artisson, and that Dame Alice was the most wicked sorceress alive. She was excommunicated and burnt alive on 3 November 1324. Several more accomplices were burnt, while others were whipped, excommunicated and banished. This was the only record of a Catholic burning in Ireland. The rest were Protestants burning Protestants.

In 1447 the Irish Parliament concluded that 'ruining or destroying any man by sorcery or necromancy...they [the two houses] think and believe impossible to be performed in art' and that 'no such art was attempted at any time in this land'. In the sixteenth century, when the rest of Europe was going up in smoke, just one case was recorded in Kilkenny. In 1578, two witches and a 'blackamoor' were executed 'by natural law, for that we found no law to try them in this realm'. This execution of a black man for witchcraft is unique in the history of the British Isles. The legal situation changed in 1586, when the Irish Parliament adopted Elizabeth I's witchcraft law, not repealed until 1821.

Then the sorcery started. In 1606, a minister invoked 'wicked and lying spirits' to discover the whereabouts of 'the most wicked traitor, Hugh of Tyrone'. There were a couple of cases of possession, divining and poltergeists, then in 1661 Florence Newton of Youghal was charged with hexing a young servant girl named Mary Longdon, who had fits, and causing the death of David Jones by witchcraft.

The story began at Christmas 1660, when Mary refused to give Florence a piece of pickled beef. Florence went away muttering evil threats. A week later, when Mary was carrying some laundry, 'the witch of Youghal' knocked the basket out of her hands and 'violently kissed her'. Soon after Mary was troubled with visions. A veiled woman appeared beside her bed, who 'a little man in silk clothes' told her was 'Goody' Newton. When she failed to obey this spectre, Mary became possessed. She gained demonic strength and suffered from hysteria, memory loss and vomited, 'needles, pins, stubs, wools and straw'. Showers of stones would 'follow her from place to place'. She and her master caught some of these, but they vanished immediately, even though she had tied one with a hole in it to her purse with a leather thong.

Throughout these torments, Mary Longdon said that she had seen Florence Newton sticking pins into her. When Florence was manacled, the fits stopped. After a preliminary hearing before the mayor, she was jailed on 24 March 1661. An amateur witch-finder then tried stabbing Florence's hand with an awl 'but could not enter it, though the awl was so bent that none of them could put it straight again. Then Mr Blackwall took a lance, and lanced one of her hands an inch and a half long, but it bled not at all. Then he lanced the other hand, and then they bled.' The story was first recorded by Joseph Glanvill, a contemporary expert on witchcraft, from the notes of the presiding judge, Sir William Ashton. Sadly he omitted the conclusion of the trial, but it is assumed she was executed.

Around the end of the seventeenth century, a 19-year-old girl who had given alms to a beggar woman received in return some sorrel leaves. As soon as she swallowed a leaf, 'she began to be tortured in her bowels, to rumble all over, and even was convulsive, and in fine to swoon away as dead'. Unable to cure her, the doctor sent for the minister, whose presence made the girl hysterical. According to a contemporary chronicler, 'She began first to roll herself about, then to vomit needles, pins, hairs, feathers, bottoms of threads, pieces of glass, window nails, nails drawn out of a cart or coach wheel, an iron knife about a span long, eggs and fish shells.'

It was concluded that the beggar woman had bewitched the girl. She was arrested, condemned and burnt.

Ireland's last witch trial took place in 1711 at Carrickfergus in the county of Antrim. Those involved were the widow of a Presbyterian minister who was staying with her son James Haltgridge and his wife on nearby Magee Islands, their young servant, a child and young urchin, either real or imaginary. The house was attacked by a 'noisy ghost' or poltergeist – or possibly one of the youngsters – who threw stones and turf at the windows, stole books, pulled the bedclothes off the beds, or make them up to look like they had corpses in them. This never happened when anyone was in the room. These attacks ended when Mr Haltridge's dog scared the poltergeist away. But it returned in February 1711. The widow Haltridge was particularly upset by these attacks. She felt a stabbing pain in her back and, a few days later, died. The rumour was that she had been killed by witchcraft.

An 18-year-old girl named Mary Dunbar, 'a very intelligent young person', was hired to look after young Mrs Haltridge in her mourning. Mary began to have fits and saw the spectres of various women who torment her. By the end of March, she had named seven local women as witches. They were arrested. Then Mary identified an eighth, who 'as soon as she came into the room the said Mary fell into such a violent fit of pain that three men were scarce able to hold her, and cried out, "For Christ's sake, take the devil out of the room!".' However, the authorities had enough witches to be going on with, so the woman was not arrested.

The trial took place between 6am and 2pm on 31 March 1711. Most of the evidence concerned Mary's fits. A vicar from Belfast named Dr. Tindall wrote a first-hand account of the proceedings:

There was a great quantity of things produced in court, and sworn to be what she vomited out of her throat. I had them all in my hand, found there was a great quantity of feathers, cotton, yarn, pins and two large waistcoat buttons, at least as much as would fill my hand. They gave evidence in court that they had seen those very things coming out of her mouth, and had received them into their hands as she threw them up.

The prisoners had no lawyer, but they were acknowledged to be 'laborious, industrious people, and had frequently been known to pray with their families, both publicly and privately; most of them could say the Lord's Prayer, which it is generally said they learned in prison, they being every one Presbyterians'.

The two judges could not agree. Judge Anthony Upton 'seemed entirely of the opinion that the jury could not bring them guilty upon the sole testimony of the afflicted person's visionary images...Had the accused been really witches and in compact with the devil, it could hardly be presumed that they should be such constant attenders upon divine service.'

But Judge James MacCartney thought they were guilty – and the jury agreed with him. They were sentenced to one year in prison and four appearances in the pillory.

With the passing of this sentence, however, the Irish witch experience was over.

More unfortunate 'witches' come to an unhappy end in another
nineteenth-century illustration. On the Channel Islands, as in
Scotland and on the Continent, witches were burnt at the stake.

Burning on the Channel Islands

THE CHANNEL ISLANDS, being close to France, suffered more from witches than any other part of the British Isles. And, following the French custom, they burnt them. Between 1558 and 1649, on Guernsey, an island with a population of only a few thousand, twenty men and fifty-eight women were tried for witchcraft and fifty convicted – in England only one in five was convicted. Three women and one man were burnt alive. Twenty-four women and four men were hanged first, then burnt. Three woman and one man were whipped and had an ear cut off. And twenty-one women and five men were banished. One woman returned and was hanged.

In Jersey, between 1562 and 1736, there were sixty-six witch trials, with at least half the accused being hanged or burnt. There were no special laws against witchcraft there, though Jersey passed a special ordinance banned inhabitants seeking 'assistance from witches and diviners in their ills and afflictions...on pain of imprisonment' for one month on bread and water. Unlike in other places, the court records stress *maleficia* – beds are infested with maggots, shirts with lice and cows stopped yielding milk, sometimes by the use of black powder.

The devil was also about. In 1617, Collette du Mont confessed to attending a sabbat. She undressed, rubbed black ointment into her back and belly and flew there. There were fifteen or sixteen other witches there, but she could not recognise them at first, because they were blackened and disfigured. Collette copulated with the devil, in the form of a black dog who stood on his hind legs and whose paws felt curiously like human hands. At the feast following there was no salt and the wine was of poor quality.

That same year, Isabel Dequet went to sabbats on the nights her husband went out fishing. She kissed the devil's backside and was rewarded with a mark on her upper thigh. This was examined by midwives who 'reported that they stuck a small pin into it and that she had not felt it and that no blood had issued'.

On the Channel Islands, the victim was tortured after the sentence of death was passed to extract the names of more suspects. The strappado was the preferred method, though the Channel Islanders had a more excruciating version. They tied the supporting rope to the thumbs of the victim, so that, when they were dropped, they could be torn off.

Although the list of accomplices compiled this way kept the courts busy, some began to have their doubts. The Lieutenant Bailiff of Jersey Philippe le Geyt, who lived from 1635 to 1715, said, 'How many innocent people have perished in flames on the asserted testimony of supernatural circumstances? I will not say there are no witches; but ever since the difficulty of convicting them has been recognised in the island, they all seem to have disappeared, as though the evidence of time gone by had been an illusion.'

The world needs more people like Philippe le Geyt.

Further Reading

A Complete Guide to Witchcraft by Teresa Moorey, Hodder & Stoughton, London, 2000

The Dark World of Witches by Eric Maple, Pan Books, London, 1965

The Devil in Massachusetts by Marion L. Starkey, Robert Hale Ltd, London, 1952

The Discovery of Witches by Matthew Hopkins, Partizan Press, Leigh-on-Sea, Essex, 1992

The Discovery of Witches by Montague Summers, Cayme Press, London, 1928

The Encyclopedia of Witchcraft and Demonology by Rossell Hope Robbins, Crown Publishers, Inc, New York, 1959

European Witchcraft by E. William Monter, John Wiley & Sons, Inc, New York, 1969

The European Witch-Craze of the 16th and 17th Centuries by H.R. Trevor-Roper, Penguin, London, 1967

Europe's Inner Demons by Norman Cohn, Heinemann, London, 1975

Enemies of God by Christina Larner, Blackwell, Oxford, 1983

The History of Witchcraft and Demonology by Montague Summers, Alfred A. Knopf, New York, 1926

A History of Witchcraft in England from 1558 to 1718 by Wallace Notestein, American Historical Association, Washington, DC, 1911

A History of Witchcraft, Sorcerers, Heretics and Pagans by Jeffery B. Russell, Thames and Hudson, London, 1980

The Lancashire Witch-Craze: Jennet Preston and the Lancashire Witches, 1612 by Jonathan Lumby, Carnegie Publishing, Preston, Lancashire, 1995

Malevolent Nuture:Witch-Hunting and Maternal Power in Early Modern England by Deborah Willis, Cornel University Press, Ithaca, 1995

Narratives of the Witchcraft Cases edited by George L. Burr, Charles Scribner's Sons, New York, 1914

A Popular History of Witchcraft by Montague Summers, Kegan Paul, Trench, Trubner & Co, London, 1937

The Scottish Witch-hunt in Context edited by Julian Goodare, Manchester University Press, Manchester, 2002

The Story of the Forfar Witches by Fiona C. Scharlau, Angus District Council Libraries and Museums Service, Forfar, 1995

The Suberversion of Women – As Practiced by Churches, Witch-Hunters and Other Sexists by Nancy van Vuuren, The Westminster Press, Philadelphia, 1973

The Triall of Witch-Craft, London 1616 by John Cotta, Da Capo Press, New York, 1968

Twelve Bad Men by Thomas Seccombe, T. Fisher Unwin, London, 1894

Witchcraft by P. G. Maxwell-Stuart, Tempus Publishing Ltd, Stroud, Gloucestershire, 2000

Witchcraft by Roger Hart, Wayland, London, 1971

Witchcraft by Walter B. Gibson, Grosset & Dunlap, New York, 1973

Witchcraft and Witch Trials by Gregory Durston, Barry Rose Law Publishers, Chichester, 2000

Witchcraft in England by Christina Hole, Charles Scribner & Sons, New York, 1947

Witchcraft in Europe 1100–1700: A Documentary History edited by Alan C. Kors and Edward Peters, J. M. Dent & Sons, London, 1972

Witchcraft in Europe and the New World 1400–1800 by P. G. Maxwell-Stuart, Palgrave, New York, 2001

Further Reading

Witchcraze: A New History of the European Witch Hunts by Anne Llewellyn Barstow, HarperCollins, London, 1994

The Witch-Cult in Western Europe by Margaret Alice Murray, Clarendon Press, Oxford, 1921

Witches in Fact and Fantasy by Lauren Paine, Robert Hale & Company, London, 1971

Witch-Finder General by Ronald Bassett, Herbert Jenkins, London, 1966

Witch-Hunt: The Great Essex Witch Scare of 1582 by Anthony Harris, Ian Henry Publications, Romford, Essex, 2001

Witch-Hunt: The Great Scottish Witchcraft Trials of 1697 by Isabel Adam, Macmillan, London, 1978

The Witch-Hunt in Early Modern Europe by Brian P. Levack, Longman, New York, 1987

Witch Hunting by C. L'Estrange Ewen, Kegan Paul, Trench, Trubner & Co, London, 1929

Index

Index